ABSOLUTE BEGINNER'S GUIDE

TO

Wi-Fi® Wireless Networking

Harold Davis

800 East 96th Street,
Indianapolis, Indiana 46240

The Absolute Beginner's Guide to Wi-Fi® Wireless Networking

International Standard Book Number: 0-7897-3115-0

Library of Congress Catalog Card Number: 029236731199

Printed in the United States of America

First Printing: April 2004

06 05   5

Trademarks

All terms mentioned in this book that are known to be trademarks or service marks have been appropriately capitalized. Que cannot attest to the accuracy of this information. Use of a term in this book should not be regarded as affecting the validity of any trademark or service mark.

Wi-Fi® is a registered trademark of the Wi-Fi Alliance.

Warning and Disclaimer

Every effort has been made to make this book as complete and as accurate as possible, but no warranty or fitness is implied. The information provided is on an "as is" basis. The author and the publisher shall have neither liability nor responsibility to any person or entity with respect to any loss or damages arising from the information contained in this book.

Bulk Sales

Que offers excellent discounts on this book when ordered in quantity for bulk purchases or special sales. For more information, please contact

U.S. Corporate and Government Sales
1-800-382-3419
corpsales@pearsontechgroup.com

For sales outside of the U.S., please contact

International Sales
international@pearsoned.com

Associate Publisher
Greg Wiegand

Acquisitions Editor
Michelle Newcomb

Development Editor
Todd Brakke

Managing Editor
Charlotte Clapp

Project Editor
Andy Beaster

Copy Editor
Margaret Berson

Indexer
Mandie Frank

Proofreader
Juli Cook

Technical Editor
Will Eatherman

Team Coordinator
Sharry Lee Gregory

Interior Designer
Anne Jones

Cover Designer
Dan Armstrong

Page Layout
Stacey Richwine-DeRome

Contents at a Glance

Table of Contents

About the Author

Harold Davis is a strategic technology consultant, hands-on programmer, and the author of many well-known books. He has been a popular speaker at trade shows and conventions, giving presentations on topics ranging from digital photography through wireless networking and programming methodologies.

Harold has served as a technology consultant for many important businesses, including investment funds, technology companies, and Fortune 500 corporations. In recent years, he has been Vice President of Strategic Development at YellowGiant Corporation, Chief Technology Officer at an expert systems company, a Technical Director at Vignette Corporation, and a principal in the e-commerce practice at Informix Software.

Harold started programming when he was a child. He has worked in many languages and environments, and has been lead programmer and/or architect in projects for many corporations, including Chase Manhattan Bank, Nike, and Viacom.

He has earned a Bachelor's Degree in Computer Science and Mathematics from New York University and a J.D. from Rutgers Law School, where he was a member of the law review.

Harold lives with his wife, Phyllis Davis, who is also an author, and their two sons, Julian and Nicholas, in the hills of Berkeley, California. In his spare time, he enjoys hiking, gardening, and collecting antique machines including typewriters and calculation devices. He maintains a Wi-Fi access point and a mixed wired and wireless network for the Davis menagerie of computers running almost every imaginable operating system.

Dedication

For Julian, Nicholas, and "Roo"

Acknowledgments

Thanks to all of those who helped make this book possible, including Todd Brakke, Phyllis Davis, Michelle Newcomb, and Matt Wagner.

We Want to Hear from You!

As the reader of this book, *you* are our most important critic and commentator. We value your opinion and want to know what we're doing right, what we could do better, what areas you'd like to see us publish in, and any other words of wisdom you're willing to pass our way.

As an associate publisher for Que, I welcome your comments. You can email or write me directly to let me know what you did or didn't like about this book—as well as what we can do to make our books better.

Please note that I cannot help you with technical problems related to the *topic* of this book. We do have a User Services group, however, where I will forward specific technical questions related to the book.

When you write, please be sure to include this book's title and author as well as your name, email address, and phone number. I will carefully review your comments and share them with the author and editors who worked on the book.

Email: feedback@quepublishing.com

Mail: Greg Wiegand
         Associate Publisher
         Que
         800 East 96th Street
         Indianapolis, IN 46240 USA

For more information about this book or another Que title, visit our Web site at www.quepublishing.com. Type the ISBN (excluding hyphens) or the title of a book in the Search field to find the page you're looking for.

INTRODUCTION

If you are new to Wi-Fi—wireless networking—I'd like to be your guide to this wonderful technology. I am no industry flak or starry-eyed gadget freak (although I do appreciate technology that makes life easier for people, like Wi-Fi).

I want to be your guide to Wi-Fi, so it is fair for you to ask (and me to answer) some questions:

- What are my qualifications?
- What is my approach?
- Who is this book for, and why an "Absolute Beginner's Guide?"

I'd like to start with my qualifications. I take qualifications in this context to be a pretty broad issue, meaning (in part) who am I?

I am a normal human being, whatever that means, who is interested in technology (among other things). I have a wife, two kids, another one on the way, and a house with a mortgage. Besides my interest in technology, I like to read, write, garden, take photographs, and hike.

I've been involved in technology as a professional for more than 20 years. (Because technology years actually compare with dog years, that probably is the equivalent of hundreds of experiential years!) I've seen technologies come on strong, grow up, mature, and burst like a star that has gone nova too soon. I like to think I know what is important, and what is not, and what technologies matter.

I've been involved with Wi-Fi since its infancy, and have lectured about Wi-Fi and taught people how to construct Wi-Fi networks. I maintain a Wi-Fi network in my home for the convenience of myself and my family. I've been a road warrior and a stay-at-home. I enjoy sharing my knowledge with people and helping them get up to speed as quickly as possible.

Well, enough about me! Perhaps you are completely new to Wi-Fi and want to quickly get up to speed so you can surf at local hotspots, or while you're on the road. This book will give you the practical information you need to buy the right equipment, get your equipment working perfectly, find Wi-Fi hotspots, and get the best deal with Wi-Fi providers.

Perhaps you already use Wi-Fi in your local coffee shop, at the airport, or in hotel lobbies, and you want to set up a small office or home network. You already know how great Wi-Fi is, so you want to enjoy the benefits where you live and work. It is truly transformational to one's lifestyle to decouple computing from the wires!

tip

A *tip* is a piece of advice—a little trick, actually—that lets you use your computer more effectively or maneuver around problems or limitations.

caution

A *caution* will tell you to beware of a potentially dangerous act or situation. In some cases, ignoring a caution could cause you problems—so pay attention to them!

note

A *note* is designed to provide information that is generally useful but not specifically necessary for what you're doing at the moment. Some are like extended tips—interesting, but not essential.

Let Me Know What You Think

I always love to hear from readers, particularly if they have nice things to say about my book! Seriously folks, I'd love to hear from you with comments, criticism, praise, and (most important) items that should be in the next edition of this book. Please write to me at WifiReader@bearhome.com.

Although I can't promise to answer every email, I will do my best to do so.

Thanks for reading my book!

PART i

Why Wi-Fi?

1

ENTERING A WORLD WITHOUT WIRES

Have you ever wanted to lounge on a beach chair at a fancy resort and surf the Internet? Connect and get your email in a coffee shop such as Starbucks, or one inside a Borders bookstore? Put together some computers in your home so that they can share files or access to the Internet without drilling holes or snaking snarled wires from one computer to another?

With Wi-Fi, you can do all these things, and more.

This book shows you how.

I don't assume you know anything about Wi-Fi, or about any of the related topics, such as how to set up a network of computers. You'll find everything you need to take your wireless computer on the road, and to set up a wireless network, right here between these pages (well, except the hardware and software, of course, but I'll tell you how to go about getting that!).

So step right up and get ready to enter a wonderful new world without wires!

What Is Wi-Fi?

The very short version is that Wi-Fi is a way for wireless devices to communicate.

Wi-Fi, short for *wireless fidelity*, is the Wi-Fi Alliance's name for a wireless standard, or protocol, used for wireless communication. I'll tell you a bit more about this wireless standard and its variations, known collectively as IEEE 802.11, in Chapter 2, "Understanding Wi-Fi." (IEEE stands for the Institute of Electrical and Electronics Engineers, which defines the standard.)

THE WI-FI ALLIANCE

The Wi-Fi Alliance is a not-for-profit organization that certifies the interoperability of wireless devices built around the 802.11 standard. The goals of the Wi-Fi Alliance are to promote interoperability of devices based on 802.11, and, presumably, to promote and enhance the standard.

For better or worse, this is no neutral organization. The members of the Wi-Fi Alliance are manufacturers that build 802.11 devices. As of this writing, there are 205 companies that belong to the Wi-Fi Alliance and more than 900 products that have been certified as Wi-Fi interoperable.

The promise that the Wi-Fi Alliance makes is that if you buy an 802.11 device with the Wi-Fi seal of certification, the device will work seamlessly with any other Wi-Fi certified device.

You can find more information about the Wi-Fi Alliance at the Alliance's Web site, `www.wi-fi.org`.

Standards and protocols are mostly of interest to engineers (however, see the sidebar "What Is a Standard?" for more information if you are curious).

WHAT IS A STANDARD?

The words *standard* and *protocol* are essentially synonymous (protocol is a slightly more technical term). When used in its engineering context, a standard means the technical form of something such as a message or a communication. In other words, a standard might specify how the communication is made.

If you know the standard, you know how to decode the message. In order to work with a standard (called *complying* with a standard), a device needs to know both how to encode into the standard and decode from the standard.

A standard for working with communications, such as the Wi-Fi standard, will generally involve specifications both at the hardware and the software level (in geek-speak, these levels are called *layers*).

You can think of the standard as a kind of secret handshake that gets you into a club. If you (or your wireless device) know how the secret handshake works, you can find out what the other people in the club (the other wireless devices) are actually saying.

But Wi-Fi has garnered a huge amount of attention from people who would normally be unconcerned about engineering details: in other words, normal human beings like you and me. Students, professionals, homemakers, English Lit majors, and office workers are all talking about Wi-Fi.

The really big question is: Why is Wi-Fi getting all this attention? I'll get to that soon. I'll also show you how Wi-Fi can change your life (for real!). But first I'd like to tell you a little bit more about what Wi-Fi is.

For now, you need to know that Wi-Fi devices are certified interoperable and run on some flavor of 802.11, a medium-range wireless networking standard. 802.11 runs at speeds roughly comparable to those of wired networks. (I'll be telling you in more detail about transmission speeds in Chapter 2.)

Wireless Spectrums

Unlike many other wireless standards, 802.11 runs on "free" portions of the radio spectrum. This means that (unlike cell telephone communications) no license is required to broadcast or communicate using 802.11 (or Wi-Fi).

The free portions of the radio spectrum used by 802.11 (and Wi-Fi) are the 2.4GHz band, and, more recently, the 5GHz band. As you may know, many household appliances such as microwave ovens and (most significantly) wireless telephone handsets also use these free spectrums.

With a wireless telephone handset, a base station is connected to the telephone line, and the handset communicates with the base station over the "free" radio frequency, so that you can roam about your home or office while talking on the phone. Clearly, these wireless telephone handsets are not the same thing as cell phones, which do not connect to a telephone wire at all and use licensed portions of the spectrum.

The 802.11 (and Wi-Fi) standard includes what is called a *physical* layer. This physical layer uses something known as Direct Sequence Spread Spectrum technology (DSSS) to prevent collisions and avoid interference between devices operating on the same spectrum. You'll find much the same kind of technology in your wireless telephone handset. The idea here is that you don't want the signal coming out of your microwave unit to interfere with your email (or vice versa).

note

In this increasingly complex world of ours, there are more and more appliances and devices that broadcast and receive wireless signals, many of them on the same "free" radio spectrums used by Wi-Fi.

In addition to its physical layer, each 802.11 Wi-Fi device has an *access control* layer. The access control layer specifies how a Wi-Fi device, such as a mobile computer, communicates with another Wi-Fi device, such as a wireless access point.

A recent addition to the Wi-Fi standard is the Wi-Fi Protected Access solution (WPA). WPA will be explained in greater detail in Chapter 19, "Securing Your Wi-Fi Network."

Together, the physical and access control layers, along with extensions intended to implement extra features (such as WAP for security) make up the 802.11 Wi-Fi standard.

> **tip**
>
> If you find that your Wi-Fi device is getting interference from some other appliance such as a microwave or wireless telephone, one of the first things to try is moving either your Wi-Fi device, or the other device, to a new physical location.

Using Wi-Fi

If you've picked up this book, you probably have a use in mind for Wi-Fi. More precisely, you have a use in mind for a device that uses the Wi-Fi standard to broadcast and receive information.

The two most common uses for these devices both involve freedom:

- You can work almost anywhere by using a mobile Wi-Fi device to connect to the Internet without wires when away from your home or office.
- You can free yourself from the need to drill holes and snake wires by creating a network at the home or office using Wi-Fi devices.

In this chapter, I'll give you a picture of the hundred-mile view of each of these important uses for Wi-Fi devices. Your perspective is going to be pretty different if you've bought this book to learn how best to take your laptop on the road (or what kind of mobile device to buy) than if you've bought this book to learn how to create a wireless network.

Some preliminary footwork is necessary to both topics. These preliminaries are explained in this first part of the book, "Why Wi-Fi?"

But if you're reading this book to learn to travel with Wi-Fi, I've got lots of information and goodies for you (see Chapter 3, "Hitting the Road with Wi-Fi," and Part III, "Going Mobile with Wi-Fi"). On the other hand, if your primary interest is in setting up a wireless network, you may just want to turn straight away to Part IV, "Creating a Wi-Fi Network."

You'll find everything you always wanted to know about buying and configuring a Wi-Fi device in Part II, "Setting Up Your Computer for Wi-Fi."

Part V, "Securing Your Wi-Fi Computer and Network," provides plentiful information about that perennially pesky topic, security and wireless computing.

Why Wi-Fi Is Important

The 802.11 standard is important because millions of people all over the world are using this standard. They use it to connect without wires to the Internet when they are on the road and away from their home or office. They are also using 802.11 to create wireless networks in their homes and offices.

Although Wi-Fi is only a few years old, it's important because it provides an assurance of compatibility for 802.11 devices. Each Wi-Fi device will "talk" to every other Wi-Fi device—and the Wi-Fi Alliance has certified that this is the case! (For more information about the Wi-Fi Alliance, see the sidebar "The Wi-Fi Alliance" earlier in this chapter.)

The Wi-Fi Alliance makes the unequivocal statement that "Wi-Fi labeled equipment will work with any other piece of wireless networking gear that also has the Wi-Fi logo." Without the assurance of Wi-Fi compatibility, you would probably go mad trying for interoperability in a world of widely divergent wireless devices.

Every device with the Wi-Fi logo is also tested for functionality and durability by an independent testing laboratory.

Finally, the Wi-Fi Alliance, and the companies that form the Alliance, are engaged in an ongoing effort to expand wireless standards, and make wireless computing a more secure and enjoyable experience.

Understanding Wi-Fi Networks

You're on the road and you've found a location with a Wi-Fi broadcast device that your mobile computer can talk to. A Wi-Fi broadcast device is variously referred to as an *access point*, an *AP*, or a *hotspot*.

With your access point located, you're ready to sit right down, establish a wireless connection, and start reading your email and surfing the Web, right? Not so fast, partner.

It's really important to understand that being able to "talk" with a wireless access point just means that you can "talk" with a wireless access point. It doesn't mean that you can connect to the Internet unless the wireless access point is itself connected to the Internet.

So if Starbucks or whoever wants to provide you with the chance to surf on their turf while you sip that latte, Starbucks needs to provide an Internet connection. Generally, this connection is wired, and uses a cable or DSL (digital subscriber line) telephone line for high speeds.

A high-speed wire brings the Internet to the location, and a Wi-Fi access point broadcasts the wireless Internet connectivity to wireless devices (in technogeek-speak, the wireless devices are generically referred to as *clients*).

Between the Internet connection and the Wi-Fi access point, there also needs to be some hardware designed to connect with the Internet and share the connectivity. There are a whole lot of different ways this can be done, depending on many factors. For example, is a wired network also involved? I'll be getting into these details in Part IV.

For now, you need to understand that connecting to the Internet via Wi-Fi involves four things:

1. Your Wi-Fi device (the client)
2. A Wi-Fi broadcast unit (the access point)
3. Network connectivity hardware (such as a router and modem)
4. The actual Internet connection (usually via cable or DSL)

A fairly typical simple Wi-Fi network setup of this sort, that lets Wi-Fi users connect to the Internet, is shown in Figure 1.1.

FIGURE 1.1

In order to connect to the Internet via Wi-Fi, the wireless Wi-Fi access point must be plugged into equipment and an Internet connection, usually cable or DSL.

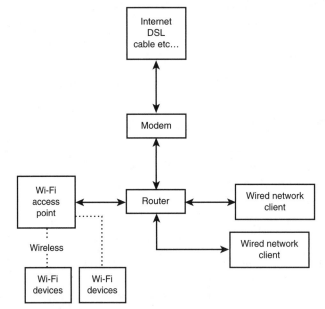

Using Wi-Fi on the Road

I'll be giving an overview of connecting on the road in Chapter 3. Part III includes a lot of detailed information, as well as tips, tricks, techniques, and information about the latest hot mobile gadgets. For now, I'd like to go over some basics related to using Wi-Fi on the road.

For starters, as I explained in the preceding section, "Understanding Wi-Fi Networks," it's not enough to find a Wi-Fi wireless access point. Behind the scenes, the wireless access points need to be capable of providing access to the Internet, usually via a high-speed cable or DSL connection.

In Figure 1.1, I showed you a pretty typical example of how this might work behind the scenes.

Connecting

With your Wi-Fi device happily chugging and ready to go, a good strong signal from a Wi-Fi access point broadcasting its way to you, and a behind-the-scenes Internet connection that the access point is plugged into, what's next?

Connecting to a public Wi-Fi access point is generally really easy. Usually all you have to do is open your Web browser. In some cases any Web browser will do, but often you need to use Microsoft's Internet Explorer. Connecting is really quite simple, but I'll be showing you some examples of how this works in Chapter 3.

Paying for It

There are two sides to Wi-Fi. One is the grass-roots peoples' movement in which propeller-headed persons (such as the author of this book) put up free Wi-Fi access points that can be used by anyone within range for free. (Of course, in my case the range is about 50 feet from my house in a quiet residential neighborhood, so it may help a neighbor or two, but is unlikely to be of much use to anyone else.) I'll talk a little more about this free Wi-Fi movement in Chapter 17, "Adding Wi-Fi Antennas to Your Network."

As a practical matter, you are far more likely to encounter the other side of Wi-Fi, which goes like this: Wi-Fi is one of the few areas in technology that has really boomed since the technology bubble burst in 2000. So let's try to build out a public infrastructure so that everyone can use Wi-Fi and charge whatever the market will bear.

The capitalistic, entrepreneurial side of Wi-Fi is what you may meet when you access the Internet via Wi-Fi in public venues such as Starbucks, Borders, hotels, and airports. There will be no free lunches in these venues! On the other hand, some businesses have found that offering free Wi-Fi is a great way to entice customers to stick around for a while and spend more money. In addition, there is a hard-core contingent of idealistic engineering types who see offering free Wi-Fi access as a worthy endeavor. So perhaps sometimes there are free lunches! And when there are, they are really tasty!

As I'll discuss in detail in Chapter 12, "Working with National Wi-Fi Networks," Wi-Fi is increasingly being rolled out by large-scale infrastructure providers.

Typically, you pay for your access based on how long you use it either with a payment plan, or as you go. If you plan to pay as you go, you'll need to have a credit card handy when you log on to the Wi-Fi network.

I'll discuss payment options and plans further in Chapter 12.

Finding Access Points

Where are the public Wi-Fi access points? Why, everywhere and nowhere, like a taxicab on a rainy day.

Actually, the picture is not nearly so bleak, and there are more and more wireless access points every day.

There are also a great number of online tools that help you find access points that meet your needs.

I'll provide an overview of how to find Wi-Fi access points in Chapter 3, and go into greater detail on the various tools and directories available in Chapter 11, "Where Can You Wi-Fi?"

The Absolute Minimum

Here are the key points to remember from this chapter:

- 802.11 is the engineer's name for a wireless standard that uses a free portion of the broadcast spectrum.

- Wi-Fi is the name given to wireless devices that are certified to be compatible and use the 802.11 standard.

- Millions of people are using Wi-Fi to connect to the Internet and private networks without wires.

- This book will explain both how to connect via Wi-Fi on the road, and how to set up a Wi-Fi wireless network at home (or in the office).

- Wi-Fi wireless Internet access requires more than just a Wi-Fi access point. To access the Internet, you'll also need an Internet connection and an intermediate layer of hardware equipment.

IN THIS CHAPTER

- The free spectrums that Wi-Fi uses for its transmissions

- The various variants of the 802.11 standard that collectively make up Wi-Fi

- Other (non-Wi-Fi) wireless standards and how they relate to Wi-Fi

- Transmission speeds

2

UNDERSTANDING Wi-Fi

You don't have to understand a whole lot about Wi-Fi to be able to make good use of it. Therefore, this chapter does not go into a great deal of technical detail about the various Wi-Fi standards. You'll find some of the gory, geeky details in Appendix A, "Wireless Standards," if you really need to know.

Still, there are a number of good reasons for you to have some basic understanding of how wireless technologies work and the alphabet soup of standards they use. A little information will help you make knowledgeable decisions when you buy equipment. It is interesting to know enough about the technical things to see which way this fast-moving technology is going. And, knowing something about this stuff (even if it is only how to pronounce "gigahertz") is a good way to impress your friends, neighbors, and co-workers.

This chapter tells you everything you really *need* to know about the wireless standards related to Wi-Fi.

The Free Spectrums

As you probably know, any signal that is sent without wires is called a *radio transmission*. A common example is that the radio in your car receives transmissions. Similarly, a standard cell phone works by receiving—and transmitting—radio signals.

Every device that broadcasts a radio transmission does so at a particular *frequency*, which is the oscillations, or movement from peak to trough, of the electromagnetic wave created by the transmission.

The entire set of radio frequencies is known as the radio *spectrum*. Contiguous portions of the radio spectrum are called *bands*, as in "the FM band."

Radio frequencies describe the oscillations of a radio wave. For example, if you are tuned to an FM radio station at 92.5, it means that the radio transmission is oscillating at 92.5 megahertz per second. 92.5 megahertz (pronounced "may-ga-hurts" and abbreviated MHz) means that the radio transmission wave oscillates, or moves from its valley to its peak, at a rate of 92,500,000 times per second. If you think of this as listening from a distance to a really rapidly vibrating tuning fork, you have the right picture.

The AM radio spectrum was developed before the FM spectrum, so it is *lower* down the spectrum, ranging from 535 kilohertz to 1.7 megahertz, or 535,000 to 1,700,000 oscillations per second. For example, 720 on the AM dial means that your radio receiver is tuned to a frequency of 720,000 oscillations per second.

There are frequencies *above*, or higher than, the FM frequency as well as below it. In fact, as I'll explain in a moment, Wi-Fi transmissions run at some of these higher frequencies.

One thousand megahertz is equal to one gigahertz (pronounced "gig-a-hurts" and abbreviated GHz). So when you refer to the 2.4GHz frequency, you are actually talking about 2,400,000,000 (2.4 billion) oscillations per second.

There are only so many frequencies in the radio spectrum that can be used for transmissions. This has inevitably led to the potential for conflicts about usage, as well as attempts to dominate particular frequencies.

As a partial answer to frequency conflicts, the government has regulated the usage of most of these frequencies. In the United States, government regulation of radio frequencies is controlled by the Federal Communications Commission (FCC).

Some frequencies are reserved for particular usages, such as the military. Others, such as the AM and FM bands, are licensed. This means that only the licensees can use the frequency for the purpose it was licensed. In addition, some areas of the

note

Although it is commonly referred to as the 2.4GHz band, the actual spectrum is 2.39GHz–2.417GHz. In the case of the 5GHz spectrum band, the band actually runs from 5.47GHz to 5.725GHz.

spectrum have been set aside for unlicensed uses. These set-aside areas include the 2.4GHz and 5GHz spectrums, which is what Wi-Fi uses.

The uses of some of the frequencies in the radio spectrum are shown in Figure 2.1.

FIGURE 2.1
Selected uses
for the radio
spectrum.

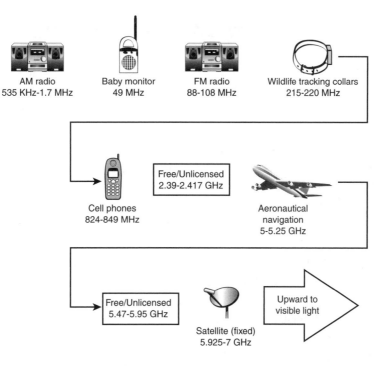

AM radio
535 KHz-1.7 MHz

Baby monitor
49 MHz

FM radio
88-108 MHz

Wildlife tracking collars
215-220 MHz

Cell phones
824-849 MHz

Free/Unlicensed
2.39-2.417 GHz

Aeronautical
navigation
5-5.25 GHz

Free/Unlicensed
5.47-5.95 GHz

Satellite (fixed)
5.925-7 GHz

Upward to
visible light

The fact that the 2.4GHz and 5GHz frequencies have been set aside for unlicensed usages does have an extremely important implication: They are cheap to use. This gives these "free" spectrums an unfair competitive advantage compared to using a spectrum that someone has paid for. But there are some legal restrictions on what you can do within the free spectrums (see Chapter 17, "Adding Wi-Fi Antennas to Your Network," for more information).

Also, the 2.4GHz spectrum has become like a shanty town in which it is cheap to live. All kinds of transmission devices have crowded into the neighborhood, from microwaves to cordless telephones. These devices can interfere with your Wi-Fi transmissions and reception. In Part IV, "Creating a Wi-Fi Network," I'll show you how to best avoid problems with competing 2.4GHz devices when

note

There are conflicts within the 5GHz band as well as the 2.4GHz band, but 5GHz band conflicts primarily concern competing usages such as radar and satellite radio, which are being ironed out by the FCC.

setting up a Wi-Fi network. (Interference is a two-way street. You also don't want your Wi-Fi network wreaking havoc on your cordless phones and other devices that use the spectrum.)

The 802.11 Standard and Its Variations

Generally, the core 802.11 standard is intended to specify a way for computers to network using the 2.4GHz and 5GHz free spectrums I just explained. (When computers network, it is said that they are forming a *local area network*, or LAN. When computers network wirelessly, it is called a Wireless LAN, or WLAN.)

The 802.11b Standard

When you say "Wi-Fi" today, you probably mean 802.11b, which is a subset of the general 802.11 standard. Most Wi-Fi devices that are currently in operation are using 802.11b. However, technology moves quickly, and 802.11g is gaining momentum fast.

The full 802.11b specification document is more than 500 pages long, but here are the key things to know about 802.11b:

- The 802.11b standard uses the 2.4GHz spectrum.
- The 802.11b standard uses a technology called Direct Sequence Spread Spectrum (DSSS) to minimize interference with other devices transmitting on the 2.4GHz spectrum.
- The 802.11b standard has a theoretical throughput speed of 11 megabytes per second (Mbps).

The 11Mbps speed compares favorably with the 10Mbps throughput of a conventional 10BASE-T wired Ethernet network, which may be what you are used to using at work. It is certainly faster than even the fastest broadband Internet connections.

However, for a variety of reasons Wi-Fi connections rarely achieve anything like its theoretical maximum (encryption slows 802.11b down, for one thing). Weak connectivity also slows Wi-Fi down. Even so, Wi-Fi connections should be fine for everyday uses such as file sharing or sharing an Internet connection. There may be some extremely demanding applications that Wi-Fi speeds are not good enough for, but I am hard put to think of any.

The most important thing you should take away regarding the speed of 802.11b Wi-Fi is that for

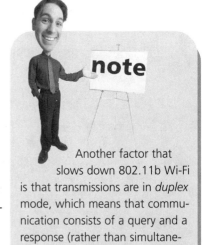

note

Another factor that slows down 802.11b Wi-Fi is that transmissions are in *duplex* mode, which means that communication consists of a query and a response (rather than simultaneous communication). This slows down speeds noticeably.

most users 11Mbps is good enough. The 802.11b Wi-Fi connection is rarely slower than other parts of the system it is in, such as the network it is connected to, or access to the Internet.

I'll be telling you a little more about transmission speeds of 802.11b related to other wireless standards later in this chapter.

The 802.11a and 802.11g Standards

The 802.11a and 802.11g standards are different variants of 802.11 that can be thought of as 802.11b's smarter, younger brothers. The 802.11a standard uses the 5GHz band for transmission, which minimizes the possibility of interference with the plethora of 2.4GHz devices out there (think microwaves, garage door openers, and so on) and promises a theoretic throughput of 24Mbps.

Still newer than 802.11a, 802.11g operates on the 2.4GHz spectrum and boasts throughput as fast as 54Mbps.

In other words, both 802.11a and 802.11g show the promise of being considerably faster than 802.11b.

The 802.11a standard poses some compatibility issues with 802.11b. But at least one vendor, Atheros Communications, makes 802.11a equipment that is backward-compatible with 802.11b. (Atheros also makes a "tri-mode" chipset that uses 802.11a, 802.11b, and 802.11g.) The chief advantage of 802.11a is that it will run into less interruption from other devices because it does not use the crowded 2.4GHz band.

Moving to 802.11a has some pluses and minuses, but moving to 802.11g is a no-brainer—because 802.11g systems are backward-compatible with 802.11b, and faster. This backward compatibility of 802.11g devices is a requirement for Wi-Fi certification.

Neither 802.11a nor 802.11g are starting to become mainstream, with prices a bit higher than for 802.11b. In fact, the 802.11g standard is replacing 802.11b as the standard for new equipment (it is preferred to 802.11a because of its backward compatibility). Pretty soon, 802.11g will be the de facto Wi-Fi standard that is at the "sweet" price point, and other, faster Wi-Fi standards—such as the proposed 802.11n—will be the new contender knocking at the door.

You'll find more information about evaluating whether 802.11a or 802.11g Wi-Fi hardware is right for you in Chapter 8, "Adding Wi-Fi to a Mobile Computer," and Chapter 13, "Buying a Wi-Fi Access Point or Router."

The 802.11i Standard

The IEEE is in the process of developing a new security standard for 802.11 that is named 802.11i. The Wi-Fi Alliance has released a subset of the 802.11i standard that the Alliance has developed called "Wi-Fi Protected Access."

Products that successfully complete the Wi-Fi Alliance testing required for meeting its version of the 802.11i standard will be called "Wi-Fi Protected Access" certified.

Wi-Fi Protected Access provides a stronger level of encryption and authentication than is built into the current Wi-Fi standards. This means that Wi-Fi networks will be better protected from unauthorized access and other security problems. Wi-Fi Protected Access is intended to replace WEP encryption built into current Wi-Fi.

The new standard is also intended to be "software implementable." This means that current Wi-Fi products should be upgradeable to Wi-Fi Protected Access by running a software patch—new hardware will not be required.

The Wi-Fi Protected Access standard is currently available, and a number of manufacturers have announced that their products will support it. However, most products on the market do not support this standard yet. For more about Wi-Fi and security, please see Part V, "Securing Your Wi-Fi Computer and Network."

Related Wireless Standards

You might also hear about some other wireless standards, and wonder how they are related to Wi-Fi. The two other wireless standards you are most likely to hear about are *Bluetooth* and *3G*.

Bluetooth is a short-range connectivity solution designed for data exchange between devices such as printers, cell phones, and PDAs. Like 802.11b, it uses the 2.4GHz spectrum. Although Bluetooth is built into a great many devices, it is a standard with some severe disadvantages, mainly that it is far slower than 802.11b (with nominal throughput of up to 721 Kilobytes per second) and with a maximum range of about 30 feet (compared to Wi-Fi's unamplified range of several hundred feet). Bluetooth's main claim to fame is that it is inexpensive, which is why it has been added to so many devices.

3G is a catch-all term for a proprietary network using spectrums leased by telecommunications carriers such as Sprint and Verizon. Although 3G would undoubtedly transmit data at faster rates than Wi-Fi—perhaps at rates as fast as 384Mbps—there is no doubt that users would be expected to pick up the tab. (After all, it uses a leased spectrum that is not free for the telecommunications companies.)

At this point, there is very little in the way of completed 3G infrastructure, nor is there any reason to expect 3G technology to be used as the backbone for ad-hoc wireless networking in the way Wi-Fi has.

Transmission Speeds

Figure 2.2 shows some comparative throughput speeds for most of the wireless standards I've discussed in this chapter.

In order to keep the comparison real-world, I've included estimated actual throughput for 802.11b as well as its theoretical maximum.

For purposes of reference, and to help you see that Wi-Fi is unlikely to slow you down much, I've included the throughput you can expect from a 10BASE-T Ethernet network in the figure (this is the kind of wired network you are most likely to find in your home or office, although many wired networks are based on the faster 100BASE-T standard).

FIGURE 2.2

Comparative speeds of wireless standards.

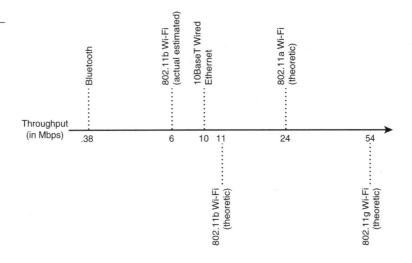

You should take away these points from Figure 2.2:

1. 802.11b Wi-Fi is a little slower in the real world than a wired network, but more than adequate for small office and home networks.

2. Wi-Fi is getting faster and better all the time.

The Future of Wi-Fi

Wi-Fi is a disruptive technology that came unexpectedly and has been growing by leaps and bounds, mainly because it is inexpensive and fills a need. Originally, Wi-Fi was just a hack so that people could connect a notebook to a network via wireless using a spectrum that didn't have to be paid for. No one expected it to grow so fast, and to become used so widely. The fact that it has spread like wildfire has caused many kinds of technology companies, from wireless cell phone providers to network hardware manufacturers, to rethink their businesses.

For sure, some telecommunications executives must be turning to each other and saying, "Hey, why should we build expensive proprietary networks when it is being done cheaply and on the fly using Wi-Fi?"

The growth of Wi-Fi has spawned all kinds of fun and useful developments and gizmos. For some examples, turn to Chapter 7, "Playing with Wi-Fi Gadgets."

As Wi-Fi grows up, it is getting better, more secure, and faster. Clearly, vendors and the Wi-Fi Alliance have listened to the users' need for security (as represented by the 802.11i standard) and interoperability. If you decide to use one of the newer flavors of Wi-Fi, you'll probably find that it will interoperate well with older versions.

The Absolute Minimum

Here are the key points to remember from this chapter:

- All radio transmissions operate on a spectrum band.
- Wi-Fi uses the unlicensed 2.4GHz and 5GHz bands.
- The 802.11b standard is the predominate flavor of Wi-Fi today.
- The 802.11a and 802.11g standards are up-and-coming faster versions of Wi-Fi.
- Wi-Fi provides data throughput that is fine for most uses.
- 802.11b will work with 802.11g and vice versa. 802.11a will only work with other 802.11a devices.

3

HITTING THE ROAD WITH Wi-Fi

One thing that is great fun to do with Wi-Fi is to connect to the Internet from a remote location such as a hotel lobby or a coffee shop. If you are on a business trip, this kind of wireless connection is not only fun and convenient, but it can help you be more productive by using your time more efficiently. The ability to connect via wireless on the road lets you pick up email, and surf for information, when you need it—on your own time.

The good news is that there is no great trick to connecting remotely via Wi-Fi.

This chapter shows you how to hit the road with Wi-Fi, even if the road is only your nearby Borders bookstore or Starbucks latte emporium!

I won't go into too many gory details at this point because I can't do everything at once, but don't worry if things don't seem quite as simple to you as they are made out to be in this chapter. There's plenty of more in-depth material later on in this book, and in this chapter I'll point you to the right place to find more detailed information on the topics covered.

The Equipment You Need

The answer to the question, "What equipment do you need to hit the road and connect?" is: not much.

Obviously, you need a mobile computing device such as a laptop, or possibly a Personal Digital Assistant (PDA). Most likely, you'll be using a laptop computer.

See Chapter 6, "Buying a Wi-Fi PDA," and Chapter 10, "Tools for the Perfect Road Warrior," for more information about using Wi-Fi with PDAs.

If your laptop features integrated Wi-Fi, such as Windows machines based upon Intel's Centrino technology or an Apple PowerBook with AirPort Extreme technology, you are home free because you've already got the necessary hardware.

⇨ You'll find more information about mobile computers that come with integrated Wi-Fi wireless technology in Chapter 5, "Buying a Wi-Fi Laptop."

Laptops that do not feature integrated Wi-Fi need a way to use Wi-Fi. Probably the most common mechanism is to add a card, called a PC card, like the one shown in Figure 3.1, to your laptop so it can connect to a wireless network.

> **tip**
>
> Another good approach is to use a USB Wi-Fi adapter with your laptop, particularly if you don't have a free slot for a PC Card. This kind of device just slips into a USB port on your laptop. For more information about using a USB Wi-Fi device with desktop or laptop computers, see Chapter 8, "Adding Wi-Fi to a Mobile Computer," and Chapter 9, "Wi-Fi on Your Desktop."

FIGURE 3.1

A Wi-Fi PC Card is the most common way to connect your computer to the Internet without wires.

PC Cards are more technically known as *PCMCIA* cards. PCMCIA is short for *Personal Computer Memory Card International Association*, which is the name of the organization that has devised the standard for cards that can be added to laptops. These cards were originally designed to add additional memory to laptops. They've come to be used for many other things as well, not the least of which is to connect to Wi-Fi wireless networks.

If you look at the PC Card shown in Figure 3.1, you'll see that one end is actually an antenna (on the left side). In some models of cards, this antenna actually can be extended, and may even resemble the old-fashioned "rabbit ears" antenna sometimes used with old television sets. This antenna is used for the transmission and reception of Wi-Fi signals.

The side of the PC Card away from the antenna slides into a laptop (as shown in Figure 3.2).

FIGURE 3.2

A Wi-Fi PC Card sliding into the expansion slot of a laptop.

The slot that the PC Card fits into on the laptop is sometimes called an *expansion slot*.

With the Wi-Fi card in an expansion slot, you'll need to be sure that the right software to make it work is loaded, and the software is set up properly. If you are running Windows XP (or Mac OS X), this will probably happen automatically.

You'll find more information about installing and configuring a Wi-Fi card's software in Chapter 8.

You will have to "tune" your Wi-Fi card to the network broadcasting the Wi-Fi signal, just as you have to tune a radio to a station to get reception. The network is identified by something analogous to call letters, called its service set identifier (SSID).

There's no equipment you need in addition to a charged-up laptop with integrated Wi-Fi, or a Wi-Fi expansion card. You *do* need to find out where to connect using Wi-Fi. I'll show you some ways to find this information next.

Much of the time, you'll also need to pay for your access. Any major credit card will do. I'll tell you how this works in the section "Payment Packages," which is located later in this chapter.

Finding Hotspots

A *hotspot* is the term used to mean an area in which Wi-Fi users can connect to the Internet. For the most part, you should expect to pay for access via a hotspot, just as you pay for Internet access via an Internet service provider (ISP), such as a cable or telephone company at home. (On the other hand, many business conventions provide Wi-Fi access as a courtesy to attendees, and it is not unheard of to find courtesy Wi-Fi access in such places as hotel lobbies.)

You may know in advance where to find Wi-Fi access on your travels. I've mentioned hotels and conventions already, because these are likely places to find Wi-Fi access. You can certainly inquire ahead of time.

If you don't have advance information about the location of Wi-Fi hotspots, you can also just turn your laptop on and wander about from location to location like a digital Ulysses looking for wireless access. (You'll find a discussion of a gadget that may help you locate Wi-Fi hotspots just by wandering in Chapter 11, "Where Can You Wi-Fi?") But assuming you'd like something a little more pinpointed than the Clint Eastwood "Do you feel lucky?" approach, using the Internet to find Wi-Fi hotspots is the best way to go.

Of course, you have to be able to access the Internet directories from a location where you have Internet access.

There are three approaches to take when making your search for a place to surf:

1. You can use the search tools provided by an organization whose branches host Wi-Fi hotspots, such as the Starbucks chain.

2. If you've signed up with a Wi-Fi provider, you can search the directory of hotspots maintained by your service provider.

3. You can search one of the many cross-provider Wi-Fi hotspot directories available on the Web.

I'll show how all three approaches might work using a test example. I live midway up in the hills in Berkeley, California. Let's suppose that I want to sip latte at a coffee shop, and need to keep on checking my email while I do.

Searching a Chain

If you know the name of the organization or chain of stores that you would like to use as a wireless destination ("I want to surf at Starbucks," or "I want to browse at Borders"), you can go directly to the Web site of the organization to find a wireless location. The first approach, since I know that Starbucks coffee shops have Wi-Fi hotspots and I like Starbucks coffee just fine, is to find a Starbucks near me that is Wi-Fi enabled.

It's easy to go to www.starbucks.com and choose the store locator by clicking the Find Your Nearest Starbucks link on the home page. With the locator page open, I can select Wireless Hotspot Stores from the Store Type drop-down list, and fill in my city, state, and ZIP as shown in Figure 3.3.

FIGURE 3.3

You can search on the Starbucks Web site for stores with Wi-Fi hotspots.

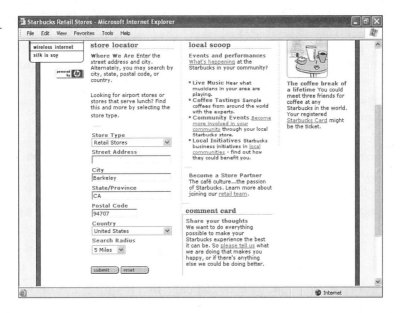

Click Submit. You'll see a page showing the nearest Starbucks that are equipped with Wi-Fi along with a handy-dandy map (see Figure 3.4).

FIGURE 3.4

The Starbucks search shows a number of local stores with Wi-Fi hotspots.

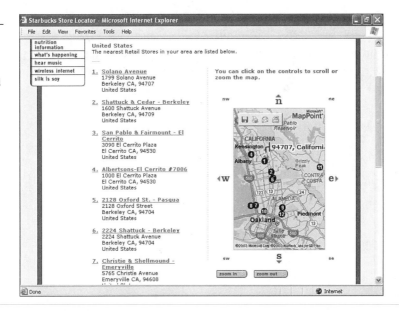

Searching a Wi-Fi Service Provider

There are about a dozen major Wi-Fi service providers in the United States alone, and hundreds of smaller, mom-and-pop, vendors. As I'll go into further in Chapter 12, "Working with National Wi-Fi Networks," there are really only a couple of big Wi-Fi service providers with national coverage. If you've signed up for a payment plan with one of these big players, you should probably stick with the hotspots they provide. Although there is no hard-and-fast rule about this, as with cell phone communications, you tend to get charged a bit more for "roaming." Because the industry is still so young and fragmented there is, indeed, no guarantee that one Wi-Fi service provider has even set up a cross-billing arrangement to cover roaming with yours.

Chapter 12 explains the structure of the Wi-Fi service provider industry, who the players are, how to pick the best one for you, and how to work with your Wi-Fi service provider. In the meantime if you're searching for a national Wi-Fi service provider, three of the biggest are Boingo, Wayport, and T-Mobile Hotspot.

- Boingo Wireless has about 2,000 live hotspots in the U.S., with a strong representation in hotels and coffee shops, and an international footprint.

- Wayport is a privately held company based in Texas that is strong in hotels, airports, and—more recently—in McDonald's restaurants.

- T-Mobile is a cell phone company that is a subsidiary of Deutsches Telekom. The T-Mobile Hotspot division provides Wi-Fi access in Borders, Starbucks, and many other locations, over 3,000 nationally.

The home page for T-Mobile Hotspot is located at `www.t-mobile.com/hotspot/`.

T-Mobile provides a number of tools for searching for hotspots, such as the clickable map and drop-down list shown in Figure 3.5.

Ultimately, if I drill down on my location using the map T-Mobile provides, I'll get the same list of Starbucks locations provided by the Starbucks chain itself for Berkeley, California.

FIGURE 3.5

You can use the clickable map to find hotspots provided by T-Mobile in your state.

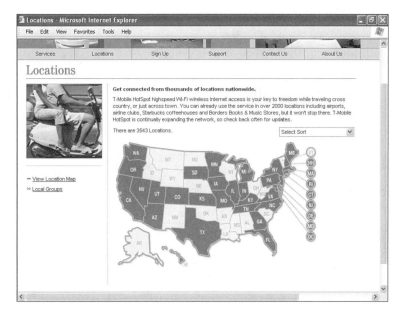

Using a Wi-Fi Directory

If you type the phrase "Wi-Fi Directory" into Google (www.google.com), you'll get many links to sites that provide this service.

At least in theory, most of these directories are not restricted to either a particular chain of stores, or to a specific Wi-Fi service provider. They should, therefore, produce the broadest array of choices.

Figure 3.6 shows WiFi411, www.wifi411.com, a directory that lists more than 11,000 hotspots, set up to do our search for coffee shops near my home.

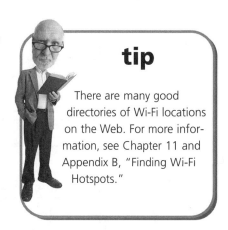

tip

There are many good directories of Wi-Fi locations on the Web. For more information, see Chapter 11 and Appendix B, "Finding Wi-Fi Hotspots."

As you can see in Figure 3.7, the search shows any nearby Starbucks with Wi-Fi hotspots. In addition, it also shows a number of unaffiliated coffee shops, which might be more to your liking, or more convenient. Each listing does show the Wi-Fi service provider that hosts access at the location.

FIGURE 3.6
You can use a general Wi-Fi site to find hotspots without reference to brands or providers.

Location Name	Type	City	State/Province	Network Provider
Ballena Isle Marina	Marina	Alameda	California	iDockUSA
Starbucks, Park Street & Central	Café/ Coffee Shop	Alameda	California	T-Mobile USA
Starbucks, South Shore Shopping Center	Café/ Coffee Shop	Alameda	California	T-Mobile USA
Starbucks, Webster & Atlantic - Alameda	Café/ Coffee Shop	Alameda	California	T-Mobile USA
Kinko's Alameda CA	Store/Retail Shop	Alameda	California	T-Mobile USA
French Hotel Café	Café/ Coffee Shop	Berkeley	California	Deep Blue Wireless
Espresso Roma Cafe II	Café/ Coffee Shop	Berkeley	California	Deep Blue Wireless
Cafe Milano	Café/ Coffee Shop	Berkeley	California	Deep Blue Wireless
Espresso Roma Café	Café/ Coffee Shop	Berkeley	California	Deep Blue Wireless
French Hotel	Hotel	Berkeley	California	Deep Blue Wireless
International House	Hotel	Berkeley	California	Deep Blue Wireless
Julies Healthy Café	Café/ Coffee Shop	Berkeley	California	Surf and Sip
Beanery Cafe	Café/ Coffee Shop	Berkeley	California	Surf and Sip
A Cuppa Tea	Café/ Coffee Shop	Berkeley	California	Surf and Sip
Brewed Awakening	Café/ Coffee Shop	Berkeley	California	Surf and Sip
Starbucks, Shattuck & Cedar, Berkeley	Café/ Coffee Shop	Berkeley	California	T-Mobile USA
Starbucks, Solano Avenue	Café/ Coffee Shop	Berkeley	California	T-Mobile USA
Starbucks, 2128 Oxford St. - Pasqua	Café/ Coffee Shop	Berkeley	California	T-Mobile USA
Starbucks, 2224 Shattuck - Berkeley	Café/ Coffee Shop	Berkeley	California	T-Mobile USA
J R Muggs	Restaurant/Bar/Pub	El Cerrito	California	Surf and Sip
Starbucks, San Pablo & Fairmount - El Cerrito	Café/ Coffee Shop	El Cerrito	California	T-Mobile USA
T-Mobile San Pablo & Fairmount	Store/Retail Shop	El Cerrito	California	T-Mobile USA
Apple Store	Store/Retail Shop	Emeryville	California	Apple Stores
Emery Cove Yacht Harbor	Marina	Emeryville	California	iDockUSA
Emeryville Marina	Marina	Emeryville	California	iDockUSA

184 location(s) found, 8 page(s) for display (Results 1 - 25 , page 1)

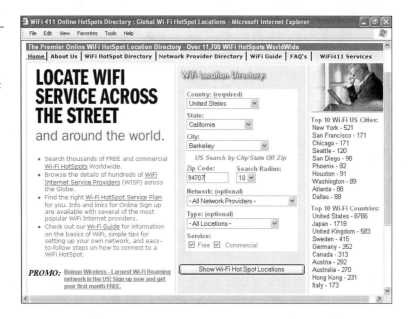

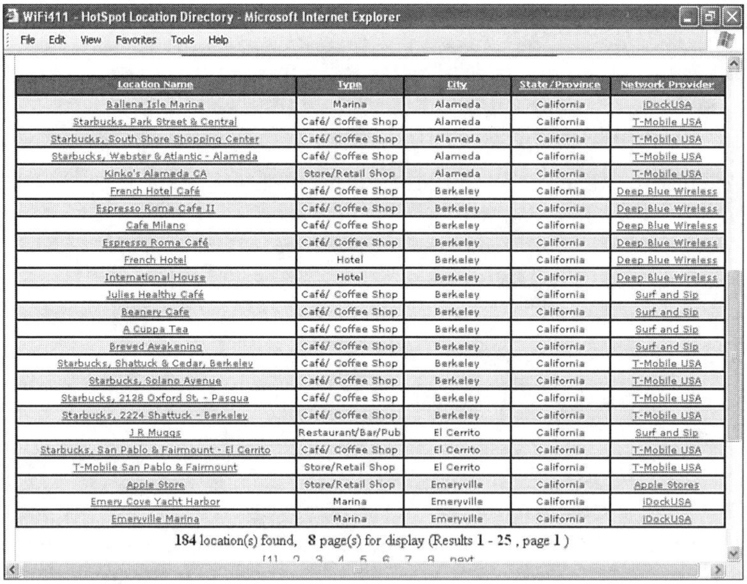

FIGURE 3.7
The WiFi411 directory shows independent hotspots, as well as the ones hosted in Starbucks locations.

Paying for Your Fun

For the most part, as the saying goes, there is no such thing as a free lunch, or a free latte. This is all too true, I'm afraid: Mostly you will need to pay to surf while you sip.

With most Wi-Fi service providers, you don't need to sign up for a plan, although it will certainly be beneficial for you to do so if you plan to make much use of the service (Chapter 12 has more information on making the best of the economics of the matter). You also don't need to enroll with a Wi-Fi service provider in advance. You can do it on the spot when you connect via your laptop (provided, of course, you've brought a valid credit card).

With T-Mobile Hotspot, you can sign up for access by the minute, the day, or for a monthly plan.

The initial sign-up screen is shown in Figure 3.8 and gives you a good idea of the different plans and costs associated with them.

tip

If you're just looking to get your feet wet in the pool of connecting to the Internet through a public hotspot, it's worth noting that Starbucks provides a promotional one-day pass that gives you a free day of Wi-Fi access using a special promotional code as explained in special brochures available in each store.

FIGURE 3.8

It's easy to sign up with T-Mobile or other Wi-Fi service providers.

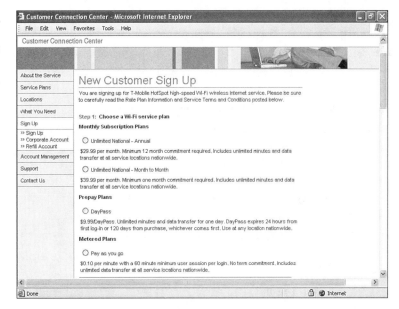

Surfing While You Sip

With a working Wi-Fi card in your computer, the next thing to do is to tune your card to the Wi-Fi frequency being broadcast at the hotspot you've decided to visit. This is essentially like tuning a radio to the frequency you want to hear. Just as a radio station has a frequency and call letters, a Wi-Fi hotspot has a network name, often called an SSID, that you can use to tune to the particular hotspot.

The specifics of setting your Wi-Fi card to a hotspot will differ somewhat depending on the software that comes with the card (see Chapter 8 for more information about this). Figure 3.9 shows Wi-Fi card software that sets up a separate profile for each hotspot. You can store settings for multiple access points and switch between them (the principle is like the preset buttons on a car radio). Generally, the application that does this is started from an icon on the system tray that is part of the Windows taskbar.

FIGURE 3.9

Using the configuration software that comes with a Wi-Fi card.

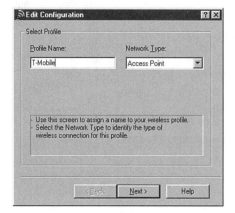

You need the network name to connect, so the crucial thing is to set the network name, also called the SSID. Setting the SSID is usually all it takes to connect to a public hotspot. An SSID is shown entered in one type of Wi-Fi card configuration software in Figure 3.10.

You might not know that the name for the T-Mobile Hotspot network is tmobile. In that case you can scan for available Wi-Fi broadcasts using the software that came with your Wi-Fi card. In the software shown in Figure 3.10, this is done by clicking the Scan button.

With the network name (SSID) set, you are ready to open your Web browser. When you do, the welcome screen for the hotspot will open (in this case, as you can see in Figure 3.11, featuring Starbucks as well as T-Mobile Hotspot).

note

In an effort to differentiate itself from everyone else offering Wi-Fi access, you'll find that providers such as Starbucks are now offering some exclusive, free content (such as games and music) in addition to the ability to surf.

FIGURE 3.10

The crucial step is setting the network name, also called (more technically) the SSID.

FIGURE 3.11

You can log on using an existing T-Mobile Hotspot account, or create a new account on the spot.

You can log on using an existing account, or create a new account on the spot. (Be sure to take advantage of any special offers such as the free day of surfing at Starbucks!)

That's all there is to it! From here, you're ready to surf the Web, download email, or whatever. A pop-up window in your browser, shown in Figure 3.12, lets you know you are connected, and provides a link that logs you off.

This is so much fun, and really very easy. Before you know it, you'll be connected everywhere (see Figure 3.13—so where does the computer end and the latte begin?).

FIGURE 3.12
A pop-up window in your browser reminds you that you are logged in (and lets you log off).

FIGURE 3.13
It's fun to surf without wires as I sip my latte!

THE ABSOLUTE MINIMUM

Here are the key points to remember from this chapter:

- You need integrated Wi-Fi, or a Wi-Fi card, for wireless access.
- There are a number of different Wi-Fi service providers.
- There are also a number of useful Wi-Fi directories on the Web.
- Expect to pay for your Wi-Fi access in advance or on the spot.
- Connections to a hotspot are made by "tuning" to the network name (SSID) of the hotspot.

IN THIS CHAPTER

- Understanding networks in general

- Hardware components of a wired network

- Adding Wi-Fi capability to an existing network versus creating a Wi-Fi network from scratch

- Equipment you'll need to add Wi-Fi capability to your network, or to create a Wi-Fi network

4

NETWORKING WITHOUT WIRES

In Chapter 3, "Hitting the Road with Wi-Fi," I gave you a taste of how easy it is to connect on the road—at coffee shops or hotels—using Wi-Fi. But perhaps you already know how to do this (it's easy enough, particularly with a mobile computer with integrated Wi-Fi, that this wouldn't be surprising). Or, maybe you don't care because, well, because you never travel.

Whatever the reason, that's fine! Wi-Fi is a great tool for more than mobile computing. You can use Wi-Fi at home or in the office to construct a network without the hassle (and expense) of dealing with wires and drilling holes through the walls. Furthermore, using Wi-Fi for your home or small office network gives you the freedom to work wherever you'd like: in the garden, in the kitchen, in bed, or maybe even in a bubble bath (where are waterproof laptops when you need them?).

This chapter provides an overview of what it takes to set up a wireless network in the wondrous world that has no snaking tangles of wire. I'll also point you in the right direction for more in-depth coverage in this book of specific topics related to wireless networking.

Understanding Home and SOHO Networks

If you are used to working on a single computer, the idea of setting up a network may seem daunting. Perhaps at work you *do* plug into the corporate network, but maintaining and configuring this network isn't your problem. Instead, it is handled by a staff of highly professional overachievers. At least, that's what the folks from corporate information technology (IT) would have you believe.

Relax! There's nothing particularly dark, deep, or mysterious about the concepts involved in setting up a small home or office network.

I'd like to step back for a moment or two and forget about Wi-Fi and wireless connectivity. This will give me the chance to explain networks to you generally. As you'll see, networks are really simple. There are no really tough concepts involved. By explaining the concepts, and showing you the relevant vocabulary, I can help make sure that you'll make the right purchasing decisions (and never be snowed by a salesperson's jargon!).

There is no real difference between wired and wireless networks except that in the former information is sent and received using the wire connections and in the latter radio transmissions are used.

In the Beginning There Was the Connection

At its most basic level, a network is simply two or more computers or devices that are connected, as shown in Figure 4.1.

Most modern networks, including the Internet itself, use a protocol called TCP/IP (Transmission Control Protocol/Internet Protocol) to standardize communications.

TCP/IP consists of a number of different so-called *layers* that specify how network transmission are broken down into units, called *packets*, and reassembled, and much more.

TCP/IP is distinct from the mechanism used to convey the communication, meaning that if your network is operating over a wired connection, such as 10BASE-T Ethernet, the TCP/IP transmissions pass "over" the 10BASE-T wires. Similarly, if your network operates using Wi-Fi, TCP/IP transmissions are occurring "on top of" the Wi-Fi signals.

note

There are many devices that can be added to a network. A good example is a network-enabled printer. However, in this chapter I'm pretty much just going to talk about computers and devices generically, and I'll be using the terms "computer" and "device" essentially synonymously.

FIGURE 4.1

The simplest network consists of two connected computers.

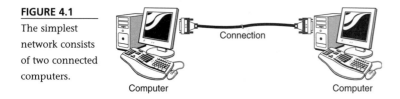

Computer   Connection   Computer

To Serve or Not to Serve

From a practical viewpoint, there are really two different ways that a network can be arranged. The arrangement of a network is called a network *topology*.

The simplest setup is one in which computers share resources such as files, printers, and Internet access on an ad-hoc basis. This is often called a *peer-to-peer* network. At a concept level, which means forgetting about things like whether the connections are made with wires or radio waves, a peer-to-peer network might look like the one shown in Figure 4.2.

FIGURE 4.2

In a peer-to-peer network computers share their resources.

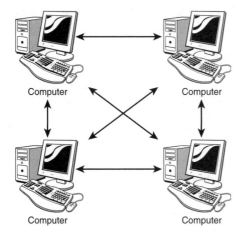

Computer   Computer

Computer   Computer

The other type of network topology, client/server, is somewhat more complex. In this kind of setup, a centralized server computer controls and polices many of the basic functions of the network. For example, the server is used to authenticate users, and to make sure that they have permission to take specific actions in respect to resources. In this kind of setup, only specific users (or kinds of users) may be allowed to modify or delete files. (Although individual computers can share resources directly, the sharing can only take place if the policies established on the server allow it.)

It's hard to enforce this kind of policy on a network without a centralized server. At a conceptual level, forgetting for the moment how the computers are actually connected, a client/server network might look like the one shown in Figure 4.3.

FIGURE 4.3

In a client/server network, a central server controls the resources shared by client computers.

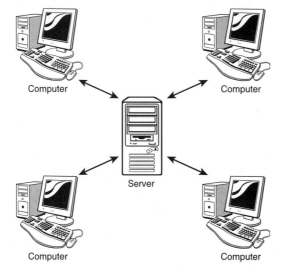

Generally, client/server networks are found in larger-scale enterprise environments. I've described them here in case you work in an environment that has this kind of network. But you probably don't need anything as complex (and expensive) to administer in your home or small office. For the sake of keeping things simple, in this chapter I'll assume you are interested in assembling a peer-to-peer network (or already have such a network that you'd like to add Wi-Fi capabilities to).

Hubs

A hub is a wired device that is the simplest way to connect three or more devices. A *hub* is basically a box that networked computers connect to via several ports. The hub simply replicates the signals coming into each of its ports and sends the signals to each of its other ports. This is another way of saying that the hub receives information from any device plugged into it and transmits the information to all other connected devices. It neither knows nor cares which devices the information is going to. It is up to each individual device to pick up the data meant for it. Plugging four devices into a hub has more or less the same result as connecting the devices to each other.

Typical wired hubs are very inexpensive and come with four or five sockets for connections to computers, but some hubs can have a great many more connections.

Switches

You may have heard the term *switch* in connection with networks. A switch is just an intelligent hub. Like a hub, a switch is a device used to connect computers. But a hub has no smarts, and simply replicates the signals coming in from each computer and passes the signal along to all the connected computers. In contrast, a switch has built-in "intelligence" that understands where to send transmissions.

Small networks usually don't need switches. The busier the network becomes, the more important it is to use intelligent switches rather than hubs.

These days, even lower-end hubs tend to have some intelligence built-in, and are called switches.

Figure 4.4 shows an inexpensive switch in use as a simple hub.

FIGURE 4.4

An inexpensive hub/switch in use.

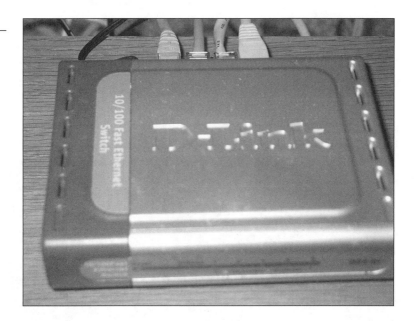

Routers

A router sits between one network and another. If you are interested in setting up a small home or office network, you are likely to use a router to connect the Internet (the largest network of all) with your small network.

Let's suppose you have a cable modem, or a DSL modem, connected to the Internet at your home. The router connects to the modem, and also to your home network as you can see in Figure 4.5.

You should know that most routers also function as hubs/switches, and provide four or five wired connection sockets. (As I'll discuss shortly, routers also come with Wi-Fi.)

If you only plan to connect a few devices to your network, in addition to your modem you may only need a router. You can always add hubs as you need them.

Figure 4.6 shows a wired router in use.

FIGURE 4.5

The router sits in between the Internet connection and your home network.

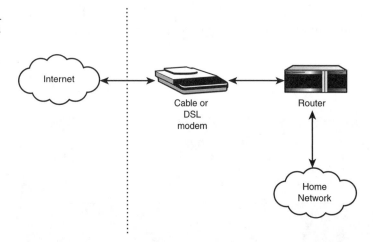

FIGURE 4.6

This wired router distributes an Internet connection across a small network.

Besides their function as a kind of gateway between networks, most routers provide some additional functionality. Routers can make Internet access possible by translating local network addresses to ones that work on the Internet, a feature called Network Address Translation (NAT), and by assigning network addresses to local machines on the fly. This allows the computer (or computers) that make up your home network to interact with servers on the Internet.

Most routers also include features that protect your data by blocking some kinds of information from accessing your network using what is known as a *firewall*. A firewall is a blocking mechanism—either hardware, software, or both—that blocks intruders from scanning for or accessing a network or individual computer. For more about using personal and network firewalls, see Part V, "Securing Your Wi-Fi Computer and Network."

What Is the Network?

How many stars are there in the sky at night, and how vast is the network? Before I wax too poetic, let me get to the point!

Small networks are created by connecting devices, usually via a hub. Larger networks are simply aggregations of small networks, with the small networks connecting to each other, and to the Internet, via routers.

Although these building blocks are very simple, it is obviously possible to create complex network topologies using them. There are also infinite varieties of the possible ways to arrange networks.

You'll have to fit the network topology you create to your physical needs. How many computers do you need, and where?

As an example, Figure 4.7 shows a fairly simple network topology that has seven connected devices and uses a router and two hubs.

FIGURE 4.7

You need to create a network topology based on your physical needs.

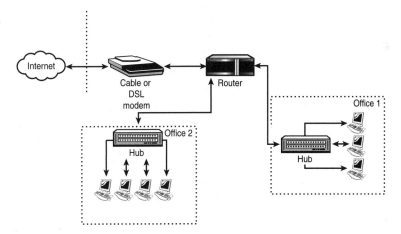

It's worth stepping back for a second and thinking about what you are creating when you string together computers to make a network. By combining computers in a network, you've created a new entity (the network) that has more computing power than any individual device on the network. Hallelujah! It gets even better when you use a router to connect your network to even more powerful external networks such as the Internet. Effectively, you've harnessed the power of many discrete networks running all over the world in every node of your home or small office.

When this kind of network has become commonplace (or "ubiquitous" as they say in marketing departments), what really is the computer? It doesn't really seem right to think of the computer as limited to a single CPU (or box and monitor) when the computer is functioning as part of a network. Maybe the network really is the computer. How much more powerful, and easy, it all becomes when you don't need wires to make the network connections, and you can take your computer (for example, the network) everywhere you go!

Different Ways to Use Wi-Fi in a Network

In the last section, I just discussed some of the implications of "stringing together" computers to make something more powerful than any individual computer on the network. But suppose you didn't have to physically "string" the computers? Well, of course, with Wi-Fi you don't.

If you are going to Wi-Fi–enable a small network, there are really two ways to go about doing it:

- You can use Wi-Fi to connect the entire network.
- You can mix wired and Wi-Fi connections.

Of course, the option of creating an entire network without wires using Wi-Fi is probably only available if you don't already have a network. If you already have a wired network that works, you most likely will not want to replace it. Instead, you'll just want to add Wi-Fi capabilities so that you can go mobile.

For a completely Wi-Fi network, assuming you want to have a shared connection to the Internet, you still need a modem for that purpose. In addition, you'll need a Wi-Fi router to connect to the modem. (You can also buy all-in-one modem and Wi-Fi routers as a single unit, as I'll explain in more detail in Chapter 13, "Buying a Wi-Fi Access Point or Router.")

A Wi-Fi network of this sort will look something like the network shown in Figure 4.8.

Perhaps you already have a working wired network. It probably makes sense to keep it. After all, there's a great saying, "If it ain't broken, don't fix it." Besides which, it probably doesn't make sense to retrofit your network devices for Wi-Fi. You simply may not be able to retrofit some devices, such as older network printers, to work with Wi-Fi. You might not want to go out and buy all new equipment that works with Wi-Fi.

caution

In some cases, household devices such as microwaves and telephones have spectrum conflicts with Wi-Fi networks. This can be another reason to maintain some wired connections in your network.

FIGURE 4.8

This network topology shows a setup that uses only Wi-Fi—and no wires—to connect to the Internet.

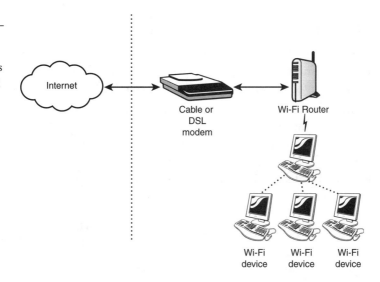

If you are adding Wi-Fi capability to an existing wire-line network, what you have to do is connect a Wi-Fi access point (AP) "after" the router. ("After" means that you need to add the access point on your side of the router, not the Internet side.)

Figure 4.9 shows what a small network with both wired and Wi-Fi capabilities might look like.

FIGURE 4.9

In mixed wire-line and Wi-Fi networks, the Wi-Fi access point needs to be connected "after" the router.

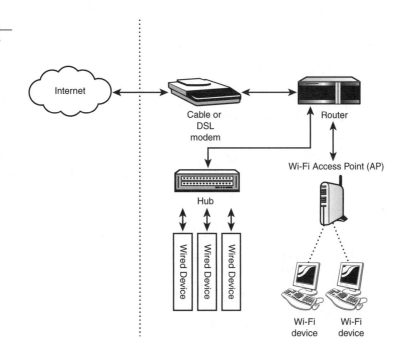

The Equipment You'll Need

Clearly, the equipment you need depends on how you want to set up your network.

If you are planning to add Wi-Fi to a wired network, in addition to all the equipment you need for the wired network, you need a Wi-Fi access point.

If you are not adding Wi-Fi but rather planning to create a completely wireless Wi-Fi network from scratch, you need a Wi-Fi router to connect to your modem. You can buy a DSL or cable modem that is integrated with a Wi-Fi router as a single unit.

tip

You should also know that you can buy a single unit that works as a router for both wired and Wi-Fi computers. See Chapter 13 for more details about this option.

In either case, you'll need Wi-Fi capability on each device that you want to connect to the Wi-Fi network. This can be achieved either by adding a Wi-Fi card to the device, or purchasing devices that come integrated with Wi-Fi already on board.

What's It Going to Cost?

It's really dangerous mentioning dollars-and-cents figures in a book for several reasons. The cost of computer-related devices is constantly changing, mostly going down over time as specific technologies become more mainstream. It's a safe bet that it will cost less to create a Wi-Fi network by the time you read this book than it cost as I was writing it.

It is also true that there are many different possible network configurations, as I've explained earlier in this chapter. Your network is unlikely to be my network. The cost of setting up your Wi-Fi network will largely depend on how many devices you need to equip with Wi-Fi.

That said, although it's still more expensive than setting up a small wired network, the bottom line is that it is relatively cheap to set up a Wi-Fi network, or add Wi-Fi to your existing network.

Here's the ballpark as of today:

- You can get good wireless Wi-Fi cards for laptops for less than $60 U.S. each.
- Adding Wi-Fi to a desktop computer should cost even less than adding it to a laptop.
- Buying a new device with Wi-Fi capabilities should add very little to the incremental cost of the device (perhaps $20–$30).

- There's a great variety in the cost of access points, starting at below $100 and going up to more than $1,000. The primary distinction is the range of Wi-Fi broadcasts. Most likely you can get a perfectly reasonable Wi-Fi access point for a good bit less than $100. By way of comparison, the incredibly nifty and easy-to-install Apple Airport Extreme (802.11g) sells for about $250.

- You can get a good Wi-Fi router for slightly less than $100.

THE ABSOLUTE MINIMUM

Here are the key points to remember from this chapter:

- Networks sound complicated, but they are really simple to understand when you realize they are made up of small building blocks that are all more or less the same.

- You can create entirely Wi-Fi wireless networks, or add Wi-Fi wireless capabilities to an existing network.

- In most cases, you'll want your Wi-Fi network nodes to connect to ordinary DSL or cable modem Internet access.

- It's inexpensive to put together a Wi-Fi network, or to add Wi-Fi capabilities to an existing network.

PART II

SETTING UP YOUR COMPUTER FOR Wi-Fi

5

BUYING A WI-FI LAPTOP

So you've read the preceding section of the book, and feel all excited about Wi-Fi. (Okay, you don't have to have read the previous section, you can be excited all on your own!) You're ready to go out and surf while you sip latte, or read your email at the airport (or better yet, poolside).

There's only one itsy, bitsy tiny problem. You don't have a laptop that works with Wi-Fi.

This chapter assumes that you are getting ready to go out and buy a Wi-Fi mobile computer. (If you want to add Wi-Fi to an existing computer, you should turn to Chapter 8, "Adding Wi-Fi to a Mobile Computer," and Chapter 9, "Wi-Fi on Your Desktop.") You'll learn about the most important considerations when buying a mobile computer, things to look out for, what's really important, and the best places to buy your computer. By the way, in this chapter, I am using the terms "mobile computer," "laptop computer," and "notebook computer" to mean exactly the same thing.

Getting to Know Your Future Wi-Fi Laptop

Laptops work in pretty much the same way as full-sized desktop computers—they just come in a smaller package. Most everything is compressed into the small familiar form factor that you can carry around with you (unlike desktop computers, which typically feature separate display devices and system units).

So when you are learning about your future Mr. (or Ms.) Laptop Computer, you should know that (just like a desktop computer) your laptop will have:

- A system unit (which includes the Central Processing Unit, or CPU)
- A display device (laptop display devices are generally LCD, or Liquid Crystal Display, screens)
- Peripheral devices, probably including a pointing device such as a trackball that takes the place of a mouse, and likely including speakers for sound

The laptop form factor typically includes the system unit, the display, and peripheral devices including a keyboard and pointing devices all in the single small, lightweight package. Essentially, these elements in the laptop are no different from the elements in a desktop computer; it is the small package size, also called the *form factor*, that makes a laptop computer what it is.

Because they are comparatively miniaturized, and require some special engineering features (such as the ability to run on low power), laptops are more expensive than comparable desktops.

The system unit is the part of the computer that makes it a computer. Just like its big brother, the desktop computer, the system unit in your laptop has a number of important components, including:

- A *microprocessor*, also called the *central processing unit* (CPU), which controls the entire computer.
- Short-term storage, called *random access memory* (RAM), which is used to temporarily store instructions and information that can be used by the microprocessor.
- Long-term storage, which is the hard disk used to permanently store important computer programs and data.
- Peripheral devices used to get information in and out of the computer; for example, CD drives, diskette drives, network cards, and Wi-Fi cards.

BATTERY LIFE AND LAPTOPS

Unlike desktop computers, mobile laptops are battery-powered. Laptop computers provide a recharging mechanism for the computer battery when the computer is plugged in.

How long a mobile computer can run on its battery is very important to users because this determines how long the computer can be used without plugging it into an electric socket.

The ability to work without network wires, thanks to Wi-Fi, is kind of undermined if you have to plug into a standard electrical outlet just to get power.

Many factors go into laptop battery life, including the kind of battery used, the power drawn by the CPU, and the power needs of the computer's peripherals. This is an area to investigate carefully before you buy your laptop, based on your needs. So review battery life specifications carefully before you buy.

Some CPUs, such as the Pentium M (sold under the Centrino brand name) from Intel Corporation and the Crusoe from Transmeta Corporation are specially designed to be used in laptops because they have low power draws. (Of course, the CPU isn't the only laptop component that draws power.) You can check to make sure that the laptop you are considering uses one of the microprocessors specially designed for laptops.

Also, rechargeable batteries do wear out, and are expensive to replace. A tip that helps to extend the life of your rechargeable battery is to make sure to fully charge and fully discharge the battery (by using the laptop) when you first get the laptop.

If you already own a laptop, you can use the software built into the operating system to find out about the microprocessor, RAM, and other components that are part of your computer.

To do this on a Windows laptop, right-click the My Computer icon on your desktop (in Windows XP you'll probably find the My Computer icon on the Start menu, not your desktop). The General tab of the System Properties dialog will open, as shown in Figure 5.1.

FIGURE 5.1

You can find information about a Windows laptop's hardware using the System Properties dialog.

The General tab of the System Properties dialog, shown in Figure 5.1, provides information about the microprocessor, RAM, and operating system in use. Using the Device Manager tab of the same Systems Properties dialog, you can find out the details of components and peripheral devices used.

If you are running Windows XP, finding the Device Manager information works a little differently. With the System Properties dialog open, click the Hardware tab (shown in Figure 5.2).

FIGURE 5.2

In Windows XP, the Hardware tab of the System Properties dialog is used to access the Device Manager.

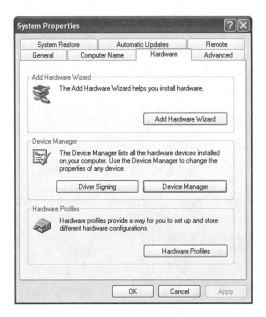

Next, click the Device Manager button. The Device Manager window, showing detailed information about your system opens as shown in Figure 5.3.

It's likely that one of the things you'll focus on most when deciding which laptop to buy is the microprocessor. This makes sense because the speed of the CPU largely determines how fast the computer can perform operations.

With laptops, the CPU is particularly important. First of all, as I mentioned earlier, CPUs specially designed for use in laptops use less power—and therefore aren't as draining on battery life. Secondly, these microprocessors—including the Centrino and Crusoe series—don't run as hot as

tip

Alternatively, you can access the System Properties dialog using the System applet in Windows Control Panel. To open the Windows 9x/Me Control Panel, open the Start menu and click Settings, Control Panel. In Windows XP, click Start, Control Panel.

CPUs intended for desktops. This is a good thing because if a microprocessor runs hot the system needs additional mechanisms, such as fans, to cool itself down. All of a sudden, your mobile laptop has become about as mobile as a brick, a heavy brick. They can throw your back out if you have to carry them very far! You certainly don't want to be lugging a heavy brick that gets hot enough to fry an egg (or your legs). Hot laptops are a hazard to themselves, and their surroundings. They have been known to start fires! So make sure your laptop is built around a central processing unit that is appropriate for mobile computing.

Just as brute brawn isn't everything in life, you probably would not be surprised to learn that the raw speed of the CPU isn't the only factor in how speedily a laptop performs its appointed tasks. For many applications, the amount of RAM available on the computer is actually more important than the CPU speed. In another example, for watching movies, besides the quality of the video screen, the most important hardware is the video display subsystem, not the CPU.

Mac users can display the same information by clicking About This Mac on the Apple menu. More extensive component and peripheral information is available by clicking the More Info button, which you'll see when the About This Mac window is open. Clicking the More Info button opens the System Profiler application, which provides extensive information about the hardware (and software) that is running.

FIGURE 5.3

In Windows XP, the Hardware tab of the System Properties dialog is used to access the Device Manager.

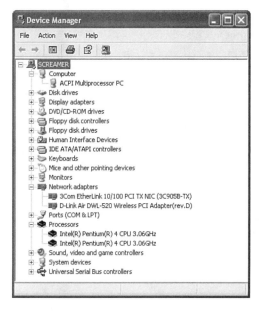

Trade-Offs

A friend of mine quipped a number of years ago that "the computer you really want always costs $5,000." Over time, the cost has come down, and you can certainly buy a high-end laptop for less than $2,000 today. But the point of the joke is still true. Unless money is absolutely no issue for you, you will have to make same trade-offs such as:

- Faster CPU or more RAM
- Lighter weight or less expensive
- Paying more for a brand name or less for an off-brand product
- Bigger and better display or less cost

For the most part, these choices will depend on your wallet. But a mobile laptop is a specialized computer, and some of the trade-offs really depend on how you will use the system. For me, it is extremely important to have a lightweight, small machine, but I also wanted a reasonable size keyboard. I chose an IBM model accordingly, and it has worked well on the road for me, and as a Wi-Fi machine—but there were trade-offs involved. For one thing, my IBM machine doesn't have a CD-ROM drive on board. If I want to read a CD, I have to connect an external drive via a USB port. (But I can leave it behind on road trips if I don't think I'm going to need it.)

The general bottom line is: do an assessment of what really matters to you, and purchase accordingly (see the sidebar "What Really Matters" for more tips on this topic).

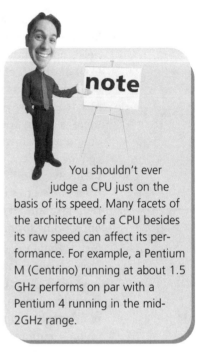

You shouldn't ever judge a CPU just on the basis of its speed. Many facets of the architecture of a CPU besides its raw speed can affect its performance. For example, a Pentium M (Centrino) running at about 1.5 GHz performs on par with a Pentium 4 running in the mid-2GHz range.

I purchased my IBM laptop a number of years ago, so the trade-off I made regarding my CD-ROM drive is by way of example. Almost any laptop purchased today will have a built-in DVD/CD drive.

WHAT'S REALLY IMPORTANT

As I've noted, you'll have to make the final decision on what's really important to you in a Wi-Fi laptop. To get another viewpoint on how to make this decision, I asked a friend of mine who is an expert consultant and has advised thousands of computer purchasers for her words of wisdom. Here's what the expert says:

- Buy a well-known name brand, such as Apple, Dell, or IBM.

- Don't be too cheap. You can expect a good piece of equipment to last a long time, so buy one that is rugged and with enough power.

- That said, you don't need the latest cutting-edge CPU.

- You should buy one with a CPU designed for mobile computing.

- If your mobile is too heavy to take with you, you'll end up leaving it at home. Pay special attention to weight.

- Buy a system with at least 512MB of RAM (by the way, 256 MB is the minimum you can get on a Mac portable).

- Get at least a 40GB hard drive.

- Ergonomics are important. Buy a model with a screen you like to look at, and a keyboard and other input devices that are comfortable for you to use.

- Forget about cute. This is a computer, not a fashion accessory. Don't buy a computer because you like its color or shape.

To Mac or Not To Mac?

It's not part of my intention here to get into religious wars. People take the question of whether to buy an Apple Macintosh or a Microsoft Windows machine with great fervor. Perhaps they should. This really may matter a great deal more than the question of which end to open an egg!

Although Macs and Windows machines have some real differences, the truth is that as microcomputers they are really far more alike than they are different.

Both Mac and Windows mobile computers work just fine with Wi-Fi!

If you are already familiar with either the Mac or Windows, you should probably stick with what you know. It doesn't really make particular sense to use the occasion of buying a Wi-Fi laptop to switch operating systems.

Sticking with what you know is good advice, and probably settles the question for you. In case it doesn't, let me give you my impressions (which are sure to anger diehards in both camps):

- Macs are more elegantly designed and engineered than Windows machines.
- Macs cost a bit more.
- There are fewer options with Macs, which is good and bad: Buying is simpler, but you have less choice about what you buy.
- Mac OS X machines work seamlessly with Wi-Fi, without any need for software configuration (this isn't always true of Windows machines).
- Mac mice don't have a second button or a wheel, which is too darn bad (particularly the wheel). Apple, please take note: We like our mouse wheels! The good news: You can buy a two-button mouse with a wheel for your Apple from third-party manufacturers.
- Some software runs only on the Mac, and other software (actually, more of it) will run on Windows but not the Mac. While most of the standard stuff (such as Microsoft Word for the MAC OS or for Windows) runs perfectly fine on either OS, you should check to make sure that there isn't some specialized program you need to run that requires one OS or the other. (Windows emulators running on the Mac work reasonably well to run an occasional Windows program on the MAC, but you won't happy with this if you need to run a lot of Windows programs.)

> **tip**
>
> Apple calls Wi-Fi "Airport" in its own material. In other words, what Apple calls Airport is just plain vanilla 802.11b. Apple's term for devices that support 802.11b and 802.11g Wi-Fi is "AirPort Extreme."

So, as always in life, the choice is yours: to Mac, or not to Mac, in other words, whether to Windows? Whichever you choose, I'm sure you'll enjoy using it with Wi-Fi.

Buying a Mac with Wi-Fi

Supposedly, Henry Ford said in regard to his Model T, "Any customer can have a car painted any color that he wants so long as it is black." (He is also supposed to have said, "History is bunk!" but that's a matter for another time.)

> **tip**
>
> Check to see if you are entitled to a student discount from Apple when purchasing your Mac. You'll find more information about the Student Program at http://developer.apple.com/students/index.html/.

It's somewhat unfair to the Mac to say that you can only have it one way because it is possible to customize systems. But for the most part there is no real reason to customize a system, and at any given time there are really only a handful of systems to choose from. This is as much good news as bad news because it makes purchasing a Mac a much less daunting proposition than purchasing a Windows computer.

There's also not as wide a choice of vendor. You pretty much may as well buy your Mac directly from the Apple Corporation. Purchasing a system online via the Internet, over the telephone, or in one of Apple's stores all work equally well, so it's just a question of which is most convenient for you.

To view the Mac laptops that are currently available, go to www.apple.com. Next, click the Store tab at the top of the screen. Apple products will be displayed as shown in Figure 5.4.

In the Portables category at the top of the screen shown in Figure 5.4 you can see iBooks and PowerBooks. Depending on your needs and personal tastes, all of the machines listed in this category are adequately equipped. All of these machines can be used with Wi-Fi, although some of them do require an additional card. You should consider this as an additional expense when comparing prices. You can add an AirPort card (802.11b Wi-Fi) to a system for $79 and an Airport Extreme card (dual 802.11b and 802.11g) to a system for $99.

Click on each of the portables shown for further description. If the detailed description says "AirPort Extreme ready," it means that the portable will work with both the 802.11b and 802.11g varieties of Wi-Fi. (See Chapter 2, "Understanding Wi-Fi," for more information about 802.11b and 802.11g.)

If the system description says that "AirPort Extreme" is built in, as for example in the two PowerBook machines shown on the right side of Figure 5.5, it means that 802.11b and 802.11g Wi-Fi are already included in the system.

note

Feel free to mix and match your retail buying experience. It makes sense to research your Mac on the Web, then order and pick it up at a store. On the other hand, if you like to have a "touch and feel" sense for things before you buy them, you can go to an Apple company store to play with the various systems that are available. (You can find an Apple retail store at www.apple.com/retail/.)

It's then up to you to decide whether it is more convenient to pick your Mac up at the store or have it delivered.

FIGURE 5.4

By clicking on the Store tab at the Apple site, you can see a catalog of currently available Macs.

FIGURE 5.5

The PowerBook 15" and 17" laptops shown on the right have AirPort Extreme (Wi-Fi) built-in whereas the 15" and smaller notebooks on the left do not.

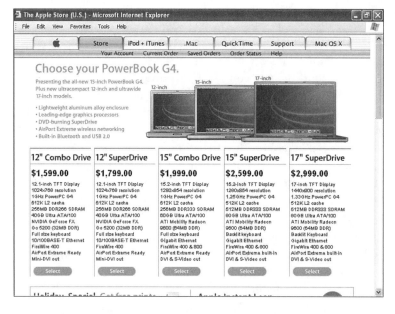

Buying a Windows Notebook with Integrated Wi-Fi

Welcome to the wild and wonderful world of buying a Windows mobile computer! Unlike the straightforward universe of the Mac, there are innumerable brands of Windows computers you can buy, in many different configurations. You can also reasonably buy these systems from a veritable cornucopia of vendors, both online and in the brick-and-mortar world.

Prices vary tremendously, so it pays to shop carefully.

The sidebar "What's Really Important" earlier in this chapter gave one expert's advice about how to shop for a Wi-Fi laptop. Because there are so many hardware options available with Windows PCs, it is worth reiterating the key advice about hardware specifications:

- Don't buy an off-brand. Stick with the majors.
- Be concerned with weight, battery life, and durability.
- Do not pay too much attention to cute design and colors.
- Buy a laptop with a CPU specially designed for mobile computers.
- Buy a laptop with Wi-Fi already integrated on board.
- Get at least 512MB of RAM with your system.
- Get a 40GB or larger hard drive.

As you do your comparison shopping, you'll see that even with these guidelines as a starting place, there's a huge variety of potential systems, vendors, and pricing. So get ready to hunker down and be your own best advocate!

Where to Buy

There are numerous options about where to buy your laptop. You can purchase a machine

- Directly from the manufacturer, using the Internet or a catalog and telephone
- Online or using a catalog from a computer reseller
- At a "real" store such as a computer manufacturer's store, a consumer electronics store, a computer store, or an office supply store

There's nothing wrong with any of these options. It all depends on what you are most comfortable with, and what works best for you. It's even okay to mix and match: You can check equipment out in a brick-and-mortar store, and then buy it online.

Do make sure you buy your Wi-Fi laptop from a reputable vendor who will make things right if there is a problem. It's a fact that the majority of hardware problems occur within the first twenty-four hours of use, so you want to be sure the matter will be easily taken care of if you do happen to buy a lemon.

It's easy to go to an online manufacturer's site to buy your Wi-Fi computer. For example, if you choose the Compare All Notebooks option on www.dell.com, you'll see the entire Dell current laptop offerings shown in Figure 5.6.

If you look at the models shown once you've clicked Compare All Notebooks, you'll see on the right side two with integrated Wi-Fi. These models are both designated with an "M" suffix (the 300M and the 600M) and use an Intel-supplied Centrino CPU. (You may have to scroll down the page to see these models.)

tip

You may be offered a floor sample, demo model, or reconditioned model (or the same thing by some other name) at a very substantial discount. This is a place for the old saying, "Buyer Beware!" to come into play. I'd recommend that you avoid any such scenario in which the laptop you are thinking of buying has been used and turned off and on, even if it is reconditioned (or factory certified, whatever that means!).

FIGURE 5.6

By choosing Compare All Notebooks on the Dell site, you can get information about all the currently available laptops.

When you configure your Dell computer, you can always elect to have one of the other models that does not come with integrated Wi-Fi equipped with a Wi-Fi card.

On www.ibm.com, the Notebook finder, shown in Figure 5.7, is an excellent way to sort through the available models.

By clicking the Wi-Fi link shown at the bottom of the Select a Feature box shown in Figure 5.7, you will be presented with a feature selection list for all the models that are Wi-Fi enabled (see Figure 5.8).

With your choices restricted to models that are Wi-Fi enabled, you can now assemble a system that otherwise meets your needs. In this example, there are so many choices of IBM laptops that are Wi-Fi enabled, it's a good idea to simplify your results by using additional criteria, like the price range you are interested in, or by specifying a particular CPU.

tip

The first thing you should do when you get your laptop is run it for 24 hours. This should disclose most latent problems in the hardware. Some of this running time should be with the laptop on battery power (discharging) and some should be spent recharging with the laptop plugged into an electrical socket. You should aim to use this time to "cure" the battery by fully discharging and recharging it twice (this will extend battery life).

FIGURE 5.7

IBM's Notebook finder helps you sort through models.

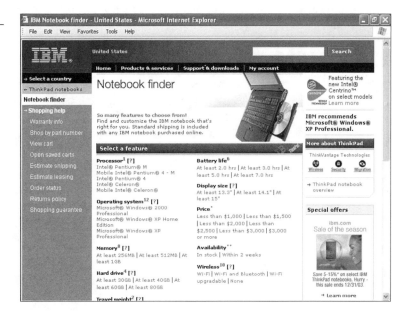

FIGURE 5.8

By selecting Wi-Fi, you can sort through all the models that are Wi-Fi enabled.

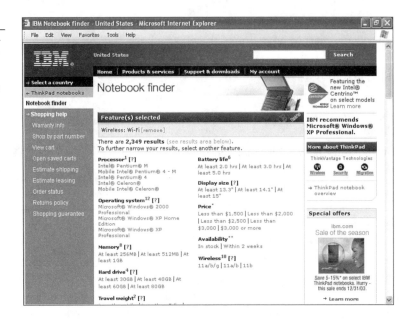

If you want to compare Wi-Fi notebook computers in general, a good resource to use is www.cnet.com. You can then enter a search term such as "Wi-Fi Notebook." The results will provide a great deal of pricing and review information about a wide variety of products (see Figure 5.9).

FIGURE 5.9

CNET provides an easy way to compare multiple brands of Wi-Fi notebooks.

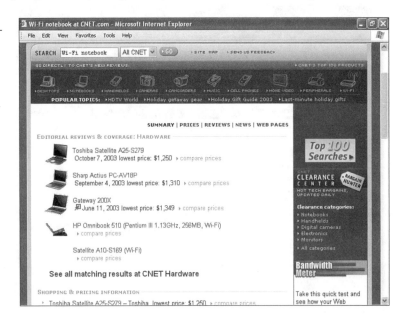

From within CNET, you can generally click on links to specific retailers to buy online at the prices quoted in the CNET comparisons.

A final point is that simply entering a phrase such as "Wi-Fi Notebook" into a Web search engine such as Google or Yahoo produces a great many links for researching Wi-Fi equipment and purchasing Wi-Fi notebooks. You should be aware that some of these links are paid for against specific keywords, such as "Wi-Fi," and amount to a purchased advertisement.

Of course, you may prefer to use Wi-Fi with a device that is really small such as a PDA (Personal Digital Assistant). You'll find information about buying a Wi-Fi PDA Pocket PC in Chapter 6, "Buying a Wi-Fi PDA."

A LAPTOP WITH INTERNAL WI-FI VERSUS ADDING WI-FI

It's better to buy a machine with Wi-Fi already onboard than to add a Wi-Fi card to an existing computer. Not only will you save a little money (specifying Wi-Fi when you buy a new computer costs virtually nothing) but there are also some other advantages. These include

- The PC slot on your laptop will not be taken up by a Wi-Fi card, a good thing if you need to use the slot for other purposes.

- Laptops intended for use with Wi-Fi generally come with external antennas that are better than the ones that come with Wi-Fi PC Cards.

- You don't have to worry about configuring Wi-Fi software because it will come already loaded on your new computer.

THE ABSOLUTE MINIMUM

Here are the key points to remember from this chapter:

- Buying a Wi-Fi laptop computer can seem daunting, but it's not really!

- Mac and Windows Wi-Fi laptops are both good, so which you choose to buy is simply a matter of your personal preference (if in doubt, try both before you buy).

- Buy your Mac directly from Apple, either over the Internet or in an Apple company store.

- Worry about weight, ruggedness, and battery life in a laptop, not cuteness.

- You can buy a Windows Wi-Fi notebook from a variety of sources including the manufacturer.

- It's very convenient to shop for a Wi-Fi laptop online, although you may want to visit a store to handle one before you buy it.

- You may need to read specifications with some care, but you should be able to tell if a notebook computer has integrated Wi-Fi.

6

Buying a Wi-Fi PDA

Compared to a desktop computer, a laptop is lightweight. But you don't even have to lug a "lightweight" laptop to take advantage of Wi-Fi.

In this chapter, I'll take a look at the category of computing devices that are far smaller and lighter than laptop computers. These devices are sometimes called **handheld** computers, or Personal Digital Assistants (PDAs).

In this chapter I'll explain what handheld computers are good for, how they differ from one another, what they can't do so well, and what you should look out for when buying a PDA or Pocket PC to use with Wi-Fi.

Understanding Handheld Computers

The main purpose of a handheld computer is to help you organize your life. All handheld computers include applications that allow you to

- Manage and organize appointments using calendar and datebook software. This is one of the most important handheld applications. You can enter meetings, appointments, and much more in a format analogous to a "Day-Timer" or similar book-style engagement calendar. Handheld calendar software also allows you to enter repeating events, a great way to track standing appointments, birthdays, and more.

- Enter notes, memos, or even random poetic musings with a memo pad application.

- Perform mathematical operations with a calculator.

- Track the things you need to do with a task list application.

- Manage your contacts and their information with an address book application.

Besides these core applications found in some form or other on all handheld computers, most handhelds also provide a fair number of games and interesting (or useful) applications. Some of the applications ship with the device, but others must be downloaded onto it, usually when the device is attached, or "synched" to a desktop (or laptop) computer, usually via a so-called cradle that is connected using a USB connection to the desktop computer. For example, I can use my Palm PDA to track the phases of the moon and—perhaps more usefully in the San Francisco Bay Area where I live—take the BART (Bay Area Rapid Transit) schedule with me.

Many people also use handheld devices to

- Send and receive email.

- Play music.

- Play games.

- Use mapping software and GPS features to navigate.

- Surf the Internet (depending on the handheld, due to display limitations, your experience of the Web won't be as rich as it is when using your desktop).

It may state the obvious, but sending and receiving email, and cruising the Internet, can only be achieved with a handheld device if the device is connected to the Internet. This is one place where Wi-Fi comes in.

You can manage email in a delayed fashion when a handheld is synched to the desktop. The process works like this: You compose your email wherever you happen to be, and then it gets sent when you connect to your computer (which has an Internet connection). The reverse also works: You can download accumulated emails when your handheld is synched to your computer, and then read the emails wherever you happen to be with your handheld.

But to send and receive emails in real time with your handheld, the handheld must be connected to the Internet using wireless transmissions. Although some devices, such as the BlackBerry, use a proprietary protocol to connect to proprietary network, mostly this means equipping your handheld with Wi-Fi and connecting to a Wi-Fi hotspot (for more about connecting to a Wi-Fi hotspot, see Chapter 3, "Hitting the Road with Wi-Fi").

WHAT IS THE BLACKBERRY?

The BlackBerry from Research in Motion is a popular wireless handheld that includes a small integrated keyboard. BlackBerry devices are primarily used by mobile professionals for secure wireless access to email, corporate data, telephone communication, and the Web.

BlackBerrys do not use Wi-Fi to connect to the Web. Instead they use private, subscriber networks on parts of the radio spectrum that are licensed.

For the most part, use of the BlackBerry is an enterprise thing. In other words, you may well be given one to use for business purposes by your company, but most people don't go out and sign up for one as individuals.

Handhelds themselves differ from laptop PCs in a number of important areas:

- Operating system (which I'll be getting to shortly)
- Size and quality of display
- Input devices (keyboards or handwriting)

In terms of input devices, some PDAs provide a miniature external keyboard that you can type on like a regular computer if your fingers are sufficiently deft. Other PDAs require that you learn a special kind of handwriting (called Graffiti on Palm OS devices) or provide written character recognition (Pocket PC). In addition, PDAs such as Palm OS devices that expect you to enter text using specially formulated characters and a special stylus also provide an alternative: an onscreen "keyboard" in which "keys" can be tapped using the stylus. Many of these devices also have the option of adding a physical keyboard, either thumb-board or collapsible full keyboard, usually manufactured by a third party.

Comparing Operating Systems

The two dominant operating systems for handheld computers are Pocket PC OS (Operating System) from Microsoft and Palm OS from PalmSource. Both operating systems are available on a wide variety of handhelds from various manufacturers.

Your preference between these two operating system is a matter of personal taste—and also, for some, just as much a "religious" issue as the choice between Mac and Windows.

It's risky to generalize in the context of a choice about which different people have strong opinions. But, treading where angels fear to go, here are my thoughts on the comparison of the two:

- Pocket PC is, well, a version of Windows, so to a great extent it looks and feels like Windows.

- Both Palm OS 5 and Pocket PC are capable of multitasking, and Palms and Pocket PCs are indistinguishable in their capabilities at this point.

- Pocket PCs are generally more expandable and can be more easily configured for wireless capabilities.

- Pocket PCs are generally somewhat larger and more expensive than Palm OS PDAs.

- Software for the Pocket PC OS has been specially created for the handheld device. It's not the same software that runs on desktop and laptop Windows computers, and tends to be a little more expensive than Palm OS software.

- Palm OS PDAs have the benefit of a sort of elegant simplicity. Although they may not have as many optional features, they can be easier to learn, and some people think they are more stable.

The Right Handheld for You

If you like Windows, and expect to try to use your handheld device in much the same way you would use a laptop, probably a Pocket PC OS is best for you. But don't expect a handheld to have the ruggedness or functionality of a full-fledged computer.

If compactness and simplicity are what is most important to you, and you realize that you will be using your handheld primarily as a portable organizer, a PDA running the Palm OS would probably suit you better.

Ultimately, when all is said and done, the best thing you can do is play with each kind of device to see which you like best. If you don't have friends who carry these, a trip to a store is the best way to try out different kinds of handheld devices.

Handhelds and Wi-Fi

With the ongoing ubiquity of Wi-Fi, it makes a great deal of sense to plan to use your handheld with Wi-Fi. If your handheld is Wi-Fi enabled, you will have the option of using it to connect on the road, in hotels, and in a wide range of places.

Pocket PCs present a slightly wider range of choices as of the present writing for Wi-Fi–enabled handhelds (although this may change by the time you read this book). You can buy Pocket PCs from HP, Toshiba, and others that feature integrated Wi-Fi. Figure 6.1 shows a popular model from HP.

FIGURE 6.1

HP's iPaq H4355 Pocket PC features integrated Wi-Fi.

Even if your Pocket PC doesn't come with integrated Wi-Fi, you can add Wi-Fi using a Compact Flash card.

Most Pocket PCs provide a Compact Flash expansion slot, originally intended for adding extra memory to the handheld device. You may be familiar with Compact Flash cards from adding one to a digital camera to add extra memory to store more photos.

By adding a Wi-Fi Compact Flash card such as the one from SanDisk shown in Figure 6.2 to the Compact Flash expansion slot, you'll be able to use the Pocket PC with Wi-Fi.

note

Compact Flash (CF) cards, which were invented by SanDisk, are the world's most popular removable mass storage devices. A Compact Flash card is about the size of a matchbook and only weighs half an ounce.

FIGURE 6.2

This Compact Flash card from SanDisk can be used to add Wi-Fi capabilities to a handheld device.

Figure 6.3 shows the Wi-Fi Compact Flash card added to a handheld device.

FIGURE 6.3

The Wi-Fi card fits in the Compact Flash expansion slot on the handheld.

There are fewer Palm OS PDAs that support Wi-Fi (at least at this point in time) than there are Pocket PCs. One Palm PDA with integrated Wi-Fi is the Tungsten C from Palm, shown in Figure 6.4.

FIGURE 6.4

Palm's Tungsten C features integrated Wi-Fi.

You might also want to consider the Sony UX50 CLIE, shown in Figure 6.5, which has been called "the Swiss Army knife of PDAs," because it has many features and functions—and a high price to match!

Besides built-in Wi-Fi, this gadget… er, device… comes with a camera, microphone, hi-fidelity sound and video, and multiple wireless communications spectrums (Bluetooth in addition to Wi-Fi). It will also do the dishes (only kidding)!

FIGURE 6.5

The Sony UX50 CLIE is an upper-end Palm OS PDA featuring integrated Wi-Fi.

Certainly, the trend is toward more Pocket PCs and PDAs that feature integrated Wi-Fi, so you should research not only what is currently available when you decide to shop for a handheld device, but also what products PDA manufacturers plan to release over the next few months (sometimes these new products are worth waiting for).

Accessing Wi-Fi

Accessing a Wi-Fi hotspot with your handheld is pretty much like accessing a Wi-Fi hotspot with a laptop (which was explained in Chapter 3). You'll need to supply a network identification, or SSID. If you don't know this in advance, your Wi-Fi software will scan for available Wi-Fi broadcasts. The details of each device's Wi-Fi software may be slightly different, but for the most part, to connect, all you need to do is activate the Wi-Fi software, generally by clicking on it, and following directions. Some Wi-Fi networks do also require an encryption code for access, as I'll explain in more detail in Part V, "Securing Your Wi-Fi Computer and Network."

It's worth saying that using Wi-Fi to access the Internet with a handheld device is not for everyone. Sure, we've all seen people using a handheld to type email at 100 words a minute, and surfing the Web with aplomb using the most miniature of Web browsing screens. But if you are like me (I sometimes think I must have all ten thumbs), I really prefer to work with a larger keyboard. (Even laptop keyboards are often awkward for me to use!) I also like to see Web sites in a large size.

Sometimes, particularly when I'm traveling, this is just not possible, and I'm glad to have any kind of device that I can use to connect. The tradeoff is that a handheld is small enough that carrying it with you is no big deal, whereas if you had to lug a bigger computer, you might not have it along when you want it.

This comes down to a personal choice. How do you like to work? Some people are probably naturally handheld people, and others are just not.

THE ABSOLUTE MINIMUM

Here are the key points to remember from this chapter:

- Handheld computers can do many things, but they are not a substitute for laptop or desktop computers.

- Personal organization is what handhelds do best.

- Handhelds come in two principal flavors: Pocket PCs running a Windows mobile operating system and Palm PDAs, running a Palm operating system. Which you prefer is very much a matter of personal taste.

- It's best to buy a handheld with integrated Wi-Fi if you plan to use Wi-Fi, but in some cases you can connect by adding a Wi-Fi Compact Flash card to the handheld's Compact Flash expansion slot.

- Connecting to a Wi-Fi hotspot with a handheld is pretty much like connecting to Wi-Fi with a laptop.

7

PLAYING WITH WI-FI GADGETS

Ubiquitous Wi-Fi: Imagine a future in which wireless connectivity is everywhere. Wi-Fi connects your computers, printers, refrigerators, home entertainment systems, burglar alarms, and more. This imagined future is very real and is just around the corner. But it's not quite here yet: Some of these applications are still the province of bleeding-edge people for whom technology is a hobby. These people want the latest and greatest. They want to have it first, and are willing to go to great lengths to be the first on their block with new technology "toys."

So a bit of caution is in order. Not all Wi-Fi applications are ready for prime time.

Bearing today's reality in mind, this chapter takes a look at the Wi-Fi home of tomorrow from two perspectives:

- What Wi-Fi applications can you use and enjoy today?

- A little further out on the curve, how is Wi-Fi likely to shape our lives tomorrow?

The Future of Wi-Fi

It's dangerous to predict the future. I'll take that chance and risk being wrong! Here's what I think is a cheap prediction.

Within 10 years, all new appliances, home electronics, and gadgets will be equipped in the factory with wireless networking, probably of a sort that meets whatever the Wi-Fi standards of the day are. This will mean that this equipment—and more, practically anything you can thing of—will be able to

- Exchange information with other devices. For example, your burglar alarm can "talk" to your smoke detector and your stove.
- Receive commands from across a network.

The benefits of these two abilities are greater than you might think. They include

- Greater automation because all kinds of machines will be better able to work with one another.
- More effective use of data because it can be shared between numerous devices.
- Better personal control of your environment using the power of your computer. You will be able to exercise this control at home using internal networks, and remotely via an Internet connection. For example, you might use Wi-Fi and an Internet connection to set the temperature in your house from your office before you come home.

As you'll see in this chapter, some of this stuff you can do right now. For example, it's easy to add a Wi-Fi receiver to your home entertainment center so that you can use your Internet connection and Wi-Fi network to stream audio and video to your amplifier and/or television.

The software and hardware that enables you to use Wi-Fi in some of these ways has yet to be manufactured. But there's a plethora of new Wi-Fi applications coming down the pike! It's clear today what some of these applications are. Others will probably be a surprise. But surprise is what to expect from Wi-Fi as a disruptive technology that has achieved many things that were never expected.

By learning now about Wi-Fi, what it is, and what it can do, you'll be ahead of the curve when new Wi-Fi applications appear.

In this chapter, I'll show you what you can do easily today. I'll also show you some things that are in the works (and which you could put together if you were a devoted hobbyist). You'll undoubtedly see commercial versions of these Wi-Fi applications in the next few years. Finally, from time to time I'll mention Wi-Fi applications that aren't really being tried yet.

Transmitting Photos with Wi-Fi

Taking pictures used to be a cumbersome affair. Well, not quite as bad as the nineteenth-century plate cameras with black cloths and back-breaking weight. But still, you had to load film into the camera, wind it, rewind it, remember not to open the camera until the film had been rewound, and get the film to a photo lab. Some time later—it might be hours, and it might be days—your photographs would be ready. If you wanted to share them with a friend, you had to go back to the photo lab and have new prints made.

The best picture is the one you take. If you have to remember to take a camera and all the accessories with you, you may never take that picture.

Digital photography has, of course, made all this much easier. Your pictures are ready for viewing as soon as you take them. You can easily make prints using a color printer either by downloading the photos to your computer or (with some hardware) directly printing from your digital camera to your printer. Best of all, you can immediately correct problems in your digital photos such as "red-eye" by using photo retouching software such as Photoshop Elements.

Wi-Fi takes the digital photography revolution to the next step.

With Wi-Fi, you can transmit your pictures for viewing anywhere from anywhere. This has implications in many different areas, including:

- Data gathering for professionals: In a variety of professional fields, such as medicine, the ability to easily transmit photographs can be used in examinations, consultations, and for general communication.

- Teaching: The ability to instantly compare visuals with someone who is not present will be very useful in many educational contexts. For example, you could show a biology sample from your course lab work to a teacher at a distant location and get immediate feedback.

- Amateur photography: The ability to send and receive images seamlessly from a wide variety of devices will change the way people use photography. People will reach for a Wi-Fi–enabled device that also takes pictures, such as a PDA or telephone, in much the way they reach for a pen and notepad today.

In this section, we'll have a look at three digital photography Wi-Fi devices that can be purchased today. They are a PDA with built-in Wi-Fi and a digital camera, a Wi-Fi network camera that lets users view a video stream, and a Wi-Fi picture frame that can be used to display your photo library.

Camera, Wi-Fi, and PDA All-In-One

For many years, I was a professional photographer. This meant that I got used to schlepping heavy bags filled with camera bodies, lenses, filters, light meters, and other gadgets wherever I went.

These days when I travel, I no longer take pictures for a living, so I don't have to carry all this stuff. Besides, I like to travel light. This means that I don't usually carry a camera. But the best picture is the one you end up taking, meaning if you don't have a way to take the picture, you won't take it. PDA and cell phone manufacturers have begun to discover that it's easy to add digital photographic capabilities to their devices.

For example, the Sony PDA shown in Figure 7.1 includes a digital camera.

The digital camera built into the Sony PDA has a maximum resolution of 0.3 megapixels. This isn't capable of producing images with the quality of even a middle-of-the-road digital camera, but it also isn't half bad. In other words, this built-in digital camera isn't of true artistic quality, but will be good enough for many uses.

FIGURE 7.1

This Sony hand-held PDA comes with a built-in digital camera and a Wi-Fi connection.

If I had this lightweight all-in-one PDA with me on the road, and I saw something worth photographing, it would be a snap to do so. I'd always have this camera with me without having to lug an additional piece of hardware!

Best of all, the next time I was within range of a Wi-Fi hotspot, perhaps at a coffee shop or in an airport, I could "beam" my photographic masterpiece to my friends right away without delay!

It's increasingly common for digital cameras to be built into cell phones. At the present time, most of these phones don't support Wi-Fi, and users are expected to transmit the photos they take using the cell phone provider's proprietary network. (For example, Sprint has been heavily promoting its networks for use with digital photos taken using a cell "phone.") However, it is undoubtedly the case that cell phones that alternatively support Wi-Fi will soon be available. These phones will likely also include digital cameras.

Streaming Video with Wi-Fi

Toshiba (and other manufacturers) sell network cameras that let users view streaming video across networks and the Internet. These video cameras, often called Web cams or Net cams, can be bought with integrated Wi-Fi. For example, the Toshiba models shown in Figure 7.2 both come with integrated Wi-Fi.

FIGURE 7.2

The Toshiba Net cams shown come with integrated Wi-Fi.

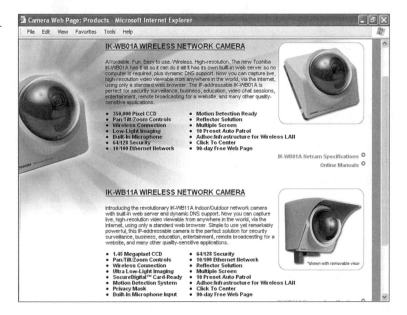

The video taken with these cameras can be viewed using Wi-Fi across a network without wires, so it's easy to place these cameras in positions that would otherwise be awkward if you had to connect a physical network cable. They are really easy to install.

One popular use for these cameras is for surveillance as part of a security system. The camera can be set to broadcast footage when motion is detected.

By the way, the camera is also equipped with a backup storage device in case the network goes down. This also limits possible security problems. (For more information about Wi-Fi and security, see Part V, "Securing Your Wi-Fi Computer and Network.")

The video from these Net cams can also be viewed across the Internet. You don't need to worry about complicated Internet configuration issues.

note

A common use of these wireless cameras is as a kind of baby monitor. Parents can use them to keep track of children (and their babysitters). Best of all, they can view the footage from the computer desktops.

Toshiba makes a variety of services available to users of their Net cams, including a directory of live cameras that can be viewed, and customizable home pages for Net cam owners. For a fee, owners can set up chat services and credit card payments. So if you've ever dreamed of setting up your own Web cam in a dormitory room, or somewhere else, it's easy to do so using Wi-Fi. Wires are not included, because you don't need them any more!

The Net cam can operate across any high-speed Internet connection.

Framing Pictures with Wi-Fi

The Wi-Fi digital picture frame is an interesting new product. Wallflower Systems, `www.wallflower.com`, is one of the pioneers in this category of product.

Here's how the Wallflower digital picture frame works. Inside the picture frame, the product includes a high-quality LCD display, a hard drive, and Wi-Fi capability. The digital picture frame displays the pictures stored on its hard drive in the way you specify, for example, as a slide show. With its Wi-Fi capabilities it scans for Wi-Fi networks. After your Wi-Fi network has been discovered, it connects to it (you may have to supply the encryption key) and copies the digital photos that have been placed in a particular folder onto its hard drive.

When you are working from a computer on the Wi-Fi network, to add an image to the digital picture frame, you just copy it into the appropriate folder.

What a great way to display your pictures in your home (for example, on the living room fireplace mantel) or in your office!

Other Nifty Gadgets

There are all manners of ways that Wi-Fi can be used to make your life more fun and profitable. In the following sections, I'll show you a few of them.

Home Entertainment

I think that some time soon all home entertainment—stereos and televisions—will be equipped with Wi-Fi from the factory. We will be able to download music and movies using our computers and zap it across our Wi-Fi networks to be played.

Of course, the home entertainment devices will also be able to download content directly via Wi-Fi through the home network's router and the high-bandwidth Internet connection.

You will also be able to use your computer to control a variety of aspects of configuring your home entertainment devices, for example, a la TIVO, without having to worry about connecting wires or the physical placement of your home entertainment assets.

In the here and now, as opposed to sometime soon, you can't buy home entertainment devices equipped in this way. What you *can* buy is a Wi-Fi multimedia receiver that can be plugged into your stereo or television. This device allows you to stream audio or video over the Internet and play it across your Wi-Fi network on your stereo or television home entertainment systems.

For example, SMC Network's EZ-Stream Universal, shown in Figure 7.3, plugs into any home entertainment center using standard audio or video cabling to input into the home entertainment device.

FIGURE 7.3

SMC Network's EZ-Stream Universal uses Wi-Fi to stream audio and video to home entertainment systems.

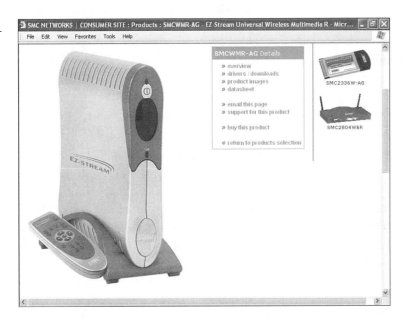

When the EZ-Stream is connected to a home entertainment device, it's easy to play audio or video streamed from the Web (or stored on your computer). You can even pop a DVD into a drive on your computer and play it on a home entertainment device connected to an EZ-Stream. (Don't blame me if other users on your Wi-Fi network start complaining about network degradation while you are watching your movie!)

Wi-Fi in the Kitchen

You may have seem some notices in the media about wired refrigerators, the so-called "Internet fridges" available in limited quantities from a number of vendors. You may even have seen television commercials for really smart fridges that clean up after themselves and introduce compatible singles (no, not really!).

However, in reality the "wired" features of these fridges don't currently offer many practical benefits. You can surf the Internet from a panel built onto the outside of the refrigerator door provided the unit is hardwired into a home network with an Internet connection, but otherwise these units don't seem to be a great deal of practical help in life.

The fact of the matter is that the digitally enabled kitchen is still in the trial and prototype stage. Undoubtedly, as these development efforts progress, Wi-Fi will come to be the most important way to connect kitchen components.

Currently, a number of major companies including General Motors, IBM, Microsoft, Motorola, and Panasonic are conducting early-stage trial and demonstration projects that involve digitally-enabled kitchens. (Some of these projects also extend to other portions of the home.) In addition, the Internet Home Alliance (IHA), an organization funded by its member companies including the companies I just mentioned, sponsors a wide variety of feasibility studies and standards initiatives around creating digitally intelligent homes. (You can find out more about the IHA and its mission at www.internethomealliance.com.)

For the time being, I can just speculate about how Wi-Fi will be used in the kitchen.

It seems clear that if every device were equipped with Wi-Fi, you could monitor your kitchen from anywhere in the home (or away from the home, for that matter). You could bring up a picture showing all available kitchen devices (for example, stoves, bread makers, and so on). The graphic would display what the device was doing, and allow you to adjust the settings. For example, you could turn down the heat on a stove burner if it looked like your soup was coming to a boil.

There's a pretty big opportunity with refrigerators to use Wi-Fi in a genuinely useful way. A fridge equipped with a Wi-Fi connection could also be provided with a bar code reader and some form of visual object recognition. You could maintain weekly shopping lists. The bar code reader and object recognition software could be used to check items in and out. When the fridge got low on food, it could simply order replacements over the Internet using its built-in Wi-Fi connectivity.

Generally, having wireless devices in your kitchen interoperating with your home network is the idea behind the standards being developed by the IHA. Sooner than you think not only your kitchen, but also your whole house, will be "unwired" to work more efficiently together, very likely using Wi-Fi for connectivity.

Voice Badges and More

"Enterprise! Come in, Enterprise!"

"Beam me up, Scottie."

I'm sure you remember the badges used for voice communication in Star Trek: The Next Generation and sequels. Well, with Wi-Fi, voice badges are no longer science fiction, they are in fact in use right here and now.

Vocera Communications makes a communications system that operates using a Wi-Fi network. The Vocera system is intended for use in a situation like a hospital, large retail operations, or a corporate campus. Vocera's early customers have primarily been hospitals, which can put to good use some of the special features of the system, like the need to locate a particular kind of specialist right away. But the badges are also being used in large retail operations where they can help customers find salespeople, and salespeople find information they need about inventory quickly.

Each user wears a small badge (this is the Star Trek part) like that shown in Figure 7.4.

FIGURE 7.4

The Vocera voice badge is worn by its user.

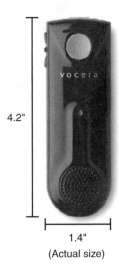

4.2"

1.4"
(Actual size)

This badge weighs less than two ounces and can be clipped to a shirt or coat or worn on a lanyard cord around your neck.

People within a campus such as a hospital use the Vocera voice badge to communicate with one another much as they would using a phone equipped with an external microphone.

However, the Vocera voice badge can do a great deal more than simple voice communications. Each badge is connected via Wi-Fi to a central Vocera server on the network. Sophisticated voice recognition software (provided by Nuance Corporation) can automatically recognize emergency calls and route them correctly. The server can also access directories to properly direct calls without human intervention. For example, suppose a doctor needs an anesthesiologist right away. Instead of having to manually identify and locate the anesthesiologist on call, the Vocera system can automatically connect the doctor to the specialist needed.

If you work as part of a team, you may be using Wi-Fi voice badges to interact with your team members—sooner than you think.

Playing Games and Having Fun with Wi-Fi

Your avatar has almost reached the inner circle. You've risen through 10 circles, made your way around monsters, and crushed machine gun nests. You are almost home free.

Bam! Bang! Suddenly you are fragged from the side and out of the game.

Welcome to the wonderful world of online multi-player gaming.

With Wi-Fi, you can be connected and play with and against players at home and across the Internet. None of this takes wires or cabling.

For example, on the Xbox gaming platform, the MN-740 wireless adapter from Microsoft, shown in Figure 7.5, uses either 802.11g or 802.11b flavors of Wi-Fi to connect an Xbox to a network. Because Xbox plays on your televisions, this is particularly convenient: It means that you don't have to wire each Xbox gaming console into your network.

note

In some cases, access to Internet multiplayer games, like Ultima Online, Star Wars: Galaxies, and others, requires a subscription fee for the service.

FIGURE 7.5

Xbox gaming consoles can be connected to Wi-Fi using this gadget from Microsoft.

You'll find that the MN-740 unit is pretty seamless to install. You won't have to worry about software options or settings: This is all taken care of for you.

At the current point in time, the Sony Playstation and Nintendo GameCube platforms seem to be a bit behind the Xbox in terms of Wi-Fi accessibility. But it is probably true that by the time you read this book, both platforms will offer an easy way to add Wi-Fi capabilities to each gaming device.

tip

The Xbox console comes with an Ethernet connection, which is what the MN-740 plugs into. So you can use any Ethernet–to–Wi-Fi connection gadget to Wi-Fi–enable your Xbox console. See Chapter 9, "Wi-Fi on Your Desktop," for more information.

THE ABSOLUTE MINIMUM

Here are the key points to remember from this chapter:

- You can do many cool things with Wi-Fi devices.
- The best is yet to come: Many of the benefits of "unwiring" with Wi-Fi are still in early stages.
- Wi-Fi makes it easier to have fun with digital photography, games, and much more.

note

If your gaming console has a standard Ethernet port, you can add wireless Wi-Fi activity using a wireless bridge device such as the one from Linksys (and other vendors). The wireless bridge can be plugged into the gaming console just as it would be into any computer with an Ethernet port. For more information, see Chapter 9.

8

ADDING WI-FI TO A MOBILE COMPUTER

Let's suppose you didn't buy your laptop with Wi-Fi preinstalled. Don't worry, be happy! It's easy to add Wi-Fi capabilities to your laptop.

In this chapter, I'll show you how to add Wi-Fi capabilities to a laptop that doesn't have Wi-Fi hardware. Step by step, I'll take you through the process necessary for adding a Wi-Fi card, installing the software necessary to make it work right, and testing it.

Before you know it you'll be using your laptop on Wi-Fi networks everywhere!

Choosing a Wi-Fi PC Card

Most Windows-compatible laptops come with slots for expansion cards. (I'll show you in detail how these slots, sometimes called expansion slots, work later in this chapter in the section "Installing the Card.")

These expansion slots are used to add hardware features to a laptop that it doesn't already have built in.

For historical reasons, the cards that fit in the expansion slots are called PCMCIA cards. PCMCIA is short for *Personal Computer Memory Card International Association*, which is the name of the organization that has devised the standard for cards that can be added to laptops. (You can find out more about PCMCIA at www.pcmcia.org.)

These days PCMCIA cards are commonly called *PC Cards*. They were originally designed to add additional memory to laptops, but have branched out to include devices ranging from dial-up modems to mini-hard drives, and more. You can see the same technology process at work today with PDAs that have a slot for CompactFlash memory cards. Wi-Fi devices can now be added to PDAs using the receptacle originally intended for the CompactFlash memory cards.

In much the same way, PC Cards have come to be used for many other things besides memory, not the least of which is to connect to Wi-Fi wireless networks. In fact, it is pretty much the case with laptops that the original function of these cards, as memory expansion devices, has been forgotten.

If your laptop is not equipped with Wi-Fi, and you want Wi-Fi (and who doesn't want Wi-Fi on their laptop?), you gotta go out and buy a Wi-Fi PC Card. Well, actually there is another possibility. You can use the USB or Ethernet ports on your laptop to connect a Wi-Fi receiver. For more information about this, see the "Other Options" section later in this chapter.

In any case, for now let's assume you are going to add a PC Card to your machine (it is certainly the least expensive way to add Wi-Fi).

A good starting place is understanding the differences between different Wi-Fi cards, and getting a handle on where you should buy one.

Wi-Fi and the PowerBook

If your mobile computer is an Apple PowerBook that is "AirPort ready" but not "AirPort enabled," your PowerBook didn't come from the factory with Wi-Fi capabilities. However, you can add a special card, manufactured by Apple, to your PowerBook.

note

Apple AirPort Extreme Wi-Fi cards work only with PowerBooks; they do not work with Windows laptops. Wi-Fi PC Cards used by Windows laptops do not work with Apple PowerBooks.

This card, called AirPort Extreme by Apple, uses a proprietary, easy-to-use, plug connection to attach to the PowerBook.

The Apple AirPort Extreme cards communicate using 802.11g Wi-Fi, which means that they also can "talk" to just plain vanilla 802.11b Wi-Fi.

Although adding a Wi-Fi card to an Apple PowerBook is a fairly straightforward process, the same cannot be said for adding one to a Windows PC. Depending on your Windows computer, it can be a fairly grueling process. However, it is generally reasonably easy to slip a Wi-Fi PC Card into the appropriate slot in a Windows laptop.

> **tip**
>
> If you are setting up a home network, you don't need an Apple AirPort Extreme Base Station to communicate with a PowerBook equipped with an AirPort Extreme card. The PowerBook will be capable of communicating with any 802.11b or 802.11g Wi-Fi base station or access point, regardless of brand.

Differences Between Cards

As you'll see when you start shopping for a Windows-compatible Wi-Fi PC Card, there is a plethora of cards to choose from.

COMPARISON SHOPPING ONLINE

If you use an online shopping comparison service such as CNET's, www.cnet.com, or Froogle, www.froogle.com, you'll need to search using a more generalized term than "Wi-Fi PCMCIA" to find most of the products available.

You'll get the most products listed at CNET if you use the search term "wireless NIC." ("Wireless" is, of course, more general than "Wi-Fi"; NIC is short for *Network Interface Card,* which refers to add-on cards used both in laptops and desktop computers.) A search using the term on CNET yields over 140 products (not all of them will work with laptops, of course).

The search term "Wi-Fi Card" works best at Froogle, yielding more than 250 distinct products. However, many of these products are not "cards" at all; this search yields access points and related Wi-Fi hardware as well as the cards you are looking for.

If you just walk into your handy-dandy computer or electronics store and demand a "Wi-Fi Card," you'll do just fine. So my point is that if you want to spend some time comparison shopping online—either to research or purchase—it's a great thing to do, but takes a bit more finesse.

So, how do you sort through all these choices? The good news is that it may not matter all that much what you choose: Wi-Fi certification means interoperability. (It also means never having to say you're sorry!)

Starting from the premise that your choice of Wi-Fi card for your notebook is not an earthshaking issue because any Wi-Fi card will work, here are the criteria you might want to consider that differentiate one Wi-Fi card from another (these are ranked roughly in order of importance, with brand being last as an essentially irrelevant consideration):

- "Flavor" of 802.11 Wi-Fi protocol supported
- Price
- Range and antennas
- Brand

I'll discuss each of these criteria briefly so that you can be a more informed shopper when you set out to buy your Wi-Fi card. But remember: Almost any Wi-Fi card designed for a laptop will do. So don't sweat it too much!

Supported Protocols

The least expensive cards are 802.11b Wi-Fi cards. Because the predominant flavor of Wi-Fi networks is currently 802.11b, it makes some sense just to go for the inexpensive option. (For more on the differences between the 802.11a, 802.11b, and 802.11g Wi-Fi protocols, see Chapter 2, "Understanding Wi-Fi," and Appendix A, "Wireless Standards.")

However, with a tip of the hat toward tomorrow, you probably should consider buying a 802.11g Wi-Fi card (these cards will also run on today's 802.11b networks). Although there is a cost difference, it is marginal and probably worth the hit to your pocketbook.

Unlike 802.11g Wi-Fi, 802.11a Wi-Fi is not backward-compatible with 802.11b. So it probably does not make sense to buy a card that just works with 802.11a. Instead, if you think you want 802.11a (probably because you intend to use your laptop with a specific network that runs on 802.11a), you should get one of a number of Wi-Fi cards that support both 802.11a and 802.11b. These cards are sometimes referred to as *dual band* wireless cards.

If you want to cover all bases (not a bad idea!), why not get a card that is compatible with 802.11a, 802.11b, and 802.11g?

note

Note that 802.11b Wi-Fi cards will operate on 802.11g Wi-Fi networks, just not at the faster 802.11g speeds.

Price

The price of computer hardware is always coming down. This implies that if you wait long enough they'll pay you to own a Wi-Fi card! If that's your plan, expect to wait a while.

Currently, you can get a generic off-brand 802.11b PC Card for as little as $25 or $30 U.S. At the other end of the scale, if you knock yourself out, you can probably find a 802.11g card that costs more than $100 (which makes it comparable to the Apple AirPort Extreme).

Range and Antennas

The primary job of a Wi-Fi card is to communicate. A Wi-Fi card's ability to communicate in a seamless fashion is limited by its range. This means that range is one specification that it might make sense to check when you are buying a card.

A typical Wi-Fi card has a range of 200–300 feet, but some are rated for communication as far as 3,500 feet. (The actual distance you should expect to obtain depends on many factors including terrain, obstacles such as interior walls, and interference from other devices.)

tip

It's only really worth worrying about range if you expect to be using your laptop more than a hundred feet or so from a Wi-Fi access point.

Most Wi-Fi cards use an internal antenna. You should know that some cards can be fitted with an external antenna that greatly extends their range. If an external antenna can be fitted to a card, it will be mentioned in the product specifications. You can also see if there is a small jack at the end of the card for the antenna. In some cards, such as the popular models made by Agere (and remarketed by Dell), this jack is covered with a small black plastic plug.

Optional antennas are explained in Chapter 17, "Adding Wi-Fi Antennas to Your Network."

Brands

I am not a great believer in brand loyalty. However, considering the overall inexpensive nature of Wi-Fi cards, it makes sense to buy a "name brand" card so that you have some reasonable expectation of support in case you run into difficulty.

Quality manufacturers of Wi-Fi cards include

- Agere
- Apple (on the Apple platform)
- Dell
- D-Link
- Linksys (owned by Cisco)
- Netgear
- SanDisk
- SMC Networks
- US Robotics

If you have feedback about this list—a good experience with a product from a vendor not on this list, or a bad experience with a vendor on this list—please feel free to contact me at wifireader@bearhome.com.

Where to Buy

You can easily buy a Wi-Fi card online at stores such as Amazon.com, Dell.com, or Buy.com. You can also use an online comparison shopping service such as Froogle, `www.froogle.com`, CNET, `www.cnet.com`, or PracticallyNetworked, `www.practicallynetworked.com`. (See the sidebar "Comparison Shopping Online" for more information.)

Almost any consumer electronics, computer, or office supply store should also be able to sell you a Wi-Fi card. However, with the exception of a specialty store like Fry's, you are unlikely to find as much selection in the "real world" as you will online.

Installing the Card

Okay, so now you have your Wi-Fi card in your hot, greedy hands and you're ready to get started with wireless networking today—either using a commercial hotspot or your own home network.

Whoa! Wait a minute there. Hold on, pardner! You still gotta add that fine new Wi-Fi card to your laptop, and get its software installed and configured to work nicely with a wireless network.

It's a good thing that there is nothing very difficult about any of this. Let's take it one step at a time.

Connections to Mr. Laptop

You probably know perfectly well what all the connections to your laptop do and what they are for. Just in case you don't, I want to show you some of the common connections on Windows laptop computers.

I know that I like everything to be explicitly named. Wouldn't it be great if all the plugs and sockets on your laptop were labeled with what they were for in plain English? Unfortunately, they are not. I'll show you all the common places to plug or connect something into a laptop, so you can be sure that you are doing the right thing.

tip

If you just want to add a Wi-Fi card to your computer, you might want to jump to the next section. But you can add Wi-Fi using a variety of connections (USB and Ethernet), so I thought I should show you the possibilities here.

They say that a picture is worth a thousand words. (And, who, may I ask, is "they?") Figures 8.1 through 8.3 identify the common plugs and sockets on a laptop.

Figure 8.1 shows the plug that goes into the power socket.

FIGURE 8.1

The laptop power socket and plug.

In Figure 8.2, you'll see the socket and plug for a USB connection.

FIGURE 8.2

USB socket and plug.

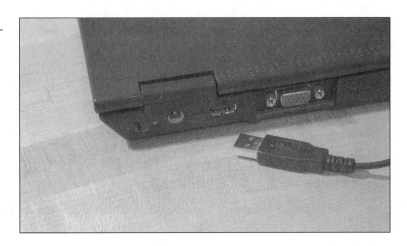

You'll see the socket for an Ethernet (wired network) connection and a Ethernet cable in Figure 8.3.

Putting the Wi-Fi Card in the Slot

Finally, we get to the socket we've been waiting for. Figure 8.4 shows the bay that a Wi-Fi PC Card slides into. (Note that this bay may be covered by a plastic plate of some kind when it is not in use.)

FIGURE 8.4
PCMCIA expan-
sion slot where
the Wi-Fi card
goes.

In the preceding section, I showed you pictures of many of the connector sockets found on a typical laptop. Finally, in Figure 8.4, I showed you the rectangular socket, about two inches long and 1/8 of an inch wide, that you'll use for your Wi-Fi card.

It's probably easier to see with a card fitting into the slot. Figure 8.5 shows a Wi-Fi card fitting into the PCMCIA expansion slot on the laptop.

FIGURE 8.5
Sliding the Wi-Fi
card into the
laptop.

There's really nothing to this. After you've identified the expansion slot on your computer, take
the Wi-Fi card out of its packaging, and slip it in
the slot. It's that simple.

Installation Software

What happens next depends, to some degree, on
what operating system you are running. Just as
when you add new hardware to a computer, the
process is somewhat simpler and more auto-
mated when you run a modern operating system
(meaning Apple's OS X or Microsoft Windows XP).
But I want to make the very important point that you can use Wi-Fi with almost
any laptop. You don't need the latest and greatest equipment, software, or operating
system to communicate using Wi-Fi for fun and profit.

If you are running an Apple PowerBook and you plug the proprietary Wi-Fi AirPort
Extreme card into its slot (remember, this is not a PC Card but rather something
designed specially by Apple for Apple computers), your PowerBook will hiccup and
automatically install the right software to make the card work. Note that the
machine may need to reboot itself at the end of the installation process.

tip

If you want to take the
card out, sometimes you just
grab the card and pull it out.
In other systems, there is a
catch button you need to
push to release the card.

If you are running Windows XP, a few moments after you place the card in position, a message box will appear above the right side of your Windows taskbar saying that new hardware has been added. The system may then open its installation wizard and prompt you to provide the software CD-ROM provided by the Wi-Fi card's manufacturer (or it may just automatically install the software for the Wi-Fi card without requiring anything further from you).

If you are running an older version of Windows—Windows 98, Windows Me, Windows NT, or Windows 2000—it is likely that you will have to install the software for your new Wi-Fi card yourself. This means putting the CD-ROM provided with the Wi-Fi card in your laptop's disk drive, and then following the instructions provided by the installation program.

Configuring Your Card for a Wi-Fi Network

With your Wi-Fi card in place, and its software installed, its time to configure your Wi-Fi card so that it will run with your network.

Fundamentally, this is a matter of setting the SSID (the name of the network you are connecting to) and the encryption key (if there is one).

Each Wi-Fi card from a different manufacturer has slightly different software that accomplishes this, but as a general matter the software all does the same thing. So I'm going to show you how this works with one Wi-Fi card, but the order in which you enter information (and the appearance of the dialogs shown in the figures) might look slightly different depending on your actual Wi-Fi card. Don't worry, just enter the information requested. It's really quite simple.

Maybe you'd want to use your Wi-Fi–enabled laptop with more than one network (this is actually quite likely). For example, you might want to surf the Web at Starbucks, and also connect to your Wi-Fi network at home. The network configuration for each of these two situations is different: The SSIDs (or network names) are different, and there is no encryption at Starbucks, but you should use encryption for my home network.

Each set of configuration data for a wireless network is called a *configuration profile*.

Most software for Wi-Fi cards allows you to store the information for multiple configuration profiles, and to switch between them. This makes it easy to connect at the coffee shop and at the home or office: You just switch between configurations.

Most software places an icon in the Windows system tray that can be used to fire up the configuration utility. If not, the Wi-Fi configuration utility can be started by clicking the program name using the Start, Programs menu.

The Wi-Fi configuration utility, also sometimes called a *Client Manager* because the Wi-Fi card makes the laptop a "client" on a network, will look something like the program shown in Figure 8.6.

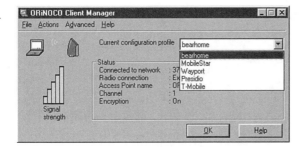

The software shown in Figure 8.6 lets you choose from existing Wi-Fi configurations
using the drop-down list shown at the upper right of the window. The configuration
manager also provides an overview of the signal strength of a selected network,
illustrated by the bars shown on the left of the window.

If you have no profiles set up (or need to add a profile to the existing ones, or to edit
an existing profile), the thing to do is to choose Add/Edit Configuration Profile from
the Actions menu. The Add/Edit Configuration Profile window will open, as shown
in Figure 8.7.

Click Add to add a new configuration. The Edit Configuration window will open,
with the Profile Name box empty. Enter a Profile Name of your choice, as shown in
Figure 8.8, ABGtoWiFi.

The Edit Configuration window, shown in Figure 8.8, is also used to set the Network
Type. The most common choice for Network Type is access point. This works both for
most SOHO (small office/home office) situations and also at public hotspots like the
one T-Mobile provides in Starbucks. But you can also choose to connect on a peer-to-
peer basis, which you can use to enable Microsoft workgroup functionality—such as
file and printer sharing—without full-fledged network support. See Part IV, "Creating
a Wi-Fi Network," for more information about this distinction.

FIGURE 8.8

Enter a new configuration name in the Edit Configuration window to provide information for a new network profile.

With a Profile Name provided, and the Network Type set to Access Point, click Next to continue adding profile information. In the next step, shown in Figure 8.9, you will be asked to identify your network.

FIGURE 8.9

The most important piece of information is the name identifying the network you want to connect to.

You may happen to know the network name (the SSID), particularly if you are setting up a profile for a hotspot belonging to a public network.

If you don't know the network name, the thing to do is to click the Scan button. Your card will scan the spectrum and produce a list of Wi-Fi networks broadcasting within range as shown in Figure 8.10.

tip

The Network Name for hotspots on the T-Mobile Hotspot Network, which is the infrastructure that serves Starbucks, is *tmobile*.

FIGURE 8.10

The Wi-Fi card scans the spectrum for Wi-Fi networks that are broadcasting within range.

Pick the network name you are looking for and click OK. The next window lets you enter the security settings (see Figure 8.11).

FIGURE 8.11

If your network is secured with encryption, you will need to enter the key.

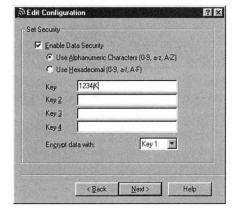

You'll then need to click Next to finish with the Wizard and accept the new settings.

The software that comes with some Wi-Fi cards doesn't support scanning. This bad idea was introduced to save us from ourselves; the thought was to aid security by stopping users from scanning for networks. If you are unlucky enough to own a Wi-Fi card whose software does not allow scanning, the good news is that you can download free scanning software. One good source is Boingo Networks, www.boingo.com. (You'll learn more about Boingo in Chapter 12, "Working with National Wi-Fi Networks.")

If you are connecting to a public network, such as a T-Mobile hotspot, most likely encryption will not be required. In this case, the Enable Data Security check box shown in Figure 8.11 should be unchecked, and the rest of the data entry fields shown in Figure 8.11 will be disabled.

If you are connecting to a private network, encryption *should* be enabled. Encryption is the first line of defense against unauthorized access. However, all too often people don't bother with encryption. This can be a big mistake. See Part V, "Securing Your Wi-Fi Computer and Network," for more information about how to use encryption and other techniques to practice safe computing with Wi-Fi.

The great words of wisdom about encryption keys on a private network are, "Check with your network administrator to find out the proper encryption settings." This is undoubtedly good advice if you have a network administrator, but what if you don't?

You'll need to check the documentation that came with your access point to learn the default encryption key, and how to change the default if you desire. (For more information about setting up an access point on a private network, see Chapter 14, "Setting Up Your Access Point.")

With the security settings omitted if encryption is not required (for example, at a T-Mobile hotspot), or the encryption key correctly entered, click Next. A window allowing you to choose power management settings for the Wi-Fi card will appear (see Figure 8.12).

tip

The default encryption key for an access point is often the network name with its first character omitted. For example, if the network name is 177fg9, the default encryption key is likely to be 77fg9.

FIGURE 8.12

Setting the Power Management features for a Wi-Fi card.

As a general matter, the more power a Wi-Fi card uses, the greater its transmission range. However, when higher power is used, the laptop's battery drains faster—an important concern when you are mobile. So you'll have to decide depending on your circumstances whether to opt for more power consumption (meaning more range but less battery life) or lower power consumption (meaning less range but less battery drain).

After you have made your Power Management selection, click Next. You will be asked whether your laptop should renew its IP (Internet Protocol) address when the configuration profile is selected (see Figure 8.13).

FIGURE 8.13

The Wi-Fi card can be set to renew its IP address when the configuration profile is selected.

It's hard to go wrong with renewing IP addresses when a new configuration profile is selected. This setting, while it may cause a slight delay, is less likely to lead to problems because a network client is "holding onto" an invalid IP address. So check the Renew IP Address When Selecting This Profile box. (For more information about IP Addresses on a network, see Chapter 15, "Configuring Your Wi-Fi Network.")

You're done! Click Finish. The main window of the Client Manager will open with your new profile selected as shown in Figure 8.14 and the Signal Strength bars (hopefully) showing a good connection.

Although you're ready now to start surfing, it's a good idea to test your card before you start. I'll show you how in the next section.

note

An IP address is the identification number used for a computer connected to a network or the Internet. Each computer that is connected to the Internet needs to have an IP address in order to be able to interact with the servers on the Web, although this IP address can be assigned dynamically, which means that it changes and is not fixed. (A fixed IP is called a *static* IP in techno-speak.)

FIGURE 8.14

The newly created profile is shown selected in the main Client Manager window.

Making Sure the Card Works

You can make sure that your Wi-Fi card is working properly by running the onboard diagnostics both for the card and its link to the network.

Generally, the same Client Manager configuration utility that is used to set up a configuration profile also provides test facilities for both.

Figure 8.15 shows the Card Check tab of a card diagnostics screen (you have to click Test Card Now to see the results).

FIGURE 8.15

You can test your Wi-Fi card to make sure it is working properly.

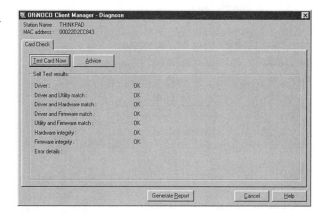

Link Test utilities, such as the one shown in Figure 8.16, test how quickly a Wi-Fi card and a network are sending and receiving messages. If any messages are shown as dropped, it indicates there is a problem.

You can click the Advice button on the Link Test utility window to get the results in plain English. A Help window screen as shown in Figure 8.17 will open with the link test results and recommendations.

Now for the final, nitty-gritty test to see if the whole thing works. If you are at a public hotspot, connect to the Internet and start surfing and downloading email (see Chapter 3, "Hitting the Road with Wi-Fi," for the basics of connecting to public hotspots, and Part III, "Going Mobile with Wi-Fi," for more in-depth information).

FIGURE 8.16

The Link Test utility tells you how good the connection between a Wi-Fi card and a network is.

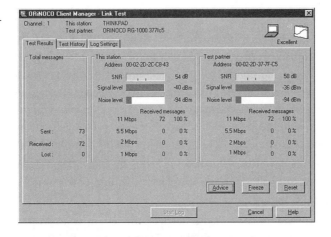

FIGURE 8.17

You can get information about how well your Wi-Fi card is communicating with the network, and what to do if there are problems.

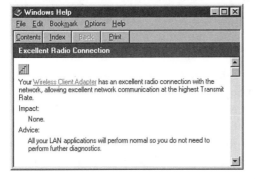

If you are connecting to a private network, such as your own home or office network, see if you can do stuff across the network with your newly networked Wi-Fi computer. Make sure that you can "see" computers on the network from the laptop, and see the laptop from computers on the network. Copy files back and forth. If you have a network printer, use it from the Wi-Fi laptop.

To see what is on your Windows network, in Windows XP click Start, My Network Places. In older versions of Windows, double-click the Network neighborhood icon located on the Windows desktop.

Everything working? That's great because it was pretty easy to set up. Wi-Fi functionality is simply way cool!

tip

As I noted at the beginning of this chapter, each Wi-Fi card and each operating system have different software for working with Wi-Fi. If your Windows laptop is running Windows XP, you will likely find installing and configuring Wi-Fi much easier than if you are running an older operating system.

Other Options

You probably want to know if there are any other options besides Wi-Fi cards. Maybe your laptop doesn't come with an expansion slot for PC Cards. Or maybe you are already using the slot with a digital storage device. The good news is that you can add external Wi-Fi capabilities to a laptop in several ways. The only downside is that you'll need to carry an additional gizmo with you because the Wi-Fi card won't be onboard your laptop—but this isn't really a big deal. (Some users also feel that external Wi-Fi access produces slightly flakier communication strengths, but there is no real reason this should be true.)

You can add an external Wi-Fi device to your computer using either an Ethernet port (shown in Figure 8.3 earlier in this chapter) or using a USB connection (shown in Figure 8.2 earlier in this chapter).

If your laptop already has a wired Ethernet connection, you can plug in a device that will bridge between the Ethernet card inside your laptop and Wi-Fi access.

One such device is Microsoft Xbox Adapter, described in Chapter 7, "Playing with Wi-Fi Gadgets." Although this device is primarily intended for use with the Xbox gaming platform, it will also provide Wi-Fi access for any computer that has Ethernet capabilities.

You'll also find a number of Ethernet–to–Wi-Fi and USB–to–Wi-Fi devices from a variety of manufacturers, including D-Link and Linksys, which enable Wi-Fi access without adding a card. These devices may seem particularly appealing when you decide you want to add Wi-Fi capabilities to a desktop computer because you don't have to open the computer up to install them. I'll tell you more about them, particularly USB–to–Wi-Fi adapters, which are likely to be more convenient than Ethernet–to–Wi-Fi adapters because you don't have to disrupt existing wired network connections, in Chapter 9, "Wi-Fi on Your Desktop."

THE ABSOLUTE MINIMUM

Here are the key points to remember from this chapter:

- Prices for Wi-Fi cards keep coming down, and it's easy to comparison shop for a good deal.
- If you look at your laptop, it's easy to see where the card goes.
- For each network you want to connect to, you'll need to configure a network profile.
- The most important part of the network profile is the network name, also called the SSID.
- You can scan to find available networks.
- You may need to provide an encryption key (particularly for private networks).
- External devices that connect via Ethernet or USB can also be used to add Wi-Fi to your laptop.

9

Wi-Fi On Your Desktop

In Chapter 8, "Adding Wi-Fi to a Mobile Computer," I showed you how to add a Wi-Fi card to your laptop computer. This chapter shows you how to add Wi-Fi to a desktop computer.

There are a number of reasons you might want to add Wi-Fi to a desktop computer. For example, you might have a Wi-Fi–enabled laptop and want to network it to a desktop computer to share files (and Internet access). (For the details of setting up a small office or home network with Wi-Fi, see Part IV, "Creating a Wi-Fi Network.")

I'll start this chapter by suggesting that if you are buying a new desktop computer, you should buy one with Wi-Fi already on board. Next, I'll show you how to add Wi-Fi, which Apple calls AirPort, to an Apple AirPort-ready desktop.

Moving back to the wonderful world of Windows, I'll show you how to add a generic Wi-Fi card to a generic Windows desktop computer.

Finally, the chapter will end with a nifty alternative for adding Wi-Fi to a desktop computer (actually any computer with a USB port). This option is, as you'll see, to use an inexpensive external USB Wi-Fi device.

Buying a New Computer

If you think you might ever want your new desktop computer to have wireless capabilities, you should buy it with Wi-Fi already built in. This won't add much to the cost and could save you a fair amount of trouble down the road. Almost every major brand has Wi-Fi available as a low-cost option when you buy a new computer.

Because you are reading this book, you probably have some interest in wireless technologies and Wi-Fi networking. But even supposing you are only planning to operate one computer, it's worth getting Wi-Fi installed when you buy it in case you add another mobile (or desktop) computer. That way you can network your computers (and share an Internet connection) without the hassle of wires. (See Chapter 15, "Configuring Your Wi-Fi Network," for a more detailed comparison of the pluses and minuses of wired and wireless networking.)

If you are buying an Apple desktop, you need to check that the machine is "AirPort ready."

For example, you might be using the Apple online store to purchase an Apple Power Mac G5 as shown in Figure 9.1.

note

"AirPort" is the Apple term for the 802.11b flavor of Wi-Fi. "AirPort Extreme" is Apple-speak for the 802.11g flavor of Wi-Fi.

FIGURE 9.1

Specifying an Apple desktop computer online at the Apple store.

If you scroll down the list of available computer options shown in Figure 9.1, you'll come to the AirPort Extreme Card option shown in Figure 9.2.

FIGURE 9.2

If you add an AirPort Extreme card to your Power Mac, it will come Wi-Fi enabled.

If you don't select the AirPort Extreme Card option, your new Power Mac will not be enabled for Wi-Fi, although it will be "AirPort ready." (I'll show you how to add an AirPort Extreme card to a Power Mac that is AirPort ready but does not have the card factory-installed later in this chapter.) If you choose the AirPort Extreme Card option, the 802.11g flavor Wi-Fi card will be factory-installed in your new computer, and your wireless troubles will be over, at least in relationship to your new desktop.

At the present point in time, things aren't so easy in the Windows world. Dell, HP, and IBM do not offer a Wi-Fi option in their online stores for their desktop models. (Desktop models from all these companies do come equipped with Ethernet-wired network connectors.)

So you'll probably have to make special arrangements with a sales rep to get your desktop Windows PC equipped for Wi-Fi "out of the box." But bear in mind that this could change quickly, as things do in technology. Wi-Fi is up and coming and everyone wants it. So by the time you read this book you may be able to specify Wi-Fi in your desktop as part of the standard online ordering process.

Adding AirPort to an Apple Desktop

If you have an AirPort-ready Apple desktop computer, and have purchased an AirPort card online, from an Apple store, or from a third-party vendor, you are ready to install the card in your desktop. Figure 9.3 shows an AirPort Extreme card fresh "out of the box."

note

As I explained earlier, "AirPort" is the Apple term for the 802.11b flavor of Wi-Fi. "AirPort Extreme" is Apple-speak for the 802.11g flavor of Wi-Fi. Despite Apple's use of proprietary terminology (for example, AirPort), there is nothing special about the Wi-Fi used in AirPort access points and cards.

Although the Apple AirPort cards are a bit more expensive than typical Wi-Fi cards used in a Windows PC, Apple makes the installation process quite painless. You cannot necessarily say this about a Windows PC: opening the case itself—let alone doing any installation—can be a trial.

If you can follow directions, you can add an AirPort card to an AirPort-ready Apple desktop! You don't need any special tools! So let's get started.

First, make sure your computer is turned off (you can choose Shut Down from the Special menu to shut the computer down).

Unplug all cables and cords from the computer.

Apple recommends that you touch one of the metal access plates on the back of the computer to discharge static electricity.

Lift the latch on the side of the computer to open the case. The latch is shown open in Figure 9.4.

Lower the side of the computer gently. Lift out the clear plastic protective cover.

The "guts" of the computer are now freely accessible, as shown in Figure 9.5.

note

The figures show an AirPort Extreme card being installed in a Power Mac G5. Positions and appearances may vary somewhat if you have a different model.

Lift latch

FIGURE 9.4

Lift the latch to open the computer.

AirPort connector is located here

FIGURE 9.5

With the side off, you have easy access to the internal parts of the computer.

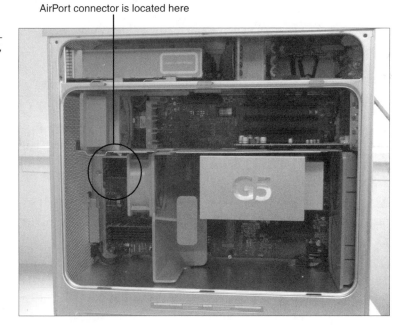

Insert the AirPort card through the opening in the PCI card guide and into the connector on the main logic board as shown in Figure 9.6.

FIGURE 9.6

Inserting the card.

You may have a little trouble finding where to plug the card in, but if you look around, you'll only find one place it can go. You may need to remove the plastic fan assembly, which easily comes out and in, to attach the card more easily.

With the card in place, connect the antenna cable to the connector on the end of the AirPort card (you'll find the antenna cable on the side of the PCI card guide).

The antenna cable is shown connected to the connector on the AirPort card in Figure 9.7.

The cool thing about this internal antenna cable is that it connects to an external Wi-Fi antenna built into the desktop.

You are done with the hardware part of the installation. Raise the panel to snap it into place and close the computer. Connect all cords and the power cable.

Restart the computer.

Locate the Assistants folder on your computer. Within the Assistants folder, check to see if the AirPort Setup Assistant is present. If it is not, you will need to install it from the CD-ROM that came with the AirPort card, or by downloading it from Apple.

With the AirPort Setup Assistant installed, launch it by double-clicking. You'll see an introductory screen like that shown in Figure 9.8.

FIGURE 9.7

The antenna cable is shown connected to the AirPort card.

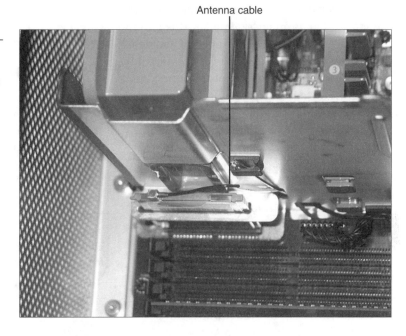

FIGURE 9.8

The AirPort Setup Assistant Introduction screen.

Make sure that the Set Up Your Computer to Join an Existing AirPort Network option is selected (I'll show you how to set up an AirPort Base Station, the other alternative, in Chapter 14, "Setting Up Your Access Point"). Click Continue.

The AirPort Setup Assistant will scan for Wi-Fi networks in the area. When it finds one, if the network is protected by encryption, it will prompt you for a password.

Note that the password you must supply here is the same thing as an encryption key (the terminology used by everyone except Apple). If you don't know the password for your Wi-Fi network, and if you don't have a system administrator (meaning, you are the system administrator), you should check the documentation of the Wi-Fi access point you are using to determine its default password.

With the password in place, click Continue. The Conclusion window will open.

When you click Continue again, your computer will be set up as a node on the Wi-Fi network. You can verify this by checking to see other computers, and seeing if you have Internet access.

With your AirPort card configured, you can also access the AirPort application, which can be found in the Apple menu. The AirPort application allows you to switch between different AirPort (Wi-Fi) networks, monitor the strength of the Wi-Fi signal, and turn the AirPort card off (see Figure 9.9).

If you select Computer to Computer from the AirPort menu, you can configure an ad-hoc peer-to-peer network as shown in Figure 9.10.

caution

If you are setting a Wi-Fi access point as explained in Chapter 14, you should be sure to change your password to something other than the default. Leaving the password at the default creates a security vulnerability. For more about the security of Wi-Fi networks, see Chapter 19, "Securing Your Wi-Fi Network."

tip

You should always run your network with encryption turned on for security reasons. See Chapter 19 for details. Clearly, making a careful note of your password (encryption key) when you set the network up is a good idea.

FIGURE 9.9

The AirPort application lets you switch between Wi-Fi networks.

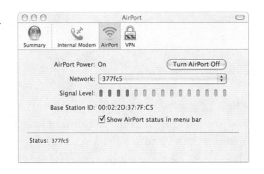

FIGURE 9.10

You can use the Computer to Computer window in the AirPort application to configure a peer-to-peer network.

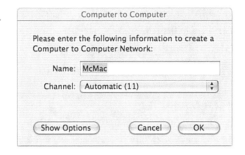

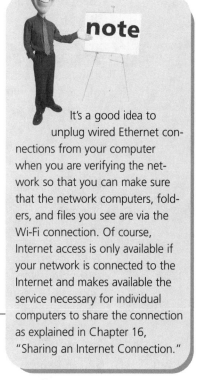

It's a good idea to unplug wired Ethernet connections from your computer when you are verifying the network so that you can make sure that the network computers, folders, and files you see are via the Wi-Fi connection. Of course, Internet access is only available if your network is connected to the Internet and makes available the service necessary for individual computers to share the connection as explained in Chapter 16, "Sharing an Internet Connection."

SYNONYMS CAN BE SLIPPERY

I am a little unhappy with Apple that they have chosen to use nonstandard terminology for their Wi-Fi products. Apart from this cavil, I have to say that the Wi-Fi products produced by Apple are examples of exemplary engineering, and quite possibly the most easy-to-use—and most foolproof—Wi-Fi equipment you can buy.

I've tried to alert you to synonyms as we've gone along in this section. Please don't let them confuse you. Table 9.1 presents some of these synonyms in one place for your convenience.

TABLE 9.1   Apple-Speak Synonyms

Apple Terminology	Common Synonym(s)
AirPort	802.11b Wi-Fi
AirPort Extreme	802.11g Wi-Fi
AirPort ID	SSID, MAC Address, wireless network name
Network Password	Encryption key

Adding Wi-Fi to a Windows Desktop

The first thing you should know about adding a Wi-Fi card to a Windows desktop computer is that, as they say, mileage will vary. By this I mean that the physical installation of the card in the computer will depend on the make and model of the

A peer-to-peer network is a simple arrangement in which two computers communicate directly without using a router to manage communications and provide shared services (such as Internet access). See Chapter 15 for more details.

computer, and the software installation procedure will vary depending on the make of the Wi-Fi card. Please read the installation instructions that come with your card carefully, and be prepared to deal with recalcitrant screws when opening up your desktop.

WHAT CONNECTIONS FOR WHICH MACHINE?

You should understand what kind of Wi-Fi card (or expansion device) you can use with what kind of computer. This will help you to specify the device you need when you are buying it from an online source, and make sure you get what you need the first time.

- PCI cards are internal cards for Windows desktop computers only.
- PCMCIA cards (also called PC Cards) and mini-PCI cards are for Windows laptops only.
- USB devices will plug into any computer with USB connectors, and will work with Windows desktop and Windows laptop computers (and also with Apple computers in many cases).

A Wi-Fi card for your desktop will fit in a PCI expansion slot, so (from a technical viewpoint) when you buy your card, you can specify it as a Wi-Fi PCI card. When fit in the PCI expansion slot, PCI cards can be accessed from the back of your computer as I'll show you, although one usually needs to remove a cover plate as part of the installation process.

You can buy an inexpensive Wi-Fi PCI card for as little as $30 to $40.

The key tool for installing the Wi-Fi card in your desktop computer is a screwdriver with a Phillips head (not a slotted head).

Figure 9.11 shows an inexpensive Wi-Fi PCI card ready to install.

If indicated by the instructions, install the drivers for the Wi-Fi card using the software provided by the manufacturer, and following the directions provided by the manufacturer.

Now you can add the card to the computer. Be sure to power the computer down and disconnect all cables before opening your computer's case.

Figure 9.12 shows the back of a fairly typical, older model, Windows desktop computer.

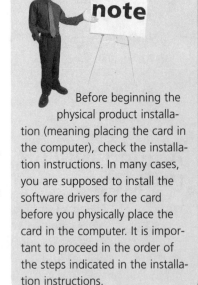

note

Before beginning the physical product installation (meaning placing the card in the computer), check the installation instructions. In many cases, you are supposed to install the software drivers for the card before you physically place the card in the computer. It is important to proceed in the order of the steps indicated in the installation instructions.

FIGURE 9.11

An inexpensive Wi-Fi card ready to go into your Windows desktop.

Pins interface with PCI slot

FIGURE 9.12

A not-so-great Windows desktop computer (rear view).

Take a close look at the lower left of the computer shown in Figure 9.12. You'll see three slots for PCI cards. The two unoccupied slots are covered with metal plates. When installed, the back of the Wi-Fi card (the part with the antenna) will stick through one of those plates.

Open the computer case (you'll probably have to use the screwdriver for this). From the inside, locate the cover plates for the empty PCI slots. To remove the cover plate, once again you'll need the screwdriver. Figure 9.13 shows the screw that needs to be removed to remove a PCI slot cover plate.

FIGURE 9.13
By removing this screw, you can take off the cover plate for the empty PCI slot.

If you look carefully at the motherboard of the computer, you'll see the slot that the connector on the Wi-Fi card fits into. If you've done this right, it should fit with a nice, solid feeling. The part of the card with the antenna (and status lights) should fit through the hole made when you took the cover plate off.

Use the screw you took off with the cover plate to firmly screw the Wi-Fi card in place, and reassemble the computer's cover. From the rear, you should now see the Wi-Fi card and antenna (see Figure 9.14).

Now it's time to install the software drivers for the card. You should check the instructions that came with your card, but most likely this means placing the CD-ROM that came with the card in the computer and turning it on. The Found New Hardware Wizard will open when the computer boots up as shown in Figure 9.15.

tip

If you are confused about which part of computer is which, and need more guidance about how to install the Wi-Fi card in your computer, take a look at one of the good books available on upgrading your PC. A good choice is *Absolute Beginner's Guide to Upgrading and Fixing Your PC* by Michael Miller (ISBN 0-7897-3045-6).

FIGURE 9.14

The Wi-Fi card is installed in an expansion slot.

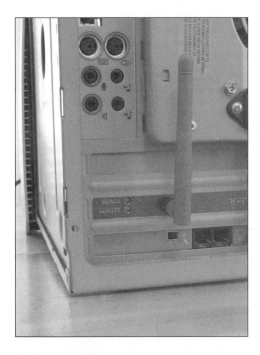

FIGURE 9.15

When new hardware, such as the Wi-Fi card, has been added to your computer, the Found New Hardware Wizard will open the next time the computer is turned on.

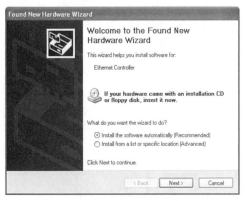

Choose the Install the Software Automatically option from the Found New Hardware Wizard screen shown in Figure 9.15, and click Next to cycle through the rest of the wizard screens (it's OK to accept the default wizard suggestions).

When installation is complete, a configuration utility will open. The precise appearance of this configuration utility will vary depending on the brand of Wi-Fi card you choose to install. But the functionality will pretty much be the same. You will be able to specify the encryption key (network password) if required, as shown in Figure 9.16.

FIGURE 9.16
You can specify
an encryption
key (network
password) if one
is required.

You'll also be able to add multiple networks so that you can switch between configurations, using a screen like that shown in Figure 9.17.

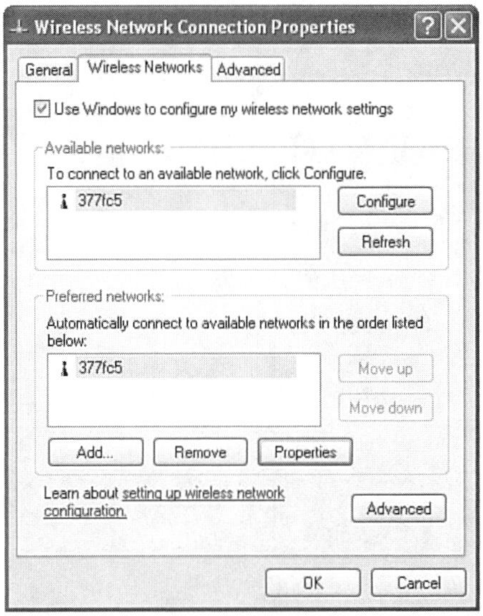

FIGURE 9.17
You can config-
ure multiple
wireless net-
works for use
with your card.

You can find more options on the Advanced tab of the Wireless Connection Network
Properties dialog shown in Figure 9.18.

You can use this dialog to configure firewall settings, and to set your computer up to
provide Internet access for a networked computer. See Chapter 19 for more about
firewalls and Chapter 16 for information about peer-to-peer Internet access sharing.

Back in the General tab of the Wireless Network Connection Properties dialog,
shown in Figure 9.19, highlight Internet Protocol in the list of items.

FIGURE 9.18

You can configure firewall settings and set your computer up to provide Internet access to a networked computer on the Advanced tab.

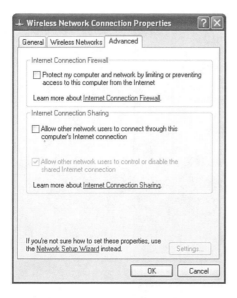

FIGURE 9.19

The General tab of the Wireless Network Connection Properties dialog.

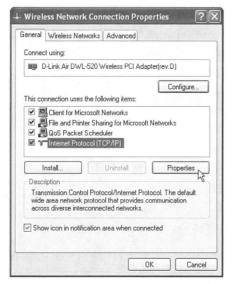

With Internet Protocol highlighted, click the Properties button. The Internet Protocol Properties dialog, shown in Figure 9.20, will open.

This dialog is used to set the network settings required for your Internet connection. I'll explain in detail the purpose of these settings in Chapter 16.

FIGURE 9.20

The Internet Protocol Properties dialog is used to establish TCP/IP settings.

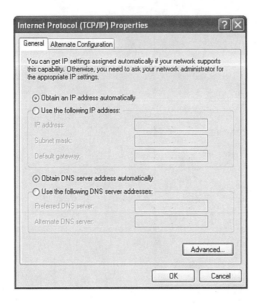

Well, you may need to tab back and forth through these configuration dialogs a bit, but actually they are quite straightforward. Your new Wi-Fi card will scan for available wireless networks. If there is more than one available, you'll need to select the one you want to use. You'll also need to provide the encryption key (network password) if required.

You should verify now that you can "see" other computers on your network, and that everything is functioning as it should.

Hip, hip, hooray! You've just added a Wi-Fi card to your desktop. If this is the first time you've opened your computer to add hardware, why then, you deserve three gold stars.

Using a USB Wi-Fi Adapter

There's an attractive alternative to opening up your desktop computer to add a Wi-Fi card. Microsoft and a number of other vendors make a Universal Serial Bus (USB) Wi-Fi adapter. These adapters fit in a USB connector, so you have to have a free USB port to be able to use one of these adapters.

Figure 9.21 shows a cute, little USB Wi-Fi connector that also doubles as a key ring (I kid you not).

USB Connector

FIGURE 9.21

An inexpensive
USB Wi-Fi adapter.

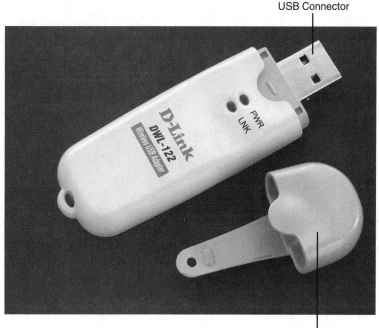

USB Connector

Connector cover

One of the best things about using a USB Wi-Fi adapter is that it should work on any computer (Apple or Windows) that has a free USB connector. It will work on laptops, or on desktops. You can carry it around in your pocket. Great for a portable world!

USB Wi-Fi and a Mac

To use a USB Wi-Fi adapter with a Mac, power the computer down. Next, plug the USB adapter into an empty USB port on the Apple computer as shown in Figure 9.22.

If it is awkward to plug the adapter directly into a USB port, you can use a USB extension cable, which may have been provided with your adapter. Also, if your USB ports are getting crowded, it's easy to buy an inexpensive USB replicator (also often referred to as a USB hub).

With the USB Wi-Fi adapter plugged in, insert the software CD-ROM that shipped with your product, and turn the computer on.

note

The text describes a fairly typical USB Wi-Fi adapter installation. Your experience will vary depending on the make and model of USB Wi-Fi adapter that you choose.

FIGURE 9.22

The USB Wi-Fi adapter is plugged into a USB outlet.

When your computer is fully booted, an icon representing the installation software CD will appear on the desktop.

Double-click the icon and drill down until you find the Mac folder. Within the Mac folder, you'll see the installation package, DlinkUsbDriver.pkg, as shown in Figure 9.23.

FIGURE 9.23

The installation package.

Double-click the installation package to open it. The Welcome screen will appear.

Click Continue to proceed through the Installer. You will be asked for a variety of information, such as where to place the files (see Figure 9.24), but you can accept the defaults and simply click Continue until the end of the installation process.

FIGURE 9.24

The installer allows you to input a number of items, but it is OK to just accept the software's suggestions.

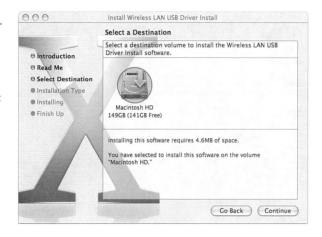

When the installation completes, the wireless adapter software will scan for available networks and show you the results (see Figure 9.25).

FIGURE 9.25

The USB Wi-Fi Adapter software scans for available networks.

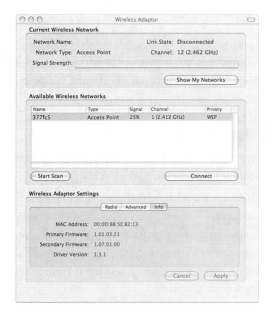

You can select a network by clicking Connect. If your wireless network requires an encryption key (network password), you will be prompted for it when you try to connect (see Figure 9.26).

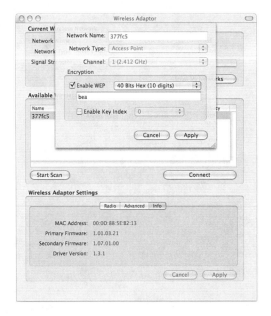

FIGURE 9.26

You will be prompted for an encryption key (network password) when you try to connect to a wireless network.

With the USB Wi-Fi adapter installed, things aren't different from any other Wi-Fi adapter (although admittedly the process is not quite as seamless as working with Apple's own Wi-Fi software for the AirPort card, as described earlier in this chapter).

USB Wi-Fi Adapter Does Windows

Figure 9.27 shows the same USB Wi-Fi adapter used with an Apple desktop plugged into the USB port of a Windows desktop.

It's important to follow the manufacturer's instructions for installing the software drivers for the USB Wi-Fi adapter.

With the software drivers installed, the USB Wi-Fi adapter on the Windows platform functions just like an internal Wi-Fi card as shown earlier in this chapter. The Wireless Network Connection Properties dialog, shown in Figure 9.28, is used to select the wireless network to connect to.

FIGURE 9.27

The USB Wi-Fi adapter is plugged into the USB port of a Windows computer.

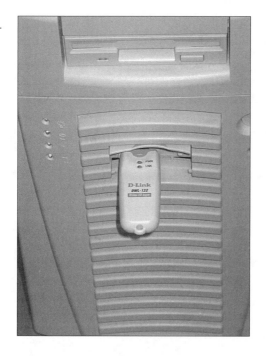

FIGURE 9.28

The Wireless Network Connection Properties dialog works the same way whether your Wi-Fi adapter is internal or connected via USB.

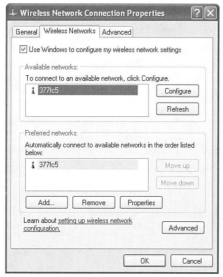

You can use the Wireless Network Properties dialog, shown in Figure 9.29, to set the encryption key (here called the network key).

FIGURE 9.29

The Wireless Network Properties dialog is used to set the encryption key.

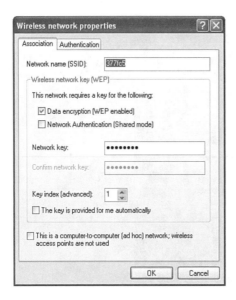

It's really fast, easy, and inexpensive to add Wi-Fi capabilities using a USB Wi-Fi adapter. I'm looking forward to putting one of these adapters on my key ring, or adding one to my pen holder using the handy-dandy clip provided, and bringing Wi-Fi access to computers of every nation and creed wherever I travel! You, too, may find that adding Wi-Fi access using an external USB Wi-Fi adapter is very easy—and, as they say, the better part of valor!

THE ABSOLUTE MINIMUM

Here are the key points to remember from this chapter:

- Installing an AirPort card in an AirPort-ready Apple desktop is fairly easy.

- Installing a Wi-Fi PCI card in a Windows desktop takes some willingness to fuss with recalcitrant hardware, but it's really not that hard.

- A USB Wi-Fi adapter can be plugged in and used regardless of operating system and without having to open the computer's case.

- Though not totally trivial, retrofitting a Windows desktop computer to work with Wi-Fi is not beyond the ability of most people.

PART III

GOING MOBILE WITH Wi-Fi

10

TOOLS FOR THE PERFECT ROAD WARRIOR

If you're going to get the best from your Wi-Fi–enabled laptop or PDA, you need to know the software and hardware accessories to bring, where to connect to a Wi-Fi hotspot, how to get the best deal from a mobile network, and much more.

This chapter starts answering these questions by discussing what to bring and what not to bring on the road with you.

Loading Software *Before* You Go

As an experienced road warrior, it is likely that you already know what software to load into your laptop (or PDA) before you leave. It's still worth observing that there is no guarantee that you will be able to access the Internet just because you have Wi-Fi–enabled equipment. You need to plan to be self-sufficient. This means loading the software you'll need before you go. At a minimum, you should probably bring on your computer or PDA:

- Drivers and related software for your Wi-Fi card (see Chapter 8, "Adding Wi-Fi to a Mobile Computer," for more information about the software that might be required).

- Wi-Fi hotspot directory information (see the next section, "Taking Hotspot Info with You," for more information).

- Software to access a Virtual Private Network (VPN) if your company operates one (see Chapter 18, "Protecting Your Mobile Wi-Fi Computer," for more information about VPNs) and if it requires special software.

- An Internet browser.

- An email program such as Outlook.

- All of the general software you will need, including contact management, word processing, presentation, and any specialized software related to your job or interests.

There's nothing more inconvenient than arriving in a strange city for an important meeting, and finding you don't have the one piece of software you need. So think carefully *before* you leave, and be sure to load anything you think you might even possibly need.

Also, particularly if you are going to be doing a lot of flying, be sure to load some recreational programs (such as music, video, or games) before you leave home.

Taking Hotspot Info with You

The perfect road warrior carries information he might need with him. For example, as you probably know if you've been on the road a great deal, it can be a lifesaver to have toll-free numbers for hotels and airlines handy.

In a similar spirit, when you travel with a Wi-Fi–enabled computer or PDA, you should certainly obtain information about Wi-Fi hotspots before you leave.

The problem with the online Wi-Fi directories, discussed in detail in Chapter 11, "Where Can You Wi-Fi?" is that you need to be online to use them. This doesn't do you much good when you are wandering the streets of some strange city looking for a place to connect.

WHICH CITY HAS THE MOST WI-FI HOTSPOTS?

Which city has the most Wi-Fi hotspots? If you are like me, you'd suspect New York or San Francisco.

Actually, as of this writing, the city with the most Wi-Fi hotspots is Vienna, Austria with about 165. San Francisco and New York are in second and third place, respectively.

Within the United States, Portland, Oregon is considered the most "unwired" city on a per-capita basis.

In determining the most "unwired" American city the study considered: the number of hotspots, or commercial Wi-Fi access points; the number of nodes, or public access points; the degree of Internet access available via cell phone companies' networks; and finally, how many people in the city actually use the Internet regularly.

Portland came out on top on a per-capita basis, with 130 active public access nodes, or 7.4 per 100,000 people. This gave Portland nearly five times the number of the next highest place—Austin, Texas, with 1.5 nodes per 100,000 of population.

Interestingly, the Portland Wi-Fi hotspots include 140 nodes put up by the all-volunteer Personal Telco Project, which does not charge for access. These free hotspots put Portland, Oregon off the charts for public Wi-Fi access.

Because it is so obvious that every road warrior needs an up-to-date hotspot directory that they can load on their mobile computing device, it seems odd that no one provides one. With no portable hotspot directory available, you need to make inquiries in advance of the hotels that you'll be staying at to make sure that they have Wi-Fi access. You can also use the directory services described in Chapter 11 to scope likely locations near where you'll be staying, or along your route. Finally, if you belong to one of the national Wi-Fi networks described in Chapter 12, "Working with National Wi-Fi Networks," you can use the search services provided by the network to locate convenient hotspots.

tip

If you are looking for help finding resources on the road, a book with good ideas is *Que's Business Travel Almanac* by Donna Williams (ISBN 0-7897-2934-2), which is intended to help road warriors on the go.

WI-FI HOTSPOTS VIA CELL PHONE

True, there's no way to download a portable Wi-Fi hotspot directory onto your laptop or PDA. But if you have a WAP (Wireless Protocol Application) cell phone, you can use your cell phone to browse a directory of Wi-Fi hotspots. You can find one such directory by pointing the browser in your WAP cell phone to `http://wap.wi-fizone.org`.

The Best of the Best

Suppose you don't already have the equipment you plan to use on the road with Wi-Fi. In this case, what's the best that you can buy?

Here are my top choices as of today's writing for an Apple laptop, a Windows laptop, and a PDA.

Apple

Apple makes it easy because there are only a few models to choose from. I'd buy a PowerBook, the most expensive one I could afford, such as the one shown in Figure 10.1.

note

For more information about buying an Apple or Windows laptop with Wi-Fi, see Chapter 5, "Buying a Wi-Fi Laptop." For more information about buying a Wi-Fi PDA, see Chapter 6, "Buying a Wi-Fi PDA."

FIGURE 10.1
The Apple PowerBook makes a mighty fine tool for the road warrior.

Windows

In contrast to the world of Apple, there is, of course, a great deal of choice when it comes to buying a Windows laptop.

For the ultimate road warrior, I'd go with an ultra-light IBM ThinkPad model in the X series with integrated Wi-Fi. The easiest way to specify a ThinkPad is to use the IBM Web site, as shown in Figure 10.2.

tip

Be sure that the PowerBook you buy is listed in the specifications with AirPort Extreme built-in.

FIGURE 10.2

You can use the IBM Web site to specify an ultra-light IBM ThinkPad in the X series with built-in Wi-Fi.

The IBM ThinkPad may not have a sexy form factor (in fact, the design of the case has been pretty static for quite a while), but it is an incredibly durable and light-weight machine with awesome capabilities.

PDA

It's a tough choice in PDAs, but if I could only go for one, I'd probably buy the Sony CLIE UX50 shown in Figure 10.3.

FIGURE 10.3

This Sony hand-held PDA has it all...

This Sony handheld PDA has great wireless connectivity, a built-in camera, and even a keyboard. At almost half a pound, it is more like a really miniature com-puter than a PDA. The only real question is whether it is too heavy for you. A lighter choice might be something you are more likely to have with you when you need it. This is a matter of lifestyle choice.

Of course, you may not want to spring for the expense of this machine. At a retail price of $600, it is probably the most expensive of PDAs that can be equipped with Wi-Fi.

To Laptop or to PDA?

As someone smart once said, the advantages of the one are not the same as the disadvantages of the other.

You can have a heavier or a lighter laptop, and a heavier or lighter PDA. Both categories of equipment vary tremendously in cost. Both categories provide devices that have been very capably integrated with Wi-Fi.

So the best advice is to consider the way you work. As much as possible, try different kinds of machines before you settle on one.

Although some road warriors like to travel light, the truth is that others feel the need to bring both a PDA and a laptop. Perhaps they leave the laptop in the hotel room (but see Chapter 18) and use their PDA for "roaming."

Whatever your choice, you can be sure that by using Wi-Fi–enabled computing devices, you'll make your time on the road more productive.

Keyboards, Mice, and Other Devices

A few accessories can make your PDA far easier to use as a sophisticated tool.

If you are planning to bring a Wi-Fi–enabled PDA as your primary computing device, you should probably consider an external keyboard. You can buy keyboards that attach to most PDAs, but the niftiest solution is to buy a wireless keyboard. These keyboards use universal infrared technology, built into most PDAs, and work with most PDAs.

These keyboards typically fold up and are pocket size. They do not add a great deal of weight to your PDA.

Road warriors find external chargers invaluable for Palm-style PDAs. These allow you to keep your PDA fully charged on the road without bringing along a heavy cradle.

The "stick-on" Targus PDA mouse, available from www.targus.com, replaces your Palm-style PDA's stylus with a more accurate mouse-like pointing device.

note

The best keyboards come from Think Outside, www.thinkoutside.com, and are made for PDAs from Palm and other manufacturers. Think Outside also has a Bluetooth version expected by the time this book is published.

Finally, a great add-on for many PDAs turns the PDA into a GPS (Global Positioning System) complete with mapping data. You don't ever have to get lost again when you are on the road!

For more information about these products, see Garmin International Inc., www.garmin.com, and Navman, www.navman.com. Garmin is one of the leading vendors of GPS equipment, and Navman offers a comprehensive product range that supports both Palm and Pocket PC operating systems as well as the Windows platform, with products such as the GPS clip on jackets for many leading handheld PDA manufacturers.

THE ABSOLUTE MINIMUM

Here are the key points to remember from this chapter:

- Load the software you'll need before you go.
- Find Wi-Fi hotspot information before you go.
- You have many choices of portable computing devices that work well on the road with Wi-Fi.
- A variety of accessories can improve your "on-the-road" experience if you are traveling with a PDA.

11

Where Can You Wi-Fi?

You've got the perfect laptop or PDA—or at least a perfectly service-able device—and you want to get out on the town and surf the Internet. Or perhaps you are about to go on a trip—for business or pleasure—and want to make sure that you can be in touch with email using Wi-Fi every step of the way. Or maybe you simply want to walk your neighborhood and see if anyone has a Wi-Fi network you can use.

This chapter shows you how you can find Wi-Fi hotspots—both those that provide free access and those you have to pay for.

Where Is Wi-Fi Likely to Be?

The answer, at least in a few years, is that Wi-Fi will be everywhere. Being able to connect to the Net wherever one wants will seem as natural as being able to breathe. Perhaps the right to surf without wires will rank right up there with life, liberty, and the pursuit of happiness (not to mention the right to chug down the freeway in a giant-size gas-guzzling vehicle).

You can find Wi-Fi in all kinds of unlikely places (see the sidebar "The Web Is a Global Village" for an example).

Nevertheless, it can take some effort to find Wi-Fi hotspots—that is, places that allow you to connect to the Internet with your Wi-Fi–enabled laptop or PDA—right where you want and need them.

In some places, it is pretty easy. For example, where I live, in Berkeley, California, there are literally hundreds of Wi-Fi hotspots. If I take out my laptop and walk in any direction, I can't go very far without hitting a place which provides Wi-Fi access.

It's a pretty safe bet that you'd find it hard to connect using Wi-Fi high up in the mountains of Wyoming. If the only occupants for hundreds of square miles are sheep, coyotes, and an occasional grizzly bear, no one will have thought to provide the infrastructure to let you connect via Wi-Fi.

A little less fatuously, if I listed the absolute minimum requirements for Wi-Fi, I'd say mostly you need to have people around. Population density is generally a necessity for public Wi-Fi access.

An important point is that Wi-Fi access requires infrastructure. There's a network "behind" Wi-Fi access, and the network provides a gateway to the Internet. Although it's theoretically possible to connect to the Internet via dial-up and then provide shared access via Wi-Fi, as a practical matter, most of the networks that provide Wi-Fi access use a broadband Internet connection.

THE WEB IS A GLOBAL VILLAGE

A number of villages in northeastern Cambodia use Wi-Fi in an unusual way to connect with the Internet. Five men on mountain motorbikes connect these villages, which are otherwise too remote for Internet access, with the world. Each motorbike is equipped with a rugged portable computer equipped as a Wi-Fi access point.

Internet search queries and email are stored on the portable devices when each bike drives past solar-powered stations near the villages, which are linked to the villages using standard Ethernet cabling. Then the content is "dropped-off," again using Wi-Fi technology, when the bike goes past a central satellite station that connects to the Internet.

The same process in reverse brings email (and answers to queries) back to the villages.

You can read more about this pioneering effort that uses Wi-Fi to bring the Internet to some of the world's most inaccessible places at www.firstmilesolutions.com/demo.htm.

Assuming that you don't live beyond the end of the Earth, where are the obvious places for Wi-Fi?

As I've already mentioned, it's probable that a Wi-Fi hotspot has a DSL or cable connection to the Internet. Most businesses have, or can get, this kind of access. In addition, for it to make sense for a business location to provide Wi-Fi access, it should be the kind of business in which one (or both) of two conditions apply:

- Revenue is generated when people decide they want to "hang out" for long periods of time.
- People are "stuck" in the place for long periods of time.

Coffee shops are, of course, the classic example of the first kind of Wi-Fi location. Airport waiting areas are probably the canonical example of the second type of place that benefits from Wi-Fi, as in, "let me check my email while I'm waiting for my flight!" (Particularly these days with the increased need to check in long before flights and the longer waits due to security concerns.)

This chapter provides information about using available tools for finding Wi-Fi hotspots. The most useful tools are online directories, with, of course, the drawback that you already have to be online to use them.

I'll also show you a neat gizmo—the Wi-Fi Finder—you can use to see if there is a Wi-Fi network broadcasting nearby.

Finally, I'll tell you what war driving and war chalking are about. These are two social movements that owe their origins to Wi-Fi and have to do with finding Wi-Fi networks.

Before I get started on this agenda, let me mention one simple, low-tech thing: It pays to ask. If you are looking for a Wi-Fi hotspot in an area far from home, just ask someone. Chances are that many people you meet can direct you to a local Wi-Fi hotspot—particularly if the person you ask is carrying a laptop!

Using Wi-Fi Directories

The best and easiest way to find Wi-Fi hotspots is to use the directories available on the Web. There are only two problems with using these directories:

- You have to be already connected to the Internet to access them.
- No one directory is comprehensive, and the information in each directory is different. This means that you may need to search multiple directories to find the hotspot you are looking for.

Where to Find the Directories

Here are some of the most widely used Wi-Fi hotspot directories and where to find them on the Web:

- China Pulse: www.chinapulse.com/wifi (hotspot locator for China)
- HotSpotList: www.wi-fihotspotlist.com
- i-Spot Access: www.i-spotaccess.com/directory.asp (currently limited to Illinois, Iowa, Missouri, and Nebraska)
- JIWIRE: www.jiwire.com
- Ordnance Survey: www.g-intelligence.co.uk/wireless/wifimap.php (great for United Kingdom hotspots)
- Square 7: www.square7.com/hotspots (great for European hotspots)
- WiFi411: www.wifi411.com
- Wi-Fi-Freespot Directory: www.wififreespot.com
- WiFinder: www.wifinder.com (one of the best all-around international hotspot directories)
- WiFiMaps: www.wifimaps.com
- Wireless Access List: wirelessaccesslist.com/wireless/u.asp (categorized by state and ZIP code, also allows sorting by network, for example, T-Mobile, Wayport, and so on)
- Zagat Survey: www.subscriberdirect.com/the_new_yorker/zagat/ (lists and reviews restaurants and hotels with Wi-Fi access in five major U.S. cities: Chicago, Los Angeles, New York, San Francisco, and Seattle)

note

If you have signed up with a national network, such as T-Mobile Hotspot, it stands to reason that you will want to use hotspots that your network provides. The best approach for finding network-specific hotspots is to use the directory provided by the network itself. For more about working with national Wi-Fi networks, see Chapter 12, "Working with National Wi-Fi Networks."

Which Directory to Use

As I mentioned earlier, if you are looking for a Wi-Fi hotspot provided by a specific network provider, that network provider is the best source of location information. See Chapter 12 for more information about national networks. Appendix B, "Finding Wi-Fi Hotspots," has a more extensive listing of national networks, along with various categories of commercial chains that provide Wi-Fi in many of their stores.

If you are looking for free Wi-Fi access, Wi-Fi Freespot is probably your best bet.

If you need to find a hotspot in a specific geographic area, a directory that targets a specific area may be the way to go. For example, China Pulse has the best listings for finding hotspots in China (yes, Virginia, there is Wi-Fi coverage in China), and the Ordnance Survey is one of the best way to find Wi-Fi hotspots in Great Britain.

If you are looking for a restaurant or hotel with Wi-Fi in one of the cities it covers, by all means use the Zagat directory.

Otherwise, I find the best all-around directories for use with commercial Wi-Fi hotspots are HotSpotList and WiFi411.

Getting Around the "You Have to Be Connected" Barrier

The JIWIRE directory, www.jiwire.com, has a partial answer to the "you can't get there from here" problem.

JIWIRE powers directories that work using the AvantGo mobile Internet service using a Palm OS PDA or a Pocket PC handheld. The JIWIRE directory can also be accessed by a WAP-enabled wireless phone.

To use the handheld directory, you need an AvantGo account (www.avantgo.com), and a wireless handheld capable of working with the AvantGo network. You download the AvantGo Hotspot Locator (powered by JIWIRE) using your desktop computer, following the instructions on the JIWIRE and AvantGo sites. The next time you synch your handheld with your desktop, the AvantGo Hotspot Locator will be downloaded onto the handheld. You will be able to use it much as you use a desktop Wi-Fi directory.

To use the WAP-enabled phone directory, you need a wireless phone with a WAP browser and a mobile Web account with your cell phone provider. You can then use the WAP-enabled phone as a Wi-Fi finder by using it to surf to www.jiwire.com. Of course, depending on your service plan, you can expect to be charged for the time you are searching.

JIWIRE's introduction of Wi-Fi locator services for AvantGo-enabled PDAs and WAP-enabled cell phones is quite innovative and probably quite useful to the intrepid road warrior. (See Chapter 10, "Tools for the Perfect Road Warrior," for more tips about the Wi-Fi equipment you need as a road warrior.) But in some ways it is a bit of a clunky solution because it requires that you carry another (non-Wi-Fi) wireless device.

Tricks and Techniques

If you've spent much time surfing the Web, you've probably learned some techniques for dealing with search engines provided by sites such as Google, Yahoo, and even Amazon. Searching a Wi-Fi directory for a hotspot is much the same: There are different tricks and techniques for using each one. In this section, I'll take a look at using my two favorite Wi-Fi directories, HotSpotList and WiFi411.

Using the HotSpotList Directory

Figure 11.1 shows the HotSpotList main window.

FIGURE 11.1

The HotSpotList search window.

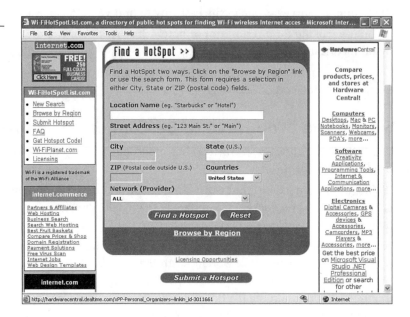

This window is used to conduct searches (you can also browse by location as I'll show you in a second).

To conduct a search, you need to enter a business name or type, and some geographic information (such as city and state, or a ZIP code). For example, a search for Starbucks in New York provides many pages of results, as you can see in Figure 11.2.

A nice feature of this search window is that it allows you to screen by network provider. When you open the search window, it is set to show all network providers, meaning that there is no network provider screening. However, you can select a network provider, such as Boingo Wireless, from the drop-down list, shown in part in Figure 11.3.

note

The HotSpotList network provider filter includes all the Wi-Fi networks you may have heard of, such as those listed in Appendix B. It also includes many "boutique" networks that you have probably never heard of.

FIGURE 11.2

The search
results window.

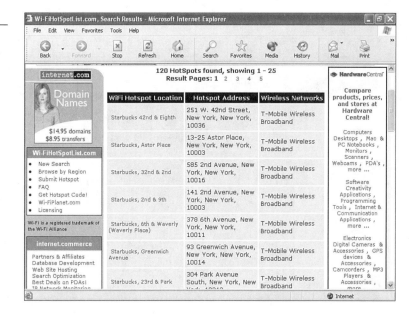

FIGURE 11.3

You can filter the
HotSpotList
search by net-
work provider.

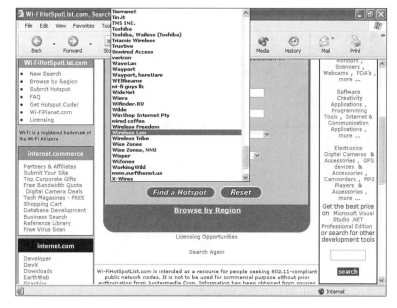

If you go back to the HotSpotList main search window and click the Browse by Region link, you can then choose a country to browse from the list.

Most of the countries shown in the list in Figure 11.4 are not further subdivided, but if you click on the United States link, you can then click a link for each state.

Drilling down the next step, if you click on a state link, you will see the cities within that state with hotspots (see Figure 11.4).

FIGURE 11.4

Each city within
the state that
has at least one
hotspot is
shown.

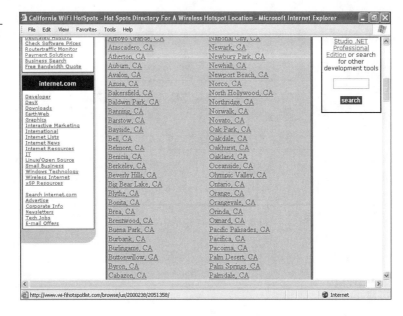

If you click on a link representing a city, you will then see the listings for that city. For example, Figure 11.5 shows the listings for my home town, Berkeley, California.

FIGURE 11.5

The HotSpotList
listings for
Berkeley,
California.

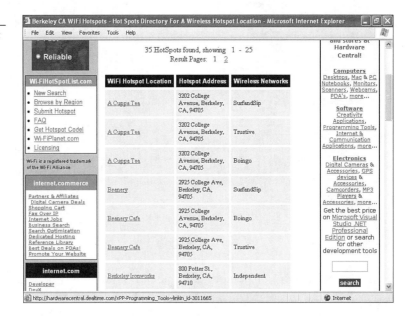

The detailed listing provides the address of the hotspot, the Wi-Fi network provider, and a link to more detailed information about the hotspot. For example, Figure 11.6 shows the listing for Pacific Ironworks, a local climbing gym that offers free Wi-Fi access.

FIGURE 11.6

Detailed listings provide further information about each hotspot.

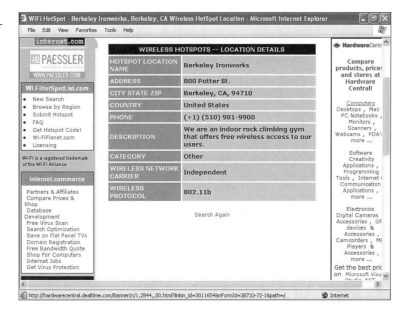

So if you ever plan to visit beautiful, downtown Berkeley, be sure to bring your mobile Wi-Fi device and visit Pacific Ironworks. Even if you don't do any climbing, you can certainly surf the Web!

Using the WiFi411 Directory

The main window of WiFi411, shown in Figure 11.7, doesn't provide a way to drill down by region (as HotSpotList does), but it does add a few useful bells and whistles of its own.

One of the most useful things about WiFi411 is that you can search by type of hotspot. Figure 11.8 shows some of the results of searching for a coffee shop in Berkeley.

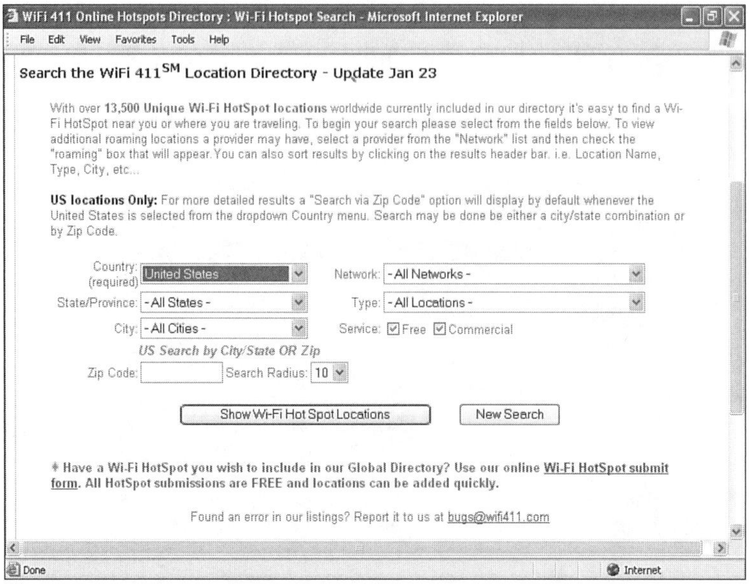

FIGURE 11.7

The WiFi411 main window.

FIGURE 11.8

Search results for a coffee shop in Berkeley.

The type of search is determined by selecting a type from the drop-down list shown in Figure 11.9 (you can also choose All types, and not filter based on type).

FIGURE 11.9

You can search for a particular type of hotspot by searching from the list.

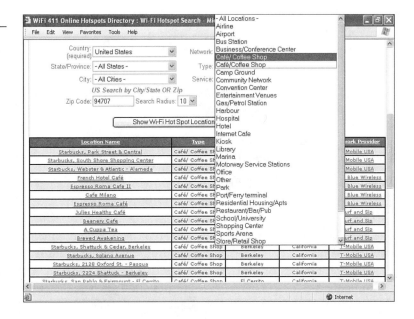

Perhaps the most useful feature of the site is the roaming feature. If you filter your search results using a Wi-Fi network provider, when the results are returned a Roaming check box is displayed (you can see this check box in Figure 11.10).

FIGURE 11.10

The Roaming check box appears when you select a network provider.

If you check the Roaming box and search again, the new results will show not only your network provider's hotspots but also hotspots that are served by any network with whom your provider has a roaming arrangement. (For more about roaming, see Chapter 12.) Very cool feature!

You may not want to roam; you may just want to stay home. Whatever your call, WiFi411 is one of the best hotspot locators of all!

I Want to Be a Hotspot

Well, I don't think you really want to *be* a hotspot—but perhaps you might want to put one up so others could use it.

If you run any kind of small business, this might make a great deal of sense. By way of comparison, Schlotzsky's, Inc., which runs deli restaurants, has stated that adding free Wi-Fi to its shops adds more than $100,000 revenue for each store per year (through added purchasing by customers who come to the store for the Wi-Fi hotspot, or who stay longer than they otherwise would).

You might also want to put up a Wi-Fi hotspot simply as a service to your fellow humans (believe it or not, this kind of altruism has largely sparked the growth of Wi-Fi!).

The technical aspects of putting up a Wi-Fi hotspot, meaning the hardware infrastructure required, don't differ that much from putting up a Wi-Fi network for personal or business use. To start with, you need a broadband connection. If you are planning to resell access via a Wi-Fi hotspot, most cable and DSL providers will require you to buy a commercial-grade account (rather than a personal use account).

For more information about putting together a Wi-Fi network, see Part IV, "Creating a Wi-Fi Network." If you are interested, I've provided some material showing the architecture of a public hotspot (which might be part of a private network) in Chapter 15, "Configuring Your Wi-Fi Network."

The problem is not the hardware so much as what is called, in the telecommunications business, *provisioning*. Provisioning means setting up the systems that provide customer service, support, and billing.

You'll want to consider provisioning issues even if you plan to give away Wi-Fi access for free. This is because it is dangerous to allow unrestricted access to your network. If access to your network does not require registration, it could be used for malicious purposes, for example, spamming, which could get your Internet address blacklisted.

Some of the national Wi-Fi network providers discussed in Chapter 12 will provide basic support and protection for IP address abuse for a reasonable fee. If you are interested in this, you should check out Surf and Sip, `www.surfandsip.com`, which specializes in Wi-Fi–enabled hotspots for providers who want to give access away for free.

> **caution**
>
> Hosting a Wi-Fi hotspot can lead to serious security risks. Even if you are not charging for access, at the very least, you should probably consider instituting a user authentication scheme. For more information about security, check out Chapter 19, "Securing Your Wi-Fi Network."

If selling access is more your cup of tea (or Java), there are any number of companies that sell turnkey packages. Generally, you purchase the hardware from the company, which then provides provisioning services, and splits the proceeds from billing using an agreed-upon percentage.

One turnkey provider of this sort is Pacific Wi-Fi, `www.pacificwi-fi.com`. Another similar product is Instant Hotspot from Advanced Internet Access (see `www.instanthotspot.com/wsg5000.htm` for more information).

When you have your Wi-Fi hotspot up, your problem is the reverse of the one primarily discussed in this chapter. You don't need to find a hotspot—you need people to find your hotspot. If you don't get the word out, no one will know about it. A hotspot that has not been promoted has a place in the world like that proverbial tree that falls in the forest—if no one knows it has fallen, what is the point? (Or is it even real?)

An essential first step in promoting your new hotspot is to make sure it appears in the directories described earlier in this chapter.

Of course, after you put up your hotspot you could "war chalk" it yourself using the standard symbols explained later in this chapter. (Traditionally, these symbols are chalked on the sidewalk, but they could also go on a permanent sign.) In a heavily trafficked area, a simple sign that says "Wi-Fi Hotspot" would probably also draw traffic.

Working with a Wi-Fi Finder

One approach to finding Wi-Fi hotspots is to use a Wi-Fi Finder, a small, inexpensive device that has appeared on the market recently.

The most commonly used Wi-Fi Finder is the one from Kensington Technology Group, model number 33063. This tiny unit measures 2.7 by 3 inches, and is about a 1/2-inch thick.

It's simple to use the Wi-Fi Finder. When you're out wandering, press the unit's button. If it detects an 802.11b or 802.11g Wi-Fi network, the green lights

note

A Wi-Fi hotspot is termed *open* when it is not encrypted. This means you do not have to supply an encryption key, which for all the world looks and acts like a password. An example of an open hotspot is the T-Mobile Hotspot hosts, which require an SSID but not an encryption key (you also have to log on to the T-Mobile network with your T-Mobile user ID and password, but that's a different issue).

A Wi-Fi hotspot is *closed* when an encryption key is required to access the node. All private Wi-Fi networks should be run in closed mode.

Wi-Fi encryption is accomplished using WEP (Wireless Equivalency Protocol), a security measure that is part of the 802.11 and Wi-Fi standards. I'll explain WEP further in Chapter 19.

light up. The more green lights, the stronger the signal. If only the red light appears, there's no Wi-Fi network in the neighborhood.

The Wi-Fi Finder blocks out competing 2.4GHz signals from devices such as cordless phones and microwaves, so that when it shows a signal, you know it is from a Wi-Fi network. It has an effective range of about 200 feet out of doors.

So far, so good. But the fact of the matter is that you can't tell from the Wi-Fi Finder what the SSID of the network is, who the network provider is, whether the hotspot is free or commercial, whether the network is open or closed, and if closed, who to contact for access.

So a Wi-Fi Finder is a fun and pretty cool thing to put on your keychain (the Kensington model comes with a ring for attachment to a key chain). But is it genuinely useful? That probably depends on the user, but you can definitely find me out cruising the neighborhood to see where the Wi-Fi is using my handy-dandy Wi-Fi Finder (see Figure 11.11).

FIGURE 11.11

The author is cruising for Wi-Fi in all the wrong places.

War Driving and War Chalking

War driving is the hobby of popping in a car and cruising around with a Wi-Fi–equipped laptop looking for open Wi-Fi nodes.

War chalking is the act of using specific chalk markings, usually on a sidewalk, to identify Wi-Fi hotspots.

Both activities show the extent to which Wi-Fi has come out of nothing as a disruptive technology, until fairly recently because of grassroots support and without the backing of major corporations. Although important companies such as Intel and others now back Wi-Fi, the "counter-culture" roots of old-time Wi-Fi and 802.11 practitioners remain an important aspect of the social history of Wi-Fi.

War driving as an activity ranges from the fun, but harmless (that is, if you find this kind of thing fun) to malicious and felonious (theft of information such as credit card numbers, and industrial spying). It's successful only because an astoundingly large number of corporations and others that deploy private Wi-Fi networks do not use even rudimentary protection such as encryption. (See Chapter 19 for advice about securing your private network.) It has been estimated that as many as 60% of the privately deployed Wi-Fi networks operate without encryption.

Supposedly, war chalking is derived in part from the marks hobos made during the Great Depression. These hobo chalk markings would point out a place to get a meal for free, a good place to sleep, and perhaps a particularly nasty railroad "bull."

In war chalking, an open node (public hotspot) is indicated by two opposing half circles marked with the SSID and the bandwidth (see Figure 11.12).

FIGURE 11.12

The war chalk marking for an open node.

A closed node (or private Wi-Fi network) is shown as a circle, along with its SSID, as in Figure 11.13.

A Wi-Fi node protected by WEP encryption is shown as a circle with a letter W within it (see Figure 11.14). Ideally, the encrypted node is marked with SSID, bandwidth, and access contact (the access contact can provide the encryption key if it is appropriate).

FIGURE 11.13

The war chalk marking for a closed node is a circle.

FIGURE 11.13

The war chalk marking for a closed node is a circle.

FIGURE 11.14

The war chalk marking for a WEP node.

FIGURE 11.14

The war chalk marking for a WEP node.

The fact that war chalking has spread as a practice is a testament to the power of the Internet to spread social habits. It also speaks to the problem of finding Wi-Fi hotspots if you are not already online. In the future, it's likely that Wi-Fi hotspot information will become more ubiquitous. Perhaps the community welcome signs that now tell the time and place for Rotary Club meetings will soon come to also provide Wi-Fi hotspot information. When travelers visiting a community can find Wi-Fi hotspot information in this kind of way, war chalking will probably fade into history like the chalk marks made by the hobos of long ago.

WHERE DOES THE "WAR" IN "WAR DRIVING" AND "WAR CHALKING" COME FROM?

Why does "war driving" use the term "war?" Admittedly, the practice of war driving is an attempt to obtain information illicitly, but a better term might be something like "Eavesdrop driving."

The term "war chalking" seems to have come along as a Johnny-come-lately term for "war driving." War driving was already firmly entrenched in the Wi-Fi counter-culture, so when the newer grass-roots activity of marking Wi-Fi hotspots came along, perhaps it seemed natural to use the "war" word. But how was "war driving" named in the first place?

The term derives from "war dialing," which was the pre-broadband hacker practice of programming a computer to dial hundreds of dial-up access numbers, hoping to find one that was not protected (or could easily be cracked). It was popularized by the movie *War Games* (1983).

THE ABSOLUTE MINIMUM

Here are the key points to remember from this chapter:

- There is no one single good way to locate all Wi-Fi hotspots.
- Online directories are a great source of information about Wi-Fi hotspots and are central to the Wi-Fi movement.
- It's problematic finding Wi-Fi hotspot information if you are not already online. Solutions range from asking people, to using a Wi-Fi Finder, to reading war chalk marks.
- Besides being a wireless protocol, Wi-Fi is a way of life, and a cultural movement!

12

WORKING WITH NATIONAL Wi-Fi NETWORKS

In this chapter, I suppose that you have your mobile Wi-Fi device ready to roll and want to sign up with a Wi-Fi network. You may primarily be interested in using Wi-Fi hotspots locally, or you may want to use them for more distant traveling. In either case, the issues are much the same as when you choose a wireless cell phone provider. You should be concerned about

- How widespread is the coverage?

- What are the costs and fees?

- Are there any discounts?

- What are the roaming policies in place?

- How good is customer service?

This chapter answers these questions. I'll start with a rundown of the major national networks. (You'll find a more complete listing of Wi-Fi networks with some of the smaller players and some non-U.S. providers in Appendix B, "Finding Wi-Fi Hotspots.")

Wi-Fi Networks

Table 12.1 shows the national U.S. networks and provides telephone numbers and Web addresses. This contact information may be useful if you want to do further research, or if you decide you want to sign up with a specific network. It could also help if you are traveling to an area that is particularly well served by a specific provider.

> **tip**
>
> The Wi-Fi industry is rapidly changing. Be sure to verify that the information in this chapter is current when doing your own research.

TABLE 12.1   Wi-Fi Networks

Network	URL	Phone	Comments
AT&T Wireless	www.attwireless.com/business/ features/communication/ servicehotspots.jhtml	888-290-4613	AT&T's Wi-Fi service is called "goport." Information about goport can be hard to find without the Web address in this table.
Boingo Wireless	www.boingo.com	800-880-4117	A pioneer Wi-Fi network, and still considered one of the best. Great roaming policies.
Sprint PCS	www.sprint.com/pcsbusiness/ products_services/data/wifi/ index.html	888-703-9514	Rolling out quickly based on existing infrastructure.
SurfHere	www.csd.toshiba.com/ cgi-bin/tais/hs/hs_home.jsp	877-429-6385	Affiliated with Toshiba, SurfHere provides access in stores including McDonald's and The UPS Store.
T-Mobile Hotspot	www.t-mobile.com/hotspot/	800-981-8563	The leading Wi-Fi provider, building infrastructure in Starbucks stores and elsewhere. T-Mobile is the one everyone else wants to beat.
Verizon	www.verizon.net/wifi/	888-842-9275	Currently provides hotspots mainly in the metropolitan NY area; most are free to Verizon DSL customers.
Wayport	www.wayport.com	877-929-7678	An early pioneer in providing Wi-Fi hotspots, now providing infrastructure in McDonald's and elsewhere.

Special Pricing, Good and Bad

You should be aware that there are likely to be all kinds of special pricing deals when you sign up for Wi-Fi access. Mostly, this is all to the good.

For example, most establishments that provide fee-based Wi-Fi access also have some special, introductory offers. In this spirit, it is typical to find a coupon at Starbucks good for a one-day pass on T-Mobile Hotspot.

However, you should also know that some Wi-Fi networks allow individual hotspot operators who are part of their network to charge more than the standard network price for access. For example, the business model of the SurfHere network is one in which it is more important to support hotspot providers than it is to create a national network for individuals. So SurfHere is quite clear that many of its hotspot providers can (and do) charge more than the standard network fees. If the location charges more than the standard network fee, your credit card will be billed for the overage.

What the Networks Charge

The charges and payment structure in this section are based upon information published by each network or on conversations I have had with Wi-Fi network company representatives. As I've noted before, they are certainly subject to change, so you should verify current pricing for yourself. I've tried to include some tips and ideas for getting the most out of each Wi-Fi network.

AT&T Wireless

AT&T Wireless (goport) offers a number of different Wi-Fi service plans as shown in Table 12.2.

TABLE 12.2 AT&T Wireless Wi-Fi Plans

Plan	Details	Price
1 Time Connect	One-time 24 hour access at the location where access was purchased.	$9.99
5 Connect Package	Five one-time connects; valid for six months (note that each connect is only good at a single location).	$29.99
10 Connect Package	Ten one-time connects; valid for six months (note that each connect is only good at a single location).	$49.99
Monthly Unlimited	"Unlimited" usage at unlimited locations. Note that this "unlimited" plan is actually limited to 150 connections per month (for "anti-fraud" reasons). Although 150 connections per month is a lot, one could easily see how it might be exceeded.	$69.99 per month

AT&T wireless has no roaming arrangements with any other Wi-Fi providers, meaning that if you buy an AT&T connection package (or monthly unlimited plan), you cannot use it on any other Wi-Fi network.

Boingo Wireless

Boingo Wireless has two kinds of payment plans available as shown in Table 12.3.

TABLE 12.3   Boingo Wireless Wi-Fi Plans

Plan	Details	Price
Boingo AsYouGo	Unlimited daily access from any number of locations	$7.95 for the first two days; $7.95 for each additional day thereafter
Boingo Unlimited	True unlimited monthly access from any number of locations	$21.95 per month for the first year; $31.95 per month thereafter

Boingo Wireless has extensive roaming arrangements with Wayport, Surf and Sip, and many smaller networks. If you download Boingo's special software, you can use roaming networks seamlessly (you won't even know you are roaming).

Otherwise, if you connect normally by scanning for an SSID (as explained in Part II, "Setting Up Your Computer for Wi-Fi"), you can enter your Boingo user ID and password to log on to the "foreign" network.

The ability to roam on other networks effectively greatly extends Boingo's Wi-Fi network.

tip

In some cases, you can save money by using Boingo for access and then roaming on a foreign (and nominally more costly) Wi-Fi network.

Sprint PCS

Sprint PCS offers Wi-Fi access on a daily basis or as part of its business data plans as shown in Table 12.4. The Sprint business data plans shown in Table 12.4 are primarily intended for business customers. Costs are based on the amount of data transferred between your mobile computer and the Wi-Fi network.

TABLE 12.4   Sprint PCS Wi-Fi Plans

Plan	Details	Price
Daily	Unlimited daily access from any number of locations	$9.00
Business Dataplan Basic	20 MB monthly of data transfer	$40 per month
Business Dataplan Unlimited	Unlimited data transfer	$80 per month

Note that if you sign up for a business data plan and go over the data transfer allotment, you will be charged for any overages.

Sprint PCS has no Wi-Fi roaming arrangements available.

SurfHere

Toshiba of America's SurfHere is primarily intended as infrastructure support for businesses that want to establish a hotspot. This means that businesses that host a SurfHere hotspot are free to mark up access prices if they want.

Access to the SurfHere network can be established in the normal fashion by using a credit card to create an account online. You can also purchase access from the vendor hosting the Wi-Fi access. The vendor will sell you a "coupon"; entering the information supplied on the coupon gets you on the SurfHere network.

Table 12.5 shows SurfHere pricing plans.

TABLE 12.5   SurfHere Wi-Fi Plans

Plan	Details	Price
One-Hour Plan	Access for an hour from any SurfHere hotspot location	$4.95
Two-Hour Plan	Access for two hours from any SurfHere hotspot location	$5.95
One-Day Plan	Access for twenty-four hours from any SurfHere hotspot location	$7.95
Seven-Day Plan	Access for seven days from any SurfHere hotspot location	$19.95
Thirty-Day Plan	Access for thirty days from any SurfHere hotspot location	$39.95

SurfHere has no roaming arrangements with other networks, so if you buy SurfHere access you cannot expect to use the access time on any hotspots except SurfHere's.

T-Mobile Hotspot

T-Mobile Hotspot is the leading provider of Wi-Fi hotspot services, and perhaps the old-line telecommunications company that is making the most effort to become a true national Wi-Fi network. (T-Mobile is a subsidiary of Deutsche Telekom.)

This effort is spearheaded, of course, by the presence of T-Mobile Wi-Fi access points in Starbucks shops.

Table 12.6 shows the T-Mobile Hotspot pricing plans.

TABLE 12.6   T-Mobile Hotspot Wi-Fi Plans

Plan	Details	Price
Metered Plan	This is a no-strings-attached, pay-as-you-go plan. No term commitment, valid at all locations.	$0.10 per minute, with a 60-minute minimum
DayPass	Unlimited access from all locations for twenty-four hours.	$9.99
Unlimited National—Monthly	Unlimited monthly access.	$39.99 per month
Unlimited National—Annual	Unlimited monthly access with a price break when you commit to a year.	$29.99 per month

T-Mobile offers no roaming facilities on other networks.

Verizon

Verizon's Wi-Fi offerings are primarily intended as a courtesy offering to existing Verizon subscribers, and the pricing reflects this fact.

Existing DSL or dial-up Internet access customers of Verizon can access Verizon's Wi-Fi hotspots at no charge. Note that Verizon states that it intends to alter this policy at some point so that dial-up subscribers are no longer allowed free Wi-Fi access.

If you have a Verizon wireless cell phone account, you can add Wi-Fi access to your account for $6.99 per day or $34.99 per month.

Wayport

Wayport offers the pricing plans shown in Table 12.7.

TABLE 12.7 Wayport Wi-Fi Plans

Plan	Details	Price
Single hotel connection	Unlimited access from a guest room or common area. Note that guest rooms and common areas are considered to be separate locations, and charged separately (you incur two fees).	$9.95 until next hotel check-in time (hotel may mark this up)
Single airport connection	Unlimited access from an airport.	$6.95 from purchase time through midnight
Prepaid connection cards	Wayport connection cards give you time-limited access (the amount of access varies by location). These cards can be bought at Wayport's Laptop Lane facilities, found in many airports (you'll also get a Laptop Lane discount when you buy one).	$25 for 3 connections $50 for 8 connections $100 for 20 connections
Month-to-month membership	Unlimited monthly access.	$49.95 per month
Annual membership	Unlimited monthly access with a price break when you commit to a year.	$29.95 per month with a one-year contract

Wayport does not offer roaming on other networks to its customers.

Comparison Shopping

Don't be thrown by the complexities of all the different Wi-Fi pricing models. It's not really as complicated as it may seem.

As a practical matter, the first time you use a Wi-Fi hotspot, you'll probably take advantage of a promotional offer, or buy one-time (or pay as you go) access. It's a good idea to stay uncommitted for a while, and to try a variety of different networks.

So start with one-off usage, and get a feel for a number of the Wi-Fi hotspot networks. You should make note of locations, access speeds, and how good the customer service is.

After you've used a number of Wi-Fi hotspots, you should begin to get the sense of your usage patterns, and you may be ready to sign up for an extended payment plan by the month (or even an annual contract). If you keep a log showing your actual usage and compare it to pricing explained in this section, you may be able to come up with the best pricing comparison.

If a particular location is vital to you, you may be stuck with one particular provider, and comparisons won't matter so much.

THE ABSOLUTE MINIMUM

Here are the key points to remember from this chapter:

- There are a limited number of national Wi-Fi networks that provide hotspots.

- A few of these networks (Boingo, Wayport) are attempting to build Wi-Fi networks from scratch.

- Other networks use the infrastructure of wireless or wireless telecommunications providers (T-Mobile Hotspot is the leader of these).

- Boingo is the network with the best roaming policy.

- Pricing is erratic and varies from network to network.

- You can generally purchase one-time access, access by the day, or monthly access.

- Some Wi-Fi network providers allow marked-up pricing; beware of retailers who overcharge for Wi-Fi access.

PART IV

CREATING A WI-FI NETWORK

13

BUYING A WI-FI ACCESS POINT OR ROUTER

Perhaps you've tried Wi-Fi on the road and have seen how great it is! It's also okay if you haven't! In any case, you are ready to "unwire" your home or small office by adding a Wi-Fi network.

You'll find that it's very easy to create a Wi-Fi network from scratch (or to add Wi-Fi to an existing Ethernet network).

This chapter gets you started building your own Wi-Fi network. There are quite a number of different pieces of hardware (or hardware combinations) you can use to do this, which can seem a bit overwhelming. But, fear not! It's all a lot simpler than it may seem.

I'll start out by clearly delineating the different kinds of hardware that you might use in creating a home or small office Wi-Fi network. There's no need for any confusion about this. Then I'll take a look at all-in-one Wi-Fi networking kits.

Finally, I'll get down to it: What access point should you buy? I'll also take a closer look at two of the most popular pieces of hardware used for this purpose: Apple's AirPort Extreme Base Station and Linksys's Wireless Broadband Router.

Understanding the Different Pieces of Hardware

So you want to set up a new wireless network in your home or office. Or, you want to extend an existing wire line network to provide wireless capabilities. In either case, relax! These are pretty easy things to do using Wi-Fi technology. You'll have your wireless network up and running in no time—and be using your computer in your living room, in your garden or on your deck, and from all kinds of unlikely places.

This chapter focuses on buying the right hardware to set up your wireless network (subsequent chapters detail other aspects of setting up and administering your wireless network).

Networking hardware can be somewhat confusing, and uses terms that overlap. Before I get down to specifics at a brand-name level, it's a good idea to spell out the different kinds of equipment that you might expect to need in a wireless network. If you take one thing away from this book, let it be clarity about the different pieces of wireless networking hardware and what they do.

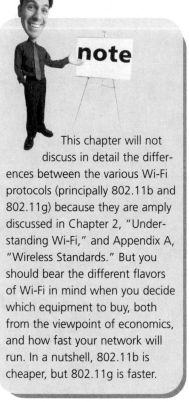

note

This chapter will not discuss in detail the differences between the various Wi-Fi protocols (principally 802.11b and 802.11g) because they are amply discussed in Chapter 2, "Understanding Wi-Fi," and Appendix A, "Wireless Standards." But you should bear the different flavors of Wi-Fi in mind when you decide which equipment to buy, both from the viewpoint of economics, and how fast your network will run. In a nutshell, 802.11b is cheaper, but 802.11g is faster.

Ad-Hoc Versus Infrastructure Modes

A basic distinction within Wi-Fi networks is between *ad-hoc* and *infrastructure* modes. In ad-hoc mode, there is no central server, and wireless nodes (meaning computers or other devices) communicate directly with each other on a peer-to-peer basis. Figure 13.1 shows an example of ad-hoc wireless networking.

In contrast, in infrastructure mode, the wireless network consists of at least one access point (sometimes called an *AP* for short) connected to a wired network as shown in Figure 13.2. The access point serves as a connection between the wired network and the wireless network, and provides a mechanism for wireless computers on the network to share access to resources such as files, printers, and Internet access.

FIGURE 13.1
These computers are networked using wireless ad-hoc mode.

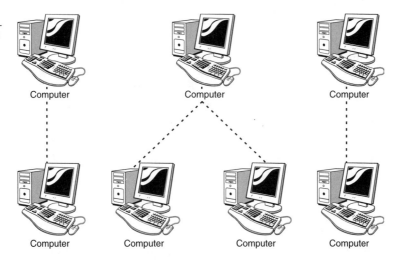

FIGURE 13.2
In infrastructure mode, at least one access point connects the wireless and wire line portions of the network.

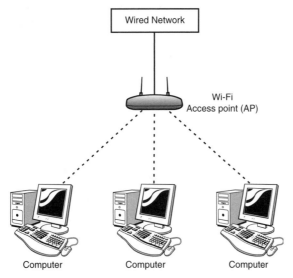

The main problem with ad-hoc mode is that it doesn't have very much range. Access points are simply better at broadcasting Wi-Fi signals than Wi-Fi cards or chips within a computer.

If you only have two computers that are not physically very far from each other, you may want to try ad-hoc mode and skip the network hardware explained in this chapter. (Ad-hoc mode can also be useful when you are on the road and want to connect to a colleague's computer.)

Ad-hoc mode can also be used to make a desktop PC wired to the Internet into an access point for another computer, assuming that both have the appropriate Wi-Fi cards. This requires that the computer that is wired to the Internet be configured to share its Internet connection, as I'll explain in Chapter 15, "Configuring Your Wi-Fi Network."

Using computers like this in the ad-hoc mode eliminates the need to purchase an access point or router (not that much of an expense these days really), but is more complicated to set up and doesn't eliminate as many wires.

caution

Note that unless one of the computers involved in an ad-hoc connection has a separate non–Wi-Fi connection to the Internet, neither computer will be able to access the Internet.

In Chapter 15 I'll show you how to configure a wireless computer to enable ad-hoc networking, and also how to share an Internet connection.

For the most part, you are less likely to be frustrated if you go ahead and set up an infrastructure mode wireless network, which is my assumption for the remainder of this chapter.

Wi-Fi Access Points

The crucial piece of equipment in your Wi-Fi network is the access point, also sometimes called a *base station*. A Wi-Fi access point

- Transmits (and receives) Wi-Fi broadcasts
- Acts as a connection between a wired computer and the Wi-Fi network

Because Wi-Fi access points come in a number of different permutations, it makes sense to take a bit of a closer look.

If you already have a wired network, you are probably using a router, which is a small device that connects to your broadband Internet modem and is connected to each of the computers on your network as shown in Figure 13.3.

note

Although your network router is most likely a small, separate device, you may be interested to know that server computers can be used for the same purpose.

FIGURE 13.3

A router sits
"between" your
Internet connec-
tion and the
computers in
your network.

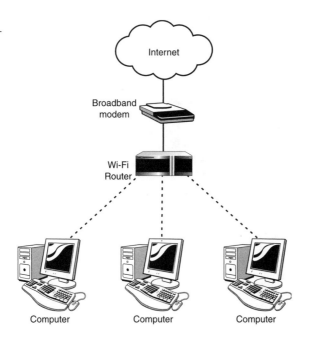

The router provides the services necessary for each computer on the network to have Internet access (explained in Chapter 16, "Sharing an Internet Connection"). It also can assign each computer on the network an Internet Protocol (IP) address so that the computers can communicate and share resources.

Small routers typically come with four or five sockets for computers to plug into; if you need to connect more computers, you can easily add hubs, which are simply wired network repeaters.

Most Wi-Fi access points provide the same services as a router, so you really don't need a router any more (but you'll need to make sure that your Wi-Fi access point can function as a router). You can eliminate your router, and instead plug in the Wi-Fi access point (which is really a combination access point and router).

The best part of it is that many access point units, such as the Linksys Wireless Broadband unit described later in this chapter, provide both Wi-Fi access for network computers, and plugs for the wired devices on your network. A network arranged using an access point/router that provides both Wi-Fi and wired connections is shown in Figure 13.4.

FIGURE 13.4

Some access points provide Wi-Fi and wired network connections.

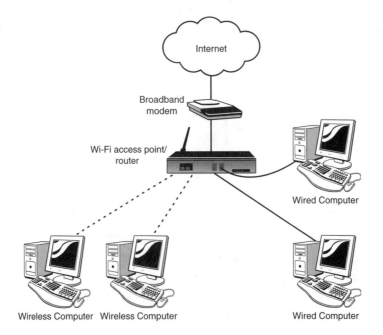

Simplicity is a good thing, and—if you are like me—it's great to get rid of all those small devices cluttering up your life near the Internet connection (in my case, that's under my desk!)

You can take the combination thing one step further, and buy a small unit that combines a broadband modem with a Wi-Fi access point and router.

For example, if you are using a cable modem to access the Internet, you could replace your cable modem with the all-in-one Wireless Cable Modem Gateway SBG1000 from Motorola, which includes a modem, router, wireless access point, and five sockets for wired network connections. This unit runs 802.11b Wi-Fi and can be had for a little more than $200 U.S.

If you make this substitution, the physical network shown in Figure 13.4 can be redrawn with one component, as shown in Figure 13.5.

tip

If you want to keep your wire-line router, you can! Depending on your network configuration, it may make more sense to plug your access point in "after" the router, rather than removing the router. As I'll discuss in Chapter 15, there are many possible ways to set up a network.

FIGURE 13.5

A Motorola
cable modem
unit includes a
Wi-Fi access
point.

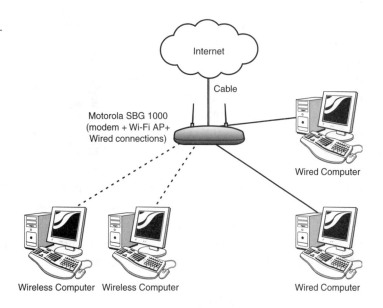

Internet

Cable

Motorola SBG 1000
(modem + Wi-Fi AP+
Wired connections)

Wired Computer

Wireless Computer   Wireless Computer

Wired Computer

Wireless Bridges

You should also know about another kind of device that can be used to extend your Wi-Fi networks or to make them more versatile. This is the wireless network bridge.

Wireless network bridges come in three flavors:

- Simple Ethernet to wireless
- A dedicated wireless bridge
- Wireless bridge access point combinations

A simple Ethernet-to-wireless bridge is intended to connect a non-wireless device to a wireless network, and you can use it to connect any device capable of networking—such as a network printer or a game box with an Ethernet port—to a wireless network.

A decent Ethernet-to-wireless bridge such as D-Link's DWL-810 can be had for a little more than $50.

Dedicated wireless bridges can be used to connect a wireless network to a wired network. They can also be used to extend the range of a wireless access point. When used this way, they are sometimes called *repeaters*. (See Chapter 15 for an example of a network setup that uses repeaters.)

High-end dedicated wireless bridges, sometimes also called *workgroup bridges*, include management and security features and can be fairly expensive. But for home or home office use as a repeater, you should be able to get a dedicated wireless bridge for about $120. A good choice at about this price point would be Linksys's WET54G

Wireless-G Ethernet bridge, which can be used to bridge or to repeat 802.11b or 802.11g Wi-Fi networks.

Finally, some access points can also be configured as wireless bridges. When an access point is configured this way, it cannot also be used as a normal access point. (An exception to this statement is that some high-end enterprise class access points can be simultaneously used as bridges.)

An access point configured as a wireless bridge is probably the least expensive repeater you can buy. If you want one of these, you can have one for as little as $50. A decent example is Linksys's WAP11.

> **tip**
>
> If you are looking to buy an access point that can be configured as a wireless bridge to use as a repeater, check that the product specifications say something like "Wireless Access Point Roaming and Bridging."

In the section in Chapter 15 that explains how Pitcairn Island was set up for Wi-Fi, I'll show you a real-world example that used wireless bridges.

Wireless Networking Kits

A number of companies produce wireless networking kits. These kits are essentially a bundle containing an access point, two wireless PC Cards or wireless USB connectors, software drivers, and instructions.

For example, for around $50 from a discount retailer, you can buy the D-Link DWL-920 kit, which includes an 802.11b access point and two USB 802.11b connectors.

Microsoft's Wireless Desktop Kit MN-610 sells for about $130, and contains "everything you need to set up a wireless 802.11b network" for two desktop computers. Essentially, the contents are the same as the D-Link kit: an access point and two USB wireless connectors. (Yes, the Microsoft USB adapters have a larger form-factor than the D-Link units, and may have a greater range.)

There's nothing particularly wrong with these networking kits, but they don't get you very far. Although the Microsoft kit is a little on the expensive side for what it is, the D-Link bundle might actually save you a little money over buying the pieces separately.

Don't get me wrong—I'm all for anything that will make life simpler for you. But in this case, wireless networking kits don't bring much to the party. You can start with one of them, and expand your network later if you want. Still, it is no more complicated to buy an access point and create your own "kit."

Choosing a Wi-Fi Access Point

A decent 802.11b Wi-Fi access point can be had for between $50 and $100 (in fact, probably for even less than $50). By contrast, an elegant 802.11g unit, the Apple Extreme Base Station, costs about $250 (a little less if you take the model without the external antenna port). Although industrial-strength commercial units can cost a good bit more, the point is that these are not hugely expensive pieces of equipment.

You'll pay more for 802.11g equipment than for 802.11b equipment because 802.11g is newer and faster. This is a choice with obvious trade-offs that you'll have to make.

Likewise, the Apple Extreme Base Station costs a little more than equipment manufactured by a vendor that is not Apple—but then again it is a wonderfully designed piece of equipment with extended range, an elegant form factor, and great ease of use.

Even if you buy your access point in the real world of bricks and mortar, it makes sense to at least comparison-shop online. For online shopping tips and tricks, see the sidebar "Comparison Shopping Online" in Chapter 8, "Adding Wi-Fi to a Mobile Computer."

I'm a firm believer in buying equipment from quality vendors that stand behind their products. Quality manufacturers of Wi-Fi access points include

- Agere
- Apple
- D-Link
- Linksys (owned by Cisco)
- Netgear
- SMC Networks

The Best of the Best

I'd like to show you the outside packaging—also called the *form factor*—of two units: Apple's AirPort Extreme Base Stations, and Linksys's Wireless Broadband Router model BEFW11S4. In Chapter 14, "Setting Up Your Access Point," I'll show you how to configure these units in your network.

The AirPort Extreme Base Station

When I look at the AirPort Extreme Base Station, shown in Figure 13.6, I see something that somehow manages to combine cute with high tech. I don't know whether you've ever seen Woody Allen's movie "Sleeper," but it reminds me of something from that retro-"Back to the Future" film.

The Apple Extreme Base Station may look cute as all get out, but it also has quite a bit of brains and brawn behind that well-designed exterior. For one thing, it runs 802.11g, so it is fast.

You can tell simply by looking at the sockets on the back of the unit that it delivers some nifty features that most other access points don't provide.

If you look at Figure 13.7, you'll see the sockets on the back of the Apple Extreme Base Station.

FIGURE 13.6

The Apple
Extreme Base
Station looks
like a prop from
the movie
"Sleeper."

FIGURE 13.7

By looking at the
sockets on the
back of the AirPort
Extreme Base
Station, you can
see that it provides
extra A couple of
the sockets shown
in Figure 13.7 bear
some elaboration.
The external
antenna port and
the connection for
a dial-up modem
are only available
on the more
expensive of the
two AirPort
Extreme models
available.

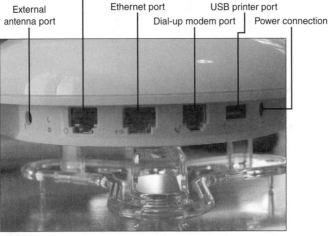

Ethernet WAN port (for
broadband Internet service)
External antenna port
Ethernet port
Dial-up modem port
USB printer port
Power connection

The Ethernet WAN (or Wide Area Network) port
is used to connect to a cable or DSL modem (or,
in some cases, to a network connected to the
Internet).

The Ethernet port can be used to connect a wired
network "behind" the AirPort Extreme Base
Station. You can connect the port to a hub or
switch, and then add quite a few wired devices.
That way, you wouldn't need a separate router.

The USB printer port provides a way to give all the
wireless devices connected via the AirPort Extreme
Base Station access to a printer with a USB port.

tip

The AirPort Extreme Base
Station provides a standard
antenna connector, so you
can add any antenna you'd
like. For more information
about antennas, see
Chapter 17, "Adding Wi-Fi
Antennas to Your Network."

The antenna for the AirPort Extreme Base Station is sold separately for about $75 at Apple stores. When it is attached to the unit, as shown in Figure 13.8, the range of the AirPort Extreme Base Station is considerably extended.

FIGURE 13.8

The optional antenna greatly extends the range of the AirPort Extreme Base Station.

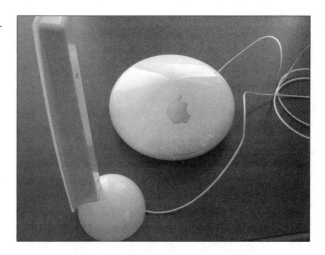

Buying a Combo Wire Line–Wi-Fi Router

Linksys's Wireless Broadband Router model BEFW11S4, shown in Figure 13.9, is a pretty typical middle-of-the-road 802.11b access point, which you should be able to buy for a street price of around $50.

Even though it's not as nifty as the AirPort Extreme, there's nothing wrong with this unit. (True, it does run the slower 802.11b protocol rather than 802.11g like the Apple.) If you want to run the faster 802.11g, you can spend a little more money and buy a Linksys model that supports it. (An 802.11g access point and router from Linksys can be had for around $100, as opposed to the AirPort Extreme Base Station for $250 and the 802.11b Wireless Broadband Router for $50.)

I'm including the Linksys here and in the next chapter to show you what the setup and configuration experience will probably be like with good equipment bought where budget is the main consideration.

Note the two antennas on either side of the unit shown in Figure 13.9. Having two antennas like this helps give this unit solid signal strength and range.

The best feature is on the back of the Linksys unit, shown in Figure 13.10.

As you can see in Figure 13.10, you can plug the Linksys Broadband Router into your cable or DSL modem, connect your wired computers to it, use the unit to connect via Wi-Fi to wireless computers, and need no further hardware. With this unit you don't need no stinking router, or even a switch or hub (provided you have four or fewer wire-line computers).

FIGURE 13.9

The Linksys Wireless Broadband Router is decent but inexpensive.

FIGURE 13.10

The Linksys Wireless Broadband unit provides four wired network sockets.

The Absolute Minimum

Here are the key points to remember from this chapter:

■ You should understand what the different pieces of wireless networking gear do before you buy one.

■ An access point, also called a base station, is the heart of a wireless network.

■ A wireless bridge can be used to connect a device with an Ethernet connection to a wireless network.

■ A wireless bridge can be used to extend the range of wireless access points.

■ Home and small office wireless access points are much less expensive than they used to be and range in cost from less than $50 to around $250 for the elegant 802.11g Apple AirPort Extreme Base Station.

14

SETTING UP YOUR ACCESS POINT

So you've taken the plunge and bought a Wi-Fi access point! This chapter tells you how to plug it in and use it both to create a network and to connect to the Internet.

What are you waiting for? Creating a wireless Wi-Fi network is usually quick and painless. This chapter provides the information you need to make it a painless experience.

Preliminaries

It's good news that usually a standard installation of a Wi-Fi access point is not much harder than plugging it in and turning it on. Typically, you'll be ready to use your wireless network (and shared Internet connection) within minutes.

But, much as I love Wi-Fi technology, I have to be honest. There can be a dark side to setting up a Wi-Fi access point. It's as if you were walking along a mountain path with steep drops on either side. As long as you can keep to the path everything is fine, but if you slip off either side, you can run into trouble.

Trouble tends to come in two forms:

- If your network is at all complicated, configuring your access point may require a little moxie.
- Access points are tricky pieces of equipment, and a small percentage of them simply ship from the factory with defects.

Regarding the first kind of trouble, network complexity, you probably won't get into it. That is, unless you already have a complicated network, or need to set up a complex network (in which case you are probably not really an "absolute beginner"). You will find more information in Chapter 15, "Configuring Your Wi-Fi Network," about different ways to set up networks, and some of the choices you can make regarding how to design and set up a network.

There's perhaps not a whole lot to be said about defective equipment. Every category of electronic device can have an occasional lemon. Your take-away from this should be that if you are following the manufacturer's directions, and the advice in this chapter, and your access point is just not working, there is a possibility that the problem is with the equipment.

Here are the general steps you need to take to get your access point working to form a network with your computers and to provide shared Internet access for the computers on the network:

- Collect information about the settings necessary to connect to the Internet
- Connect the access point to your cable or DSL modem
- Plug in the access point
- Configure the access point
- Set your wireless Wi-Fi devices to communicate using the access point
- If you have any wired devices using the access point/router, you'll need to make sure that their settings reflect the new hardware

Voilà! It's not very hard, and you'll be up and running with your Wi-Fi network very quickly—usually in less than half an hour.

For the most part, in the remainder of this chapter I'll assume that you are creating a network from scratch using your wireless access point (which I'll also assume includes router functionality). This is probably the most common situation for a Wi-Fi beginner, and in many ways the most straightforward setup scenario. You'll find more information on more complicated networking situations in Chapter 15.

I'm also assuming the simplest and most common Internet connection settings. For more information about using an access point to share an Internet connection, see Chapter 16, "Sharing an Internet Connection."

note

Some access points are not set up quite in this order. If the directions from the manufacturer differ from the steps I've outlined, you should, of course, follow their directions.

ADDING WI-FI TO AN EXISTING WIRED NETWORK

If you are adding Wi-Fi to an existing wired network with a router, from a hundred-mile view there are two ways you might go about it:

- Replace the router with the router functionality built into the Wi-Fi access point, or
- Add the access point "behind" your existing router

If you are replacing an existing router, you'll need to plug your current wires into the Ethernet socket (or sockets) provided on most access points/routers (or replace your wired network cards [NICs] with Wi-Fi cards).

You Need a Working Internet Connection

It may seem obvious, but the first prerequisite to setting up a Wi-Fi access point that will let the computers on your network connect to the Internet is a working Internet connection.

This is true for the obvious reason: You can't connect to the Internet without a connection. But there are a couple of other points involved as well.

If you are setting up Apple's AirPort Extreme Base Station to use as your access point, the AirPort Setup Assistant copies the settings from your computer to configure the access point (see "AirPort Extreme" later in this chapter for more details).

You'll need to know some of the settings to put into the access point so that it can connect to your Internet service provider (ISP). One of the easiest ways to find these settings is to read them off your Internet-connected computer. (See the following section, "Collect Your Settings," for details.)

Most cable and DSL service providers will only support one computer connected to their service. If you have a network attached to the service, for the most part they don't want to know about it, and won't help you support it. The good news is that since they have no very practical way of knowing how many computers you have connected to the Internet, they aren't going to begin charging you for each device. (Don't they just wish!)

So you need to have your computer up and connected to the Internet first to collect the settings, and also to make sure that the connection is working properly. Finally, if down the road there seems to be a problem with your Internet connection, and you need to call your ISP for support, they will almost certainly make you unplug your access point, reconnect your single computer, and debug the problem with one computer connected to the Internet.

You can skip this step if you are setting up an AirPort Extreme Base Station to work with an Apple computer because the AirPort Setup Assistant automatically collects the settings for you.

Collect Your Settings

You need to know the settings you should use to tell the access point how to connect to the Internet. The easiest way to find out these settings is to read them off your computer.

Collecting setting information is a little different in Windows XP and Windows 2000 as opposed to Windows Me and 98, so I'll show you each.

You'll notice that in the figures in the examples, the options Obtain an IP Address Automatically and Obtain DNS Server Address Automatically are selected. Today, the cable or DSL provider you work with is likely to have you use these settings, which are also the easiest. But if you have entries for IP and DNS server addresses, you'll need to make note of them and transfer them to the access point/router. (See Chapter 16 for more details about setting up Internet connectivity.)

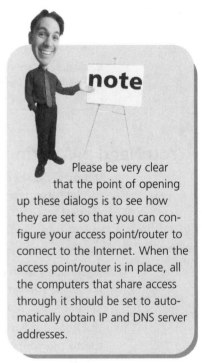

Please be very clear that the point of opening up these dialogs is to see how they are set so that you can configure your access point/router to connect to the Internet. When the access point/router is in place, all the computers that share access through it should be set to automatically obtain IP and DNS server addresses.

Windows XP and Windows 2000

Open the Windows Start menu, right-click on My Network Places and select Properties from the context menu. The Network Connections window will open, as shown in Figure 14.1.

FIGURE 14.1

The Windows XP Network Connections window lets you select a network connection.

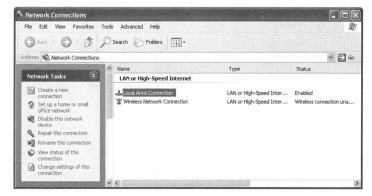

Highlight your computer's connection to the broadband modem. Most likely this will be something like "Local Area Connection." Right-click the connection and select Properties from the context menu. The Properties window for the connection will open, as shown in Figure 14.2.

In the items list, choose Internet Protocol (TCP/IP) and click the Properties button. The Internet Protocol (TCP/IP) Properties window, shown in Figure 14.3, will open.

The Internet Protocol (TCP/IP) Properties window is where you should note the settings

tip

You can also open the Network Connections window by selecting it from the Control Panel.

required for your Internet connection. Quite likely, the settings in this window will be set to automatically obtain IP and DNS server addresses as in Figure 14.3, and you should make note if this is the case. Otherwise, if your setting requires specific IP and DNS information, you should write down what it is because you will need it to configure your access point/router. If you have a static IP, you should also make note of the gateway being used, which you will also see in the Internet Protocol (TCP/IP) Properties window shown in Figure 14.3.

FIGURE 14.2

The Properties window for the Local Area Connection shows a number of items.

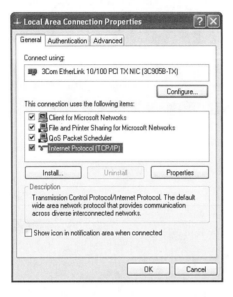

FIGURE 14.3

You can determine your settings for connecting to the Internet using the Internet Protocol (TCP/IP) Properties window for the device that connects to your broadband modem.

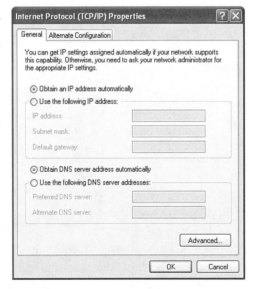

Windows Me and Windows 98

Determining your network settings in older Windows versions works pretty much in the same way as under Windows XP, but the interface is a little different.

Open the Network window, shown in Figure 14.4, either by selecting the Network application in the Control Panel (click Start, Settings, Control Panel), or by right-clicking on the My Network Places icon on your desktop, and selecting Properties from the context menu.

FIGURE 14.4

The Network window is used to select a combination of protocol and device.

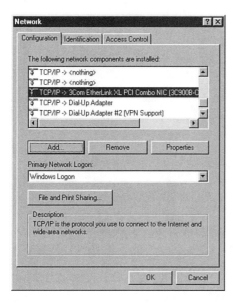

In the Network window (make sure the Configuration tab is selected), scroll down the list of installed network components until you find an entry in the list that combines the TCP/IP protocol and the device (such as a network card) that you use to connect to the Internet. A typical entry of this sort, shown selected in Figure 14.4, combines TCP/IP with a 3Com Etherlink Network Interface Card (NIC).

With the combined protocol and device selected, click the Properties button. The TCP/IP Properties window will open, with the IP Address tab displayed, as you can see in Figure 14.5.

FIGURE 14.5

The IP Address tab of the TCP/IP Properties window shows you the IP settings you should use.

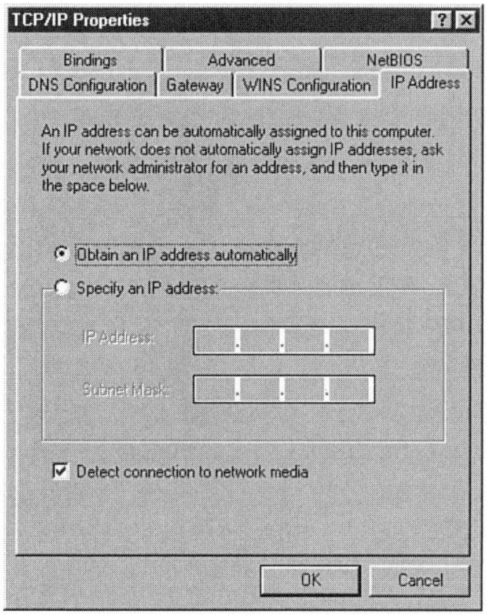

Make a note of the IP settings, and if they are anything other than Obtain an IP Address Automatically, write down the numbers you see.

Next, click the DNS Configuration tab, which you can see in Figure 14.6.

FIGURE 14.6

Make note of the DNS settings you can find on the DNS Configuration tab.

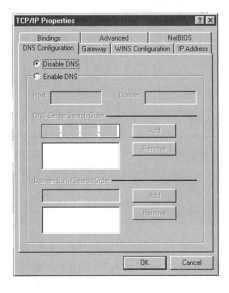

If these settings are anything other than Disable DNS, you should make note of the DNS settings because you will need them to configure the access point/router.

If you are not obtaining IP and DNS settings automatically, you will also need to note the gateway being used, which you can find on the Gateway tab.

Plugging in the Hardware

Now that you've collected your current settings, you are ready to rock and roll, er, plug and unplug things.

The first thing to do is to power down the computers on your network, any hubs, switches, or routers, and your cable or DSL modem. You may have to unplug the modem to turn it off because many of these devices don't come with power switches.

If an Ethernet cable is plugged into the back of the modem, unplug it.

tip

Remember that with the AirPort Extreme Base Station, you need an Apple computer that is both connected to the Internet and has an AirPort Extreme card before plugging in the AirPort Extreme Base Station.

Next, using an Ethernet cable (you'll probably find one provided by the access point manufacturer), connect the cable to the appropriate socket on the access point. This socket will probably be labeled "Internet" or "WAN." (WAN is short for Wide Area Network; one way of looking at the Internet is that it is a great, big WAN.)

Now, connect the wired computers and other devices (such as printers) in your network (if you plan to include wired devices) to the appropriate ports on the back of your access point/router.

If your access point/router has a number of wired sockets, like the Linksys model used as an example in this chapter and Chapter 13, "Buying a Wi-Fi Access Point or Router," the Ethernet ports may simply be numbered. Otherwise, if your access point has routing capability (as most do today), there will probably be a least one Ethernet socket for your wired network.

If it is a single Ethernet socket, it may be labeled "Ethernet" or "LAN" (short for Local Area Network). On the Apple Extreme Base Station, the Ethernet out port is designated with this special symbol:

←--→

If there is only one port for your wired devices, or if the number of ports provided on a combo wired-wireless unit is not sufficient, you may have to use a hub, or switch, to add additional Ethernet ports to the wired portion of your network. Don't worry, you can easily find very cheap hubs (or switches) that are fine for this purpose. See Chapter 4, "Networking Without Wires," for an explanation of hubs and switches.

When everything is wired up, it should look like the diagram shown in Figure 14.7: The modem is connected to the Internet; the access point is connected to the modem; and the internal, wired network (if there is one) is connected to the access point.

tip

The port, or socket, for the Ethernet cable on the modem will probably be marked, logically enough, "Ethernet." Ignore the USB socket, which you will also find on many broadband modems.

tip

The port for the Internet connection on the AirPort Extreme Base Station is marked with this special symbol:

note

Try to position the access point somewhere where it is off the floor. It should also not be covered by any bulky, particularly metal, objects. Finally, it should be located away from anything that might interfere with its broadcasts, such as microwaves, cordless phones, and other Wi-Fi access points.

FIGURE 14.7

The Internet is connected to the modem, which is connected to the access point, which is connected to your wired network (if you have one).

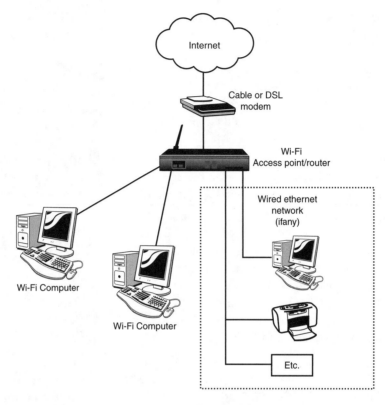

Configuring Your Access Point

When you've got your Wi-Fi access point connected to your cable or DSL modem, plugged in, and turned on (as explained in "Plugging in the Hardware," the next steps are to configure your access point and the computers in your network (sometimes but not necessarily in that order!).

Of course, you should follow the directions provided by the manufacturer of your access point device. In this chapter, I'll show you—as good illustrative examples of how to get up and running with a Wi-Fi access point—how to configure a Linksys Wireless-Broadband Router and an AirPort Extreme Base Station.

I picked these two (which are also featured in Chapter 13) because

■ The Linksys unit is fairly typical of a quality but inexpensive 802.11b Wi-Fi combination access point and router (Linksys is part of the networking giant, Cisco).

■ In the case of the AirPort Extreme, Apple's configuration procedure is sufficiently different from that of the typical Wi-Fi router that it deserves special mention.

Linksys Wireless-Broadband Router

With your Internet settings collected as explained in "Collect Your Settings," and your devices connected as explained in "Plugging in the Hardware," and your Linksys Wireless-Broadband Router turned on, you are ready to configure it.

With a computer connected to the Ethernet port of the Linksys Wireless-Broadband unit, open a Web browser. In the Web browser, enter the address `http://192.168.0.0/`. The user name and password box shown in Figure 14.8 will open.

Leave the user name blank and enter `admin` for the password, and then click OK. The primary administration screen for the access point/router will open, shown in Figure 14.9.

Have a look at the screen shown in Figure 14.9 and the information you collected about your Internet settings. If your Internet settings use automatic IP addressing, you can probably leave the default settings as they stand, and have your Wi-Fi network up and running (although I do suggest you make a few changes for the sake of security, as I'll explain in a second).

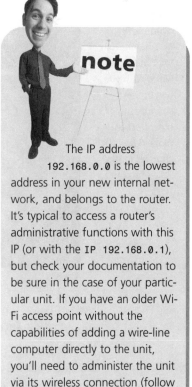

The IP address 192.168.0.0 is the lowest address in your new internal network, and belongs to the router. It's typical to access a router's administrative functions with this IP (or with the IP 192.168.0.1), but check your documentation to be sure in the case of your particular unit. If you have an older Wi-Fi access point without the capabilities of adding a wire-line computer directly to the unit, you'll need to administer the unit via its wireless connection (follow the manufacturer's directions).

FIGURE 14.8

When you enter the URL for the access point/router in a browser, you will be prompted for the administrator's user name and password.

If you use a static IP, you need to select this from the drop-down list shown at the bottom of Figure 14.9. Next you'll need to use the data you collected to enter the IP and DNS server address information you collected in the fields that will now appear.

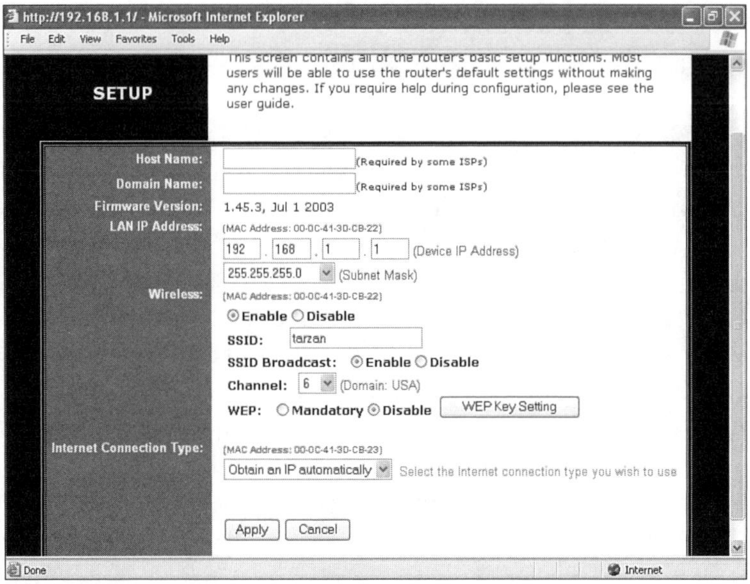

FIGURE 14.9

If you use dynamic IP addressing, your Wi-Fi network will work if you accept the default settings, but you should make a few changes for the sake of security.

As I said, assuming that you use automatic IP addressing, which is most likely, you should make a few changes just to make your network more secure.

First, make sure that Wireless is set to Enable. If the Disable button is selected instead, your wireless network will not work.

Next, you should change the SSID (or network name) to something other than the default. In Figure 14.9, you can see that I changed the default name for the network (which is linksys) to something I made up, namely tarzan.

You may want to disable SSID broadcast (the default is to enable this feature). If SSID broadcast is enabled, the scanning feature available in most Wi-Fi cards will let them see your network name. So running disabled is a security measure, because you are in kind of a stealth mode. For my own part, I tend to enable SSID broadcast because I find it useful to be able to see the SSIDs that are broadcasting when I connect a computer to one of our networks.

However you set SSID broadcast, you should certainly turn on WEP (wired equivalent privacy). This protects your Wi-Fi network with encryption. The default mode is to disable WEP.

tip

The default password for most routers is admin. I suggest you leave your password at the default for now so that you won't forget it. When you are comfortable with your Wi-Fi network, it is a good idea from a security viewpoint to change the default password. For more about Wi-Fi networks and security, see Chapter 19, "Securing Your Wi-Fi Network."

To enable WEP, select the Mandatory option next to the WEP Setting, and click the WEP Key Setting button. The WEP Key Setting window will open, shown in Figure 14.10.

In the WEP Key Setting window, enter a passphrase (in Figure 14.10, I entered the phrase mejane). Next, click Generate. The four default hexadecimal keys will be generated, as shown in Figure 14.10.

Next click Apply to accept the key and close the WEP Key Setting window. Back in the main setup window for the access point/router, click Apply to accept the changes you've made to the settings.

note

With some Wi-Fi cards and operating systems, you'll just need to enter the first key to access the network (this is most common). Other cards and operating systems will require all four keys.

FIGURE 14.10
Your Wi-Fi network is more secure if you use a WEP key.

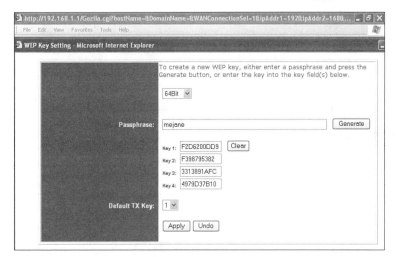

Connecting to the Wi-Fi Network

It's time to connect to your new network. Now that you have the devices and wires in place, and with your access point/router configured, it is time for the final step: setting up each computer to work on the network.

See Chapter 8, "Adding Wi-Fi to a Mobile Computer," and Chapter 9, "Wi-Fi on Your Desktop," for information about how to add a

caution

Don't forget to write down the first hexadecimal key so that you'll be able to connect your Wi-Fi computers to the access point.

laptop or desktop computer to a Wi-Fi network. You'll need to know the SSID and password you used for the network when you configured the router.

The access point/router is now doing the job of "speaking" to your ISP and the Internet for you. It has taken over the task of assigning addresses for nodes within your internal network. So, even if you use a fixed IP within the access point/router to communicate with your ISP, the computers within your network (wireless as well as wired) should be set to obtain their IP address and DNS server address automatically.

See "Collect Your Settings" earlier in this chapter for information about how to open the Network dialog used to set these items. If your computer is not set to obtain IP and DNS server addresses automatically, change the settings, and restart your computer.

Connecting to the Encrypted Network Using XP

With a Windows XP machine, open the Wireless Network Connection Properties window, shown in Figure 14.11.

One way to open the Wireless Network Connection Properties window in Windows XP is to open the Network Connections applet from the Control Panel. Next, select Wireless Network Connection, right-click, and choose Properties from its context menu. When the Wireless Network Connection Properties window opens, select the Wireless Networks tab. A window like the one shown in Figure 14.11 will open.

FIGURE 14.11

You can see if your new wireless network is broadcasting using the Wireless Network Connection window.

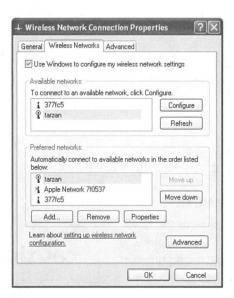

First, use the Wireless Network Connection window to verify that the new network is running (as you can see in Figure 14.11, the tarzan Wi-Fi network is broadcasting loud and clear).

Next, select the network and click Configure to open the Wireless Network Properties window, shown in Figure 14.12, and use it to enter the WEP encryption key for the network (the first key generated by the access point).

FIGURE 14.12

The Wireless Network Properties window is used to enter the encryption key for a Windows XP node on the Wi-Fi network.

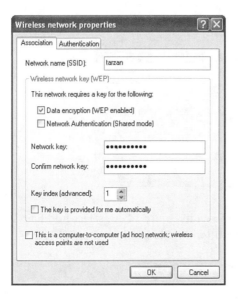

In the Wireless Network Properties window, make sure that the check box labeled "The Key Is Provided for Me Automatically" is unchecked. Next, check Data Encryption (WEP Enabled). Finally, enter (and confirm) as the network key the first of the four hexadecimal keys you generated in the access point/router's setup program (this was shown in Figure 14.10). Click OK to accept the settings, and click OK in the Wireless Network Connection Properties dialog to accept the changes and close the window.

You can test that you have access to the encrypted wireless network by using your browser to open an Internet site such as www.google.com.

tip

If you aren't able to access the Internet, you may need to reboot your computer for the new settings to take hold.

Connecting to the Encrypted Network Using Windows 98/Me

Depending on the operating system and Wi-Fi card, you may need to enter all four encryption keys, rather than the first key as in Windows XP.

Figure 14.13 shows the Wi-Fi client manager software for a mobile computer running Windows 98. This software can usually be opened by double-clicking an icon in the Windows system tray that usually shows bars for the strength of the Wi-Fi signal. Alternatively, you can choose the program that was installed along with your Wi-Fi card from the Windows Start menu.

FIGURE 14.13

Under Windows 98/Me to add a new Wi-Fi network, you start by opening the client manager software.

In the Wi-Fi client software shown in Figure 14.13, select Add/Edit from the Actions menu. The Add/Edit Configuration Profile window, shown in Figure 14.14, will open.

FIGURE 14.14

Use the Add/Edit Configuration Profile window to start the process of adding a new profile.

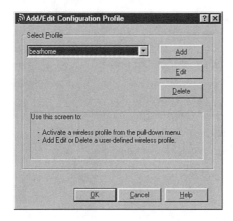

Click the Add button. The Edit Configuration window, shown in Figure 14.15, will open.

In the Edit Configuration window, enter a name for the new profile (I've given it the same name as the new network in Figure 14.15, but it doesn't have to be named the same; it can be anything you like).

When you've given the new network a name, click Next. It's time to identify the new network, as shown in Figure 14.16.

FIGURE 14.15

Use the Edit
Configuration
window to name
the new profile.

FIGURE 14.16

You can enter
the network SSID
or click the Scan
button to scan
for a network.

There are two ways to identify the network. If you happen to know the SSID, or network name, you can just enter it. Alternatively, you can click the Scan button, and
then choose the network from the list of Wi-Fi networks available.

Click Next to enter the security settings, as shown in Figure 14.17.

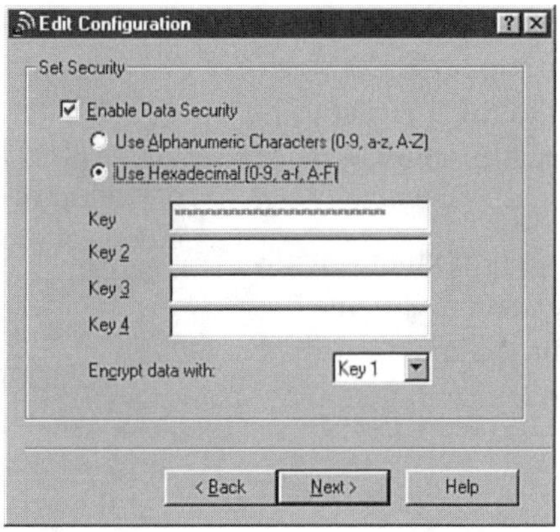

FIGURE 14.17

Enter the encryp-
tion keys to
allow access to
the network.

As shown in Figure 14.17, make sure that Enable Data Security is checked and the Use Hexadecimal option is selected. Next, enter the first security key as it was generated for you in the setup program for the access point/router (refer to Figure 14.10). Click Next a few more times, accepting default values, and then click Finish to create the new profile. Click OK to make it the active profile. As you can see in Figure 14.18, the tarzan Wi-Fi network gets a strong signal worth a jungle yodel, and encryption is turned on.

FIGURE 14.18

The tarzan Wi-Fi network is going as strong as a yodel in the jungle, and encryption is turned on!

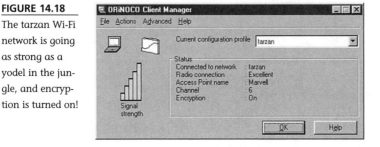

Unlike Windows XP, which has a uniform way of managing Wi-Fi cards and access as part of the Network Connections windows built into the operating system, how it will work under Windows Me/98 is really dependent on the software that shipped with your Wi-Fi card. But it won't be very difficult to access a Wi-Fi network (provided you have the encryption key you need). I'd encourage you to make older equipment part of your Wi-Fi network!

AirPort Extreme

To configure an AirPort Extreme access point, you first need to have an Apple computer, equipped with AirPort Extreme and running MAC OS X version 10, that you can connect to the Internet using either the computer's Ethernet connection or its internal dial-up modem.

The Apple computer that is AirPort Extreme–ready will be used to administer the AirPort Extreme Base Station. (For information about adding an AirPort Extreme card to an Apple desktop computer, see Chapter 9.)

note

Apple is preparing an administration program for Windows 2000 and Windows XP, which you can download from www.apple.com/airport. In theory, with this utility you don't need an Apple to administer the AirPort Extreme Base Station. Currently in Preview (meaning, pre-official release), this software is not ready for prime time. It crashed the XP systems that I tried to run it on, but it might be ready by the time you read this.

The computer must be able to connect to the Internet using some non-AirPort access method because later in the process the AirPort Setup Assistant software will use your computer's active Internet settings (the ones you can see on the Network tab of the System Preferences dialog) to configure the AirPort Extreme Base Station.

With the Internet connection tested, it's time to connect the AirPort Extreme Base Station as explained in "Plugging in the Hardware."

Fire up the AirPort Extreme Base Station by plugging it in. When the middle light of the three on the front of the AirPort Extreme Base Station comes on, you are ready for the next step.

On your computer, open up the AirPort Setup Assistant application. (You can find it in the Applications/Utilities folder.)

The AirPort Setup Assistant will first configure the AirPort Extreme Base Station, using the network settings from your computer, and then configure your computer to work with the base station.

When prompted, you should provide a name for the base station (and Wi-Fi network) and a password that is not the default. By the way, it is possible that you may need to know the default password to enter these new settings; if so, it is `public`.

When you've clicked through all the screens in the AirPort Setup Assistant, your AirPort Extreme Base Station and computer are good to go! See, wasn't that easy?

tip

If you can't find AirPort Setup Assistant on your computer, you should use the installer for it that is on the CD-ROM that came with your AirPort Extreme Base Station.

note

Of course, you can add any computer with Wi-Fi capabilities to the network you are creating with AirPort Extreme Base Station. It doesn't have to be an Apple computer.

For information about how to connect other computers to the Wi-Fi network you have created, see Chapters 8 and 9.

Apple computers that are equipped with AirPort Extreme will connect to the new Wi-Fi network automatically (they will prompt you for the password if you've protected the network). Windows machines connect to the new Wi-Fi network the way they would to any other Wi-Fi network (they don't have to know that Apple manufactures the AirPort Extreme Base Station!).

THE ABSOLUTE MINIMUM

Here are the key points to remember from this chapter:

■ Ninety percent of the time getting a Wi-Fi network going is really easy.

■ You need to have a working Internet connection with a computer connected to a broadband modem before you start.

■ You must know the settings your ISP requires before you can set up your Wi-Fi network.

■ The Wi-Fi access point is connected to the Internet modem, and your wired computer or network is also plugged into the access point.

■ Most Wi-Fi access points are administered using a Web browser, but the AirPort Extreme units are set up with a special Apple program.

■ You should change the default network name, and enable WEP encryption for security reasons.

■ After the Wi-Fi access point has been configured, you'll need to set your computers up for access to the Wi-Fi network.

■ If the Wi-Fi unit doesn't work, and you think you are doing everything right, the unit may be defective.

caution

Bear in mind that if your access point isn't working smoothly, it may be defective. From this viewpoint, make sure that you get your equipment up and running quickly enough so that it is still under warranty and can easily be returned if there is a problem.

15

Configuring Your Wi-Fi Network

In Chapter 14, "Setting Up Your Access Point," I showed you how to set up a very simple network using a Wi-Fi access point/router combination. The equipment needed for that kind of network has become quite inexpensive, and it should do for a great many home and small office applications. This chapter fills in some gaps in Chapter 14, and discusses some of the other topics that can come up in networks that involve Wi-Fi. I'll start by showing you how ad-hoc, or peer-to-peer, networking works with Wi-Fi. Next, I'll go on to a number of topics that are involved in setting up networks and show you some of the theory of different ways to arrange networks. I'll finish the chapter with two case studies showing you how Wi-Fi networking has been used to solve some specific problems.

Ad-Hoc Networking

Ad-hoc networking means that each computer talks to each other directly without the "supervision" of a device such as a router. This arrangement is sometimes called peer-to-peer networking.

⇨ Refer to Figure 13.1 on p. 165 in Chapter 13 for an example of an ad-hoc network.

If there are enough computers involved, an ad-hoc, or peer-to-peer network, can begin to form a kind of grid, or mesh. This gives peer-to-peer networks in some applications a great deal of power, although there's no really good way to administer a peer-to-peer network, and security remains an issue.

The Wi-Fi standards specify two different configuration modes, infrastructure and ad-hoc. The access point/router style network that I showed you in Chapter 14 is an example of using Wi-Fi in infrastructure mode, while (as you'd probably expect) peer-to-peer Wi-Fi access uses ad-hoc mode.

In infrastructure mode, communication between two nodes on the network flows through the access point. Computer A actually "talks" to the access point, which in turn talks to Computer B. The access point also performs a number of other roles, such as connecting the nodes to the Internet or other WAN (Wide Area Network), connecting multiple wireless networks, connecting the wireless nodes to a wired network, and providing management and security functionality (such as a firewall).

In contrast, in ad-hoc mode, Computers A and B communicate directly without an intermediary, and none of the other functionality provided by the access point is present.

The primary drawback of using Wi-Fi in ad-hoc mode is signal strength and range. Ad-hoc mode might make sense to use if you had two computers close to one another that you didn't expect to move much, the advantage being that you wouldn't need to spend $50 on an access point.

I wouldn't maintain a fixed Wi-Fi network using ad-hoc connections with more than two computers, and I wouldn't expect to be able to maintain an ad-hoc connection if one of my computers were mobile. When my wife carries our Wi-Fi laptop out to the garden, it goes way out of ad-hoc range, but well within the broadcast range of our routers.

Ad-hoc connectivity is good for, well, ad-hoc situations in life. Using Wi-Fi's ad-hoc mode, you can connect two computers when you are on the road even though no wireless networks are present, which can be very useful. For example, a colleague might have a wired network connection and access to the Internet, which I might be able to share using an ad-hoc connection with my colleague. (Sharing an Internet connection is explained in Chapter 16, "Sharing an Internet Connection.")

Ad-hoc networks are also good for quickly and easily setting up a Wi-Fi network in situations where flexibility is essential and a wireless infrastructure is not available (or needed). An example of this might be a temporary meeting or convention, or perhaps a group of consultants working on-site but without access to the "official" network might decide to set up an ad-hoc network.

Later in this chapter I'll also show you a hybrid form of networking, which uses a Wi-Fi access point and an ad-hoc mesh to blanket a large area and extend the range of the core configuration.

Ad-Hoc Apple

To turn on ad-hoc networking, with an AirPort Extreme–equipped Apple computer, open the AirPort menu by clicking the AirPort icon in the menu bar. Select Choose Network. From the drop-down list, select Create Computer to Computer Network.

In the Computer to Computer window, enter the name of the network you want to create. Click More Options if you want to password-protect the ad-hoc network.

You connect to the ad-hoc network as you would to any Wi-Fi network within range. On an Apple machine, this means selecting the ad-hoc network by name from the AirPort menu and supplying the password, if one is required. Barring obstructions and interference from other wireless devices such as microwaves and cordless phones, connection should be possible within about one hundred feet.

note

If you do not assign password protection to the ad-hoc network, there is no security mechanism other than any protections you have assigned to file sharing generally. Anybody with Wi-Fi capability within range can access your ad-hoc network.

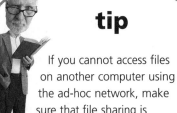

tip

If you cannot access files on another computer using the ad-hoc network, make sure that file sharing is turned on in the other computer's System Preferences control panel.

Ad-Hoc Mode on Windows

The process of establishing an ad-hoc network involves two steps:

■ Setting up the network on one machine

■ Connecting to the ad-hoc network from one or more other machines

As you may know, setting things up on Windows XP tends to be cosmetically different than doing so on older versions of Windows. It's also true that some setting up under Windows 98/Me depends largely on the software that came with the Wi-Fi card you are using.

Whichever operating system you are using, connecting to an ad-hoc network is no different than connecting to an infrastructure access point Wi-Fi network from the viewpoint of the device doing the connecting.

Even so, as an example, I'll show you how to set up an ad-hoc network using a Windows XP machine and connect to it using an older Windows 98 machine.

WHO CARES ABOUT THE OS SO LONG AS THERE'S WI-FI?

By the way, you can certainly mix and match Apple and Windows operating systems. A Windows computer can join an infrastructure network where the access point is an AirPort Extreme Base Station (which is made by Apple). Similarly, you can set up an ad-hoc network with a Windows machine, and Apple users can join it. Or, you can set up an ad-hoc network with an Apple and join it from a Windows machine.

The operating system doesn't matter; it could be Linux for all Wi-Fi cares. The only requirement is that the computers on the ad-hoc network be Wi-Fi–capable.

Of course, sharing files and resources across operating systems is a different—and potentially more painful—matter (that goes beyond the scope of this book).

Setting Up an Ad-Hoc Network on XP

Open the Network Connections window either by right-clicking on My Network Places in the Windows Start menu, or by selecting Network Connections from the Windows Control Panel. Within the Network Connections window, select Wireless Network Connection, right-click, and choose Properties from the context menu. The Wireless Network Connection Properties window, shown in Figure 15.1, will open.

FIGURE 15.1

The Wireless Network Connections Properties window is the starting place for creating an ad-hoc network.

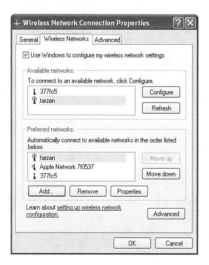

Highlight the Wireless Networks tab, which you can see active in Figure 15.1, and click the Add button. The Wireless Network Properties window, shown in Figure 15.2, will open.

FIGURE 15.2

The Wireless Network Properties window is used to assign properties to a wireless network.

In the Wireless Network properties window, enter a name for the ad-hoc network (the wireless network's SSID). (In Figure 15.2, I've given the ad-hoc network the name "theHoc".) Next, select the check box at the bottom of the window labeled "This Is a Computer-to-Computer (ad-hoc) Network; Wireless Access Points Are Not Used." Check the Data Encryption check box if you want to provide WEP encryption protection for the ad-hoc network. Finally, click OK to create the ad-hoc network.

If you were to connect to this network from a Windows XP machine, you would do so like connecting to any other Wi-Fi network, using the Wireless Network Connection Properties window. But note that if you click the Advanced button in the Window, the Advanced dialog, shown in Figure 15.3, determines which kinds of networks are displayed.

FIGURE 15.3

Using the Advanced dialog, you can display all wireless networks, only infrastructure networks, or only ad-hoc point networks.

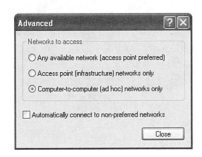

Using the Advanced dialog, you can decide to display all kinds of networks, only access point networks, or only ad-hoc networks. It might make it easier to see the ad-hoc networks if you select Computer-to-Computer (Ad-Hoc) Networks Only, as in Figure 15.3.

With Computer-to-Computer (ad-hoc) Networks selected in the Advanced dialog, it's easy to spot the new ad-hoc network in Figure 15.4.

FIGURE 15.4

The new ad-hoc network is shown in the Wireless Network Connection properties window.

Connecting to the Ad-Hoc Network from Windows 98

Now it's time to connect to the new ad-hoc network from a Windows 98 machine within range of the machine that created the ad-hoc network.

As opposed to Windows XP, where you make a connection to the ad-hoc network using Windows dialogs in the same way you would connect to any other wireless network, in older Windows operating systems the connection specifics are dependent on the client software that comes with your Wi-Fi card.

Generally, the client software can be launched from a taskbar icon (see Chapter 8, "Adding Wi-Fi to a Mobile Computer," for more details).

Figure 15.5 shows using the typical client software for one Wi-Fi card to start adding a configuration profile for an ad-hoc network.

note

The new ad-hoc network isn't shown as active in Figure 15.4 because there's nothing connected to it, and no other ad-hoc node broadcasting to connect to. If there were a node broadcasting, the ad-hoc network would appear in the Available Networks pane shown in Figure 15.4, and you would connect to it normally (by clicking the Configure button).

FIGURE 15.5

You can add a configuration profile for an ad-hoc network by selecting Peer-to-Peer.

The configuration is given a name—theHoc—which should not be confused with its network name, and "Peer-to-Peer Group" is selected from the drop-down list (rather than Access Point).

Next you need to enter the network name (SSID), as shown in Figure 15.6.

FIGURE 15.6

The network name is needed to connect to an ad-hoc network.

You'll see in Figure 15.6 that a channel needs to be entered. The default for this setting, unless you set it differently when the ad-hoc network was created, is Channel 1.

If the ad-hoc network uses encryption, the key should be entered in the Set Security screen shown in Figure 15.7.

Because I set the ad-hoc network named theHoc up without security (a pretty poor idea usually), to connect to the Hoc, the Enable Data Security box shown in Figure 15.8 should be unchecked.

With the configuration information completed, the client computer (the one running Windows 98) can easily connect to the ad-hoc network, which is shown in Figure 15.8.

FIGURE 15.7

If the ad-hoc network uses encryption, you'll need to enter the key in the Set Security screen.

FIGURE 15.8

The Windows 98 client configuration software shows a peer-to-peer (ad-hoc) connection.

Meanwhile, back at the Windows XP ranch, the computer that created the ad-hoc network now has something to connect with. Figure 15.10 shows the ad-hoc network connection from the viewpoint of Windows XP (note the details of the connection in the lower left of Figure 15.9).

FIGURE 15.9

The Network Connections and the Wireless Network Connection Status windows show the strength of the ad-hoc network connection, as well as details about the connection.

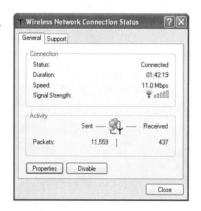

Troubleshooting a Network Using Ipconfig

Most of the time, if you are deploying a simple Wi-Fi network like the infrastructure style network described in Chapter 14, or a one-to-one ad-hoc network like the one explained so far in this chapter, you won't have any problems setting up a network. But sometimes networks go bad.

WHAT DOES IT MEAN FOR A NETWORK TO GO BAD?

You know you are having network problems when… one or more nodes on the networks stop being able to "see" other nodes on the network, or some (or all) of the nodes on the network stop being able to access the Internet.

Although many network problems are easy to find and fix—for example, an unplugged cable—others can be more subtle.

It can be very difficult to diagnose network problems (although fixing the problem when you find it can be fairly straightforward). The first thing you should suspect in a wireless network is that your node is out of range of the access point. You should also check the connections in the wired part of a network. I've wasted much time in fruitless network debugging when the problem all along was a network cable that had come unplugged. Defective network cables are another problem. (I'm mentioning cables and wires here because in a mixed wireline-wireless network, problems with cabling can cause problems in the Wi-Fi part of the network.)

You may also be having problems with the way IP addresses (the way nodes are identified on the network) are being assigned. In this case, the Ipconfig program is a very valuable tool.

If you are trying to diagnose and fix a network problem, you should know about the Ipconfig program as one of the troubleshooting arrows in your quiver.

Ipconfig can be used to display TCP/IP network configuration values, discard the current IP and DHCP settings for a device, and renew the DHCP settings for a device. (For more about working with DHCP, see Chapter 16.)

If your computer is connecting to the Internet or your local network properly, an easy thing to try is to use Ipconfig to release (meaning, discard) its current settings and then renew itself with new settings.

tips

The Windows Me and Windows 98 equivalent to the Ipconfig program is Winipcfg.

If a network cable has been crimped or damaged in any way—for example, the casing broken by a staple when you are positioning cables—you should not take any chances, but just throw the network cable out and start over with another cable.

Ipconfig is a command-line program. To see the results of the program, you should run it from a Command Prompt box. To open a Command Prompt box, select the Command Prompt icon in the Accessories program group from the Windows XP Start menu.

Next, at the command line, type the command you want to run. Here are some of the most important ways you can use Ipconfig.

The command Ipconfig /? displays all the Ipconfig commands and the syntax of the program. So this is the command to run if you want to learn more about what Ipconfig can do, and how to use it.

The command Ipconfig /all displays the network settings for a TCP/IP device on the network, as you can see in Figure 15.10. You can use this information to track the IP addresses assigned to computers on your network, and make sure that there is no conflict caused by two computers having been assigned the same address. You can also use the IP address of a device on the network to access the device directly without knowing its name.

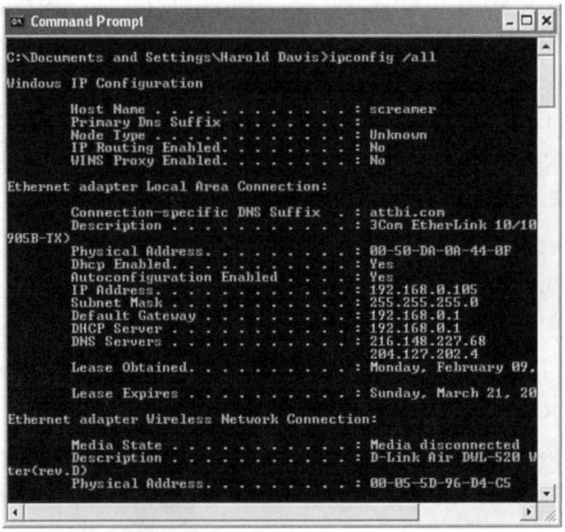

FIGURE 15.10

Ipconfig /all shows the network settings for a computer on the network.

The command Ipconfig /release sends a message to the DHCP server to release the current IP address for a device on the network.

The command Ipconfig /renew sends a message to the DHCP server to renew the IP address of your computer, provided your computer is set up to automatically obtain its IP address. The results of running this command on my computer are shown in Figure 15.11.

FIGURE 15.11

Ipconfig /renew assigns a new IP address to a computer that obtains its IP addresses automatically.

Advanced Networks: Topologies for Larger Networks

Your small office or home network may be small right now, but it may grow over time (which is what happened to me!). This section explains some of the ways to look at larger, more complicated networks. This material is somewhat advanced, and may be something to keep in the back of your mind when you are setting up your first Wi-Fi access point. But you may find it provides a useful perspective even as you are getting started.

A network *topology* means the way a network is arranged and how the devices on the network communicate with each other. A network's *physical* topology is the way devices are laid out (meaning which devices are connected to each other, and so on).

In contrast, a network's *logical* topology is the way that the signals act on the network media, meaning the way that the data passes through the network from one device to the next independent of the physical interconnection of the devices. If you diagrammed the physical and logical topology for a network, the diagram might look the same, but then again, it might not.

I've already shown you some examples of network topologies. For example, the mesh pattern created by an ad-hoc wireless network used by a number of devices is a network topology.

An infrastructure wireless network that uses an access point is operating in a star topology, as shown in the diagram in Figure 15.12.

In a true mesh topology, every node on the network is connected to every other node on the network.

FIGURE 15.12

An infrastructure Wi-Fi network that uses an access point is an example of a star topology.

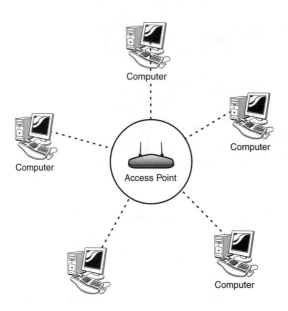

Two other common kinds of network topologies are the bus topology and the ring topology, shown in Figure 15.13. In the bus topology, all the devices on the network are connected to a central cable or bus (also called backbone). In the ring topology, all the devices are connected to one another in the shape of a closed loop, so that each device is directly connected to the two devices on either side of it, and only those two devices. (Does the ring topology "rule them all?")

As a practical matter, most even reasonably complex networks are hybrids that have features of a variety of topologies. For example, one common hybrid is called the *tree* topology, in which groups of star topology networks are placed along a bus-topology backbone. This is a common arrangement for Wi-Fi networks that cover a large area. Each Wi-Fi access point manages a star topology group, and the Wi-Fi access points are connected using a backbone.

note

Networks based on a star topology are probably easier to set up and manage than any other kind of network.

From the viewpoint of Wi-Fi, another interesting hybrid topology involves creating a full mesh network. Yes, as I explained at the beginning of the chapter, you can create a kind of mesh using Wi-Fi devices in ad-hoc mode. But what you have isn't necessarily very reliable, and it also doesn't facilitate full mesh computing in which every device speaks to every other device. (The devices don't necessarily have to speak to each other at the same time, or in real time.)

FIGURE 15.13

In a bus topology, all devices are connected to a central cable, whereas in a ring, the devices are arranged in a loop, so each device communicates with the two devices next to it.

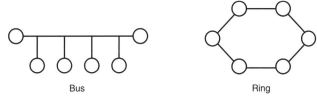

A useful Wi-Fi mesh network needs to be able to respond to devices entering and leaving the network, it needs to be able to operate with devices in infrastructure mode as well as ad-hoc mode, and it needs to be able to switch access points into bridges as required. Figure 15.14 shows what a mesh network of this sort might look like.

FIGURE 15.14

A true Wi-Fi mesh network has a great many advantages.

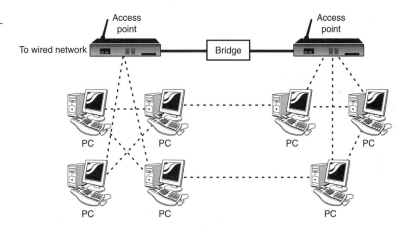

A true Wi-Fi mesh network of the sort shown in Figure 15.14 has a great many advantages. It has no single point of failure, and is therefore self-healing. This kind of network can easily get around obstacles—such as water-laden foliage and barriers to sightlines—that are problematic for other kinds of Wi-Fi networks.

However, to work properly, a Wi-Fi mesh topology requires some specialized software that provides routing functionality and has the ability to switch radios between infrastructure and ad-hoc modes as required.

Because of the benefits of Wi-Fi mesh networking, there's a lot of work going on right now in this area. For an effort to bring Wi-Fi meshes to the third world using open source technology, you might be interested in the Wireless Roadshow project, www.informal.org.uk/wirelessroadshow/. Closer, perhaps, to home, a startup company named Firetide, Inc., www.firetide.com, based in Hawaii, is making the hardware and software needed to deploy robust true mesh topology Wi-Fi networks.

Setting Up a Hotspot with a DMZ

Suppose you have a small office with a network, and want to set up a public Wi-Fi hotspot. The single most important requirement is that people who use the Wi-Fi hotspot should *not* be able to access the office network.

There are many ways to set up a network to do this, depending on the functionality that is required. Also, if you are setting up a commercial hotspot, you should get the advice of the Wi-Fi network provider you will be working with in planning the hotspot (unless you expect to be doing service provisioning yourself). You should also know that there are a number of turn-key "put up a hotspot" kits available, which you can buy and not have to think about further.

In any case, the key concept to protect the private network is the *DMZ*. DMZ is a term borrowed from the military that is short for *demilitarized zone*. In networking terms, it means a computer or subnetwork that sits between an internal network that needs to remain secure and an area that allows external access, for example a Web server or a Wi-Fi hotspot.

Figure 15.15 shows a simple model of a DMZ that uses firewalls to protect the private network both from the Internet and from users of the public Wi-Fi hotspot.

FIGURE 15.15

You can use a DMZ to protect a private network from users who have access to the public hotspot connected to the network.

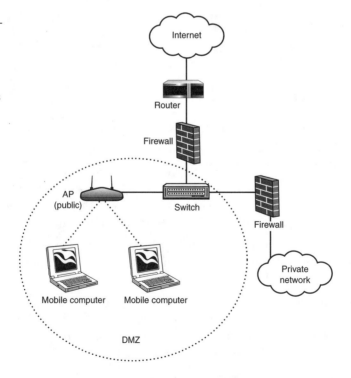

Connecting Pitcairn Island to the Internet with Wi-Fi

Understanding networking concepts can help to resolve real-world problems with setting up Wi-Fi networks. Here's an example that shows how some advanced networking concepts were used to set up a Wi-Fi network on Pitcairn Island.

Pitcairn Island is a remote, rugged speck of land in the south Pacific Ocean, thousands of miles from anywhere. Pitcairn was the last refuge of the mutineers from the HMS *Bounty*, which was seized from the infamous Captain Bligh in 1789.

Following the seizure, the mutineers, led by Fletcher Christian, fled to Tahiti, where several were eventually captured by the British navy and brought home for trial and execution. Christian and some other mutineers, along with Tahitian companions, fled in the *Bounty* to Pitcairn, where they eventually burnt the *Bounty* to avoid detection by the British navy.

Today, almost 50 people live on Pitcairn, which is administered from New Zealand. Most of these 50 people have computers.

Thanks to the Albuquerque Seismological Laboratory and the USGS (United States Geologic Survey), Pitcairn Island also has Internet access. It seems that Pitcairn is located near an area of intense earthquake activity, and the USGS needs to keep seismologic monitoring equipment on the island. The USGS is kept connected to its seismic equipment via an Internet connection provided by satellite provider Inmarsat (www.inmarsat.org). Some of the extra bandwidth on this rather expensive connection is used by the Pitcairn Island residents.

A team including Chris Hopper and Bill Haigh used Wi-Fi to extend the Internet access from the concrete bunker containing the seismic equipment and Inmarsat link to the Pitcairn Island residents using off-the-shelf components. This involved many challenges due to the ruggedness of the terrain, the tropical climate, and the remoteness of Pitcairn itself, but I'd like to highlight two issues here.

First, the distance along the road from the access point connected to the satellite to the school (the farthest point that needed access) was about a kilometer (a thousand meters). It would have been ideal to use a fixed wired backbone along the road from the bunker to the school, creating a kind of tree topology. But the problem with this was that the standard Ethernet wire that was available has a maximum range of 100 meters. So the distance was covered by adding wireless access points configured as bridges along the line-of-sight road to cover substantial portions of it, connecting the bridges with hundred-meter lengths, and then jumping via wireless to the next bridge, and so on, covering the required distance.

note

If fiber optic cable had been available, laying down a backbone of the length required would not be an issue. The 100-meter limitation is a limitation of standard 10BASE-T Ethernet cable.

Figure 15.16 gives a rough idea of the physical topology of the Pitcairn installation.

FIGURE 15.16

The problems in creating a network topology for Pitcairn Island's Wi-Fi network included a backbone distance too long for standard Ethernet cable, and a dense foliage area.

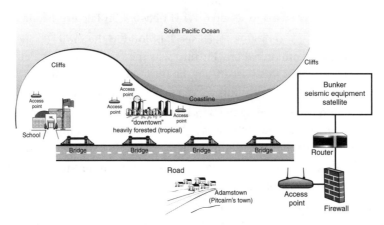

If you look at the "downtown" area shown in Figure 15.19 (the "town" in "downtown" being Adamstown, the only town on Pitcairn Island), you'll see that I've marked it as heavily forested. In fact, the vegetation is tropical foliage, dense with water. The problem with this is that water almost completely absorbs Wi-Fi broadcasts on the 2.4GHz spectrum. (This is the physics-based reason that microwaves use the 2.4GHz spectrum: The microwave signals are used to stir the molecules in food items, most of which are very high in water content.)

As a practical matter, this meant that quite a few access points needed to be positioned in the dense foliage area (more access points were needed because the tropical foliage absorbed the signals). Each access point connected to the wireless bridges along the "backbone" running along the road. In addition, each access point was equipped with an external antenna to better amplify its signals. (For more on antennas and other signal boosters, see Chapter 17, "Adding Wi-Fi Antennas to Your Network.")

THE ABSOLUTE MINIMUM

Here are the key points to remember from this chapter:

- It's easy to create ad-hoc Wi-Fi connections between Wi-Fi–equipped computers.
- Ipconfig can help you resolve Internet configuration issues with your computers on your network.
- Simple star-topology access point networks are easy to set up and manage, but when your networks start getting complicated, there are many things to think about.

16

SHARiNG AN iNTERNET CONNECTiON

This chapter gives you more information about sharing your Internet connection. I'll show you how to set up a single computer to share an Internet connection. Next, I'll revisit the settings you need to use to connect your home or small office network to the Internet. (Chapter 14, "Setting Up Your Access Point," provides basic information about this.)

It's a good idea to know something about the basic technologies that make the connection between the Internet and your home or small office network work. In this chapter, I'll explain static versus dynamic IP addressing, Dynamic Host Configuration Protocol (DHCP), Network Address Translation (NAT), and DNS (Domain Name System).

Finally, I'll show you a good alternative way to set up a mixed wired-wireless network that differs from the scenario I explained in Chapter 14.

Sharing a Connection through a Computer

It's sometimes very useful to share your computer's existing Internet connection with another computer. You might want to share an AirPort Internet connection with other computers on your wired network. Alternatively, if you've set up an ad-hoc Wi-Fi connection, as explained in Chapter 15, "Configuring Your Wi-Fi Network," and you have Internet connectivity, you might want to share your connection with your wireless friends.

caution

Sharing, as I tell my kids, is good. And sharing an Internet connection can be very useful. But it does pose some security concerns. So if you are not actively sharing your Internet connection, you should run as a default with sharing turned off.

Sharing an Internet Connection on an Apple

To share an Internet connection using an Apple computer, click System Preferences on the Apple menu. With the System Preferences window open, launch Sharing (located in the Internet & Network category).

In the Sharing window, click the Internet tab. Using the Internet tab of the Sharing window, shown in Figure 16.1, choose a Port (which means the Internet connection that is to be shared) and with whom you want to share the connection (from the Share Your Connection From drop-down list).

FIGURE 16.1

The Internet tab of the Sharing window is used to share an Internet connection.

Sharing

Computer Name:

Other computers on your local subnet can reach your computer at .local   Edit...

Services   Firewall   Internet

Internet Sharing On: Sharing your AirPort connection

Stop   Click Stop to prevent other computers from sharing your connection to the Internet. You need to stop Internet Sharing to change your settings.

Share your connection from: AirPort

To computers using:

On Ports
☑ Built-in Ethernet

AirPort Options...

⚠ If your computer is set to sleep, open Energy Saver preferences and turn sleep off. If your computer goes to sleep you need to restart Internet sharing.   Energy Saver...   ?

🔒 Click the lock to prevent further changes.

Finally, click the Start button. You will see a message saying that Sharing has been turned on. (When sharing is on, the Start button is turned into a Stop button.)

To turn sharing off, click the Stop button.

Sharing an Internet Connection on Windows XP

Open the Control Panel from the Windows XP Start menu. In the Control Panel, double-click Network Connections (if you're using Category view, click Network and Internet Connections and then the Network Connections icon).

With the Network Connections window open, highlight the connection to the Internet you want to share. With the connection highlighted, open the Properties dialog for the connection either by right-clicking the connection and selecting Properties from the context menu, or by choosing the Change Settings of This Connection option under Network Tasks on the Network Connections window.

With the Properties dialog for the connection open, click the Advanced tab. The Advanced tab for the Properties dialog is shown in Figure 16.2.

FIGURE 16.2

The Advanced tab of the Properties dialog for the connection is used to enable or disable Internet connection sharing.

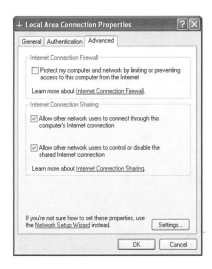

To enable Internet connection sharing, check the Allow Other Network Users to Connect Through This Computer's Internet Connection box.

Click OK. Your Internet connection is now shared.

To reverse the process, and disable Internet connection sharing, simply clear the Allow Other Network Users to Connect Through This Computer's Internet Connection check box.

Connecting to a Cable or DSL Modem

As I explained in Chapter 14, the key steps to connecting a network to a broadband (cable or DSL) modem are

- Making sure that your connection works with a single computer
- Knowing what your settings are
- Unplugging the wire that leads from the modem to your computer, and plugging it into the access point/router
- Plugging the wired portion of your network into the socket (or sockets) on the access point/router
- Entering the settings required for an Internet connection in the access point router

However, the things I showed you in Chapter 14 assume the very simplest of settings for your Internet connection, namely that your node on the Internet is dynamically assigned an IP using DHCP. (For more on what the heck is DHCP, anyway, see "Understanding Dynamic Host Configuration Protocol (DHCP)" later in this chapter.)

In this section, I'll take a look at some other settings you may have to use to connect to the Internet, depending on your ISP.

DIALING THE INTERNET

I'm assuming that you are using a cable or DSL modem, but the fact of the matter is that some access points—such as the AirPort Extreme Base Station—can be set to work with a good old-fashioned dial-up modem (remember them? I do, but barely).

To do this, you'll need to enter the phone number you need to dial, and logon information (such as your user name and password).

As your mom may have said to you, just because you can do something doesn't mean you should do it. I personally can't imagine funneling our home network's Internet connection through a slow dial-up connection (even "high-speed" Internet connections frustrate me enough), and I don't imagine you'd be happy doing this either.

Dynamic IP Addressing Versus Fixed IP Assignment

If your Internet connection works using a dynamic IP (Internet Protocol) address, it means that every time your computer starts up, it is assigned an IP address from the pool of available addresses. The same thing is true when your IP is released and renewed as discussed in Chapter 15. In other words, you don't have a fixed IP address on the Internet. You can think of dynamic IP addressing as kind of like time-sharing at a holiday resort: You can pack more travelers in because nobody owns anything specific, but you don't know for sure who exactly will be at a specific location at any given time.

Dynamic IP addressing is the most common way ISPs such as your cable or DSL provider use to assign you an IP address on the Internet. It's what I showed you in Chapter 14. The IP address that the ISP provides you dynamically is used by your computer to identify itself on the Internet. It's also used by an access point/router to identify your whole network to the Internet (the router also assigns IP addresses within your network, but that's a different story).

But there are some things you can't do with a dynamic IP. For example, in order to host a Web site based off your computer (as opposed to a site that an ISP hosts), you need to have a fixed (or static) IP address. This is because you need a "location," meaning Internet IP address, at which your Web site can always be found.

So for this reason, and for other reasons known only to themselves, some ISPs provide you with one or more fixed IPs, rather than dynamically generated IPs.

If you have a fixed IP, you will need to enter it in your access point/router, or it will not be able to access the Internet. If you are configuring an AirPort Extreme Base Station, the AirPort Setup Assistant will do this for you automatically, provided your IP is set correctly in the computer you are running the AirPort Setup Assistant on.

You can ask your ISP about the IP settings you need. Alternatively, if you are running Windows XP and are connected to the Internet, you can read the fixed IP settings from the Internet Protocol (TCP/IP) Properties dialog, as shown in Figure 16.3. (For an explanation of how to open your Internet Protocol (TCP/IP) Properties dialog, see Chapter 14.)

note

Generally, if you are setting a static IP address for your network, you'll also need to provide an address for a DNS server. DNS is explained further later in this chapter.

caution

It's really important to understand that after the access point router has been loaded with your fixed IP settings, you need to set each computer on your network to accept dynamic IP addressing. You can think of the access point/router as acting on behalf of all the computers on your network. It connects to the network using whatever settings—fixed or dynamic IPs—and then, on its own initiative, it assigns IP addresses to your computers within your network.

FIGURE 16.3

You can read your fixed IP and DNS settings off your computer connected to the Internet using the Internet Protocol (TCP/IP) Properties dialog.

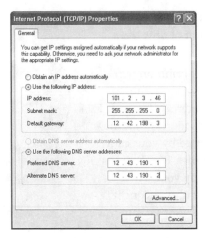

Now that you've gotten the IP (and DNS) settings required by your network, you can open up the administrative application for the access point/router as explained in Chapter 14. Figure 16.4 shows configuring the Linksys Wireless Broadband Router by selecting Static IP as the Internet Connection type, and then entering the information you gathered in the previous section. Click Apply to enter these new settings in the access point/router.

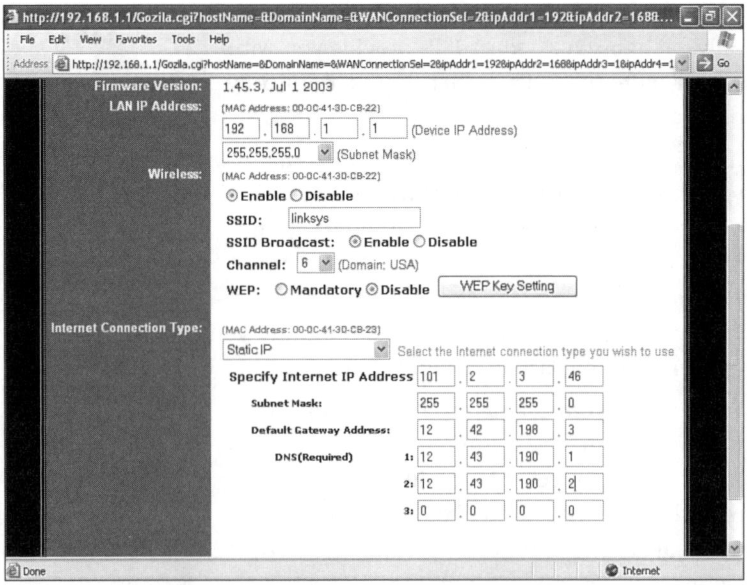

FIGURE 16.4

The static IP settings are entered in the access point/router, using the device's administration panel.

Other Settings That May Be Needed

Depending on your ISP, you may be required to enter some other settings using the administration panel for your access point/router. Some ISPs (particularly cable operators) require a host name and domain name. Figure 16.5 shows these being entered in the Linksys Wireless Broadband Router administration panel.

FIGURE 16.5

If required, the host name and domain name are entered in the access point/router, using the device's administration panel.

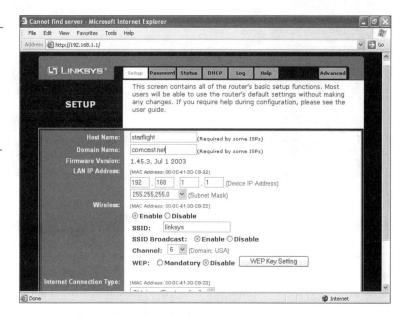

Click Apply at the bottom of the administration panel to keep these settings.

Many DSL providers use PPPoE (Point-to-Point Protocol over Ethernet). If your ISP uses PPPoE, you need to select PPPoE from the Internet Connection Type drop-down list in your access point/router's administration panel. Figure 16.6 shows PPPoE selected in the Linksys Wireless Broadband Router.

With PPPoE selected as the connection type, you'll need to enter your user name and password, as shown in Figure 16.6. Click Apply to save the settings.

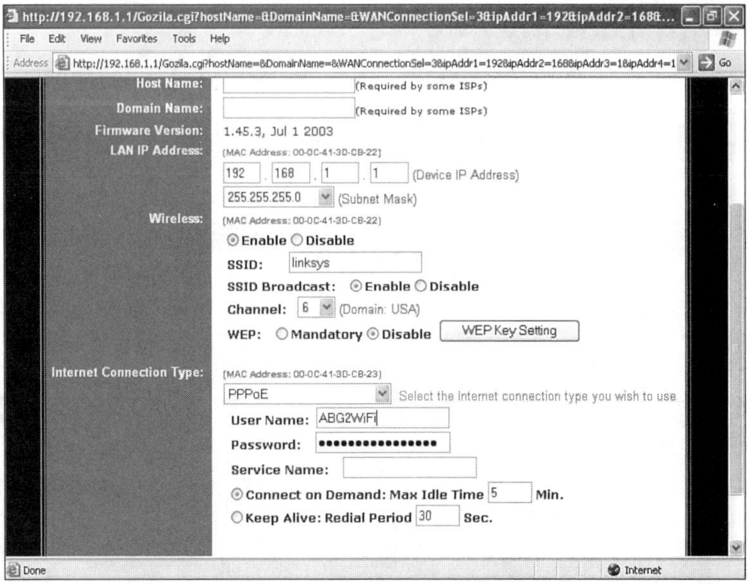

FIGURE 16.6

Many DSL ISPs use PPPoE; if yours does, you need to select it as the connection type.

Understanding Dynamic Host Configuration Protocol (DHCP)

You've read a lot in the last few chapters about DHCP, and you may be wondering what it really is. As my grandpa would have said, here's the five-cent version.

DHCP (Dynamic Host Configuration Protocol) is an agreed-upon standard for assigning variable Internet Protocol (IP) addresses to devices on a network. These variable addresses are called *dynamic* IPs.

Dynamic addressing makes network administration easier because the software keeps track of IP addresses rather than requiring a human being to perform the task. It greatly simplifies things to be able to add a new computer to a network without the hassle of manually assigning it a unique IP address. For whatever it's worth, you also don't need to have as many IPs with dynamic IP addressing—because not everyone will be on the network simultaneously.

With dynamic addressing, a device can have (and most likely will have) a different IP address every time it connects to the network. In some situations, the device's IP address can even change while it is still connected, for example, when you release and renew your IP settings using Ipconfig, as I explained in Chapter 15.

You may have noticed that so far I've said "a network," not "the Internet." From a conceptual viewpoint, the Internet is just a great, big, fat network. As a general matter, great, big, fat networks are called WANs (or Wide Area Networks). So from one viewpoint, your router is simply performing a gateway function between your local area network (LAN) and the WAN that is the Internet. The DHCP servers provided by your

ISP give your router a dynamic IP so that it can communicate with the WAN (the Internet). Within your own network (the LAN), the router assigns dynamic IPs to each node on the private network. Using Ipconfig, as described in Chapter 15, you can see the IP assigned to each of your computers. A technology called Network Address Translation (NAT) allows a single device, such as your router, to act in this way as an agent between the public network (the Internet) and your local, private network. This is what allows a single IP address to represent an entire group of computers.

DNS

You may have had to enter settings for a DNS server, or set your access point router to obtain a DNS server address automatically. In either case, you are probably curious about what DNS actually is.

DNS is short for Domain Name System (sometimes called Domain Name Service). DNS translates more or less alphabetic domain names into IP addresses. Because domain names are in English (or some other language), they're easier to remember than the tuplets that make up an IP address. For example, it is really easier to remember www.google.com than it is to remember Google's IP address, 66.102.7.99, isn't it?

Because the Internet is really based on IP addresses, every time you use a domain name a DNS server must translate the name into the corresponding IP address. In fact, there is a whole separate network of DNS servers that in aggregate provide DNS services.

The way this network works is that if one DNS server doesn't know how to translate a particular domain name, it asks another one, and so on, until the correct IP address is returned.

DNS is one of the important pieces that makes the Internet function.

More About Mixed Wired-Wireless Networks

Back in Chapter 14, I explained one good way to configure a mixed Wi-Fi and wired network using a combination Wi-Fi access point/router such as the Linksys Wireless Broadband Router or the Apple Extreme Base Station. What this amounted to was the simplest possible topology, namely plugging the wired part of the network into the access point/router as shown in Figure 16.7.

However, the topology shown in Figure 16.7 is not the only way to do things. As I showed you in Chapter 15, complicated networks can get pretty, well, complicated.

One change to the topology shown in Figure 16.7 that sometimes makes a lot of sense is to use a standalone router for your network's routing and DHCP functionality, rather than using the Wi-Fi access point/router to do these things. A reason for this change might be if your standalone router had more sophisticated firewall capabilities than those built into the Wi-Fi access point/router. (For more about firewalls, see Chapter 19, "Securing Your Wi-Fi Network.")

FIGURE 16.7

The easiest way to set up a mixed Wi-Fi and wired network is to plug the wired devices into the Wi-Fi access point/router.

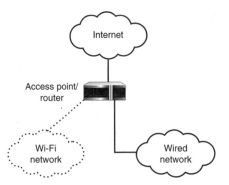

FIGURE 16.7

The easiest way to set up a mixed Wi-Fi and wired network is to plug the wired devices into the Wi-Fi access point/router.

If you made this change, the Wi-Fi access point, whose router functions would no longer be used, would be plugged into the standalone router along with the wired portion of the network as shown in Figure 16.8.

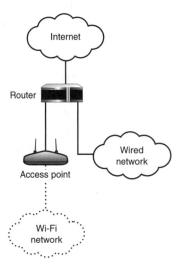

FIGURE 16.8

You might prefer to use a stand-alone router and plug your access point into it.

If you'd like to use your access point/router as shown in Figure 16.8 just as an access point (and not as a router), you need to turn off its DHCP functionality. Figure 16.9 shows disabling the DHCP functionality of the Linksys Wireless Broadband Router using the DHCP tab of the device's administration panel.

note

Quality standalone routers that include firewall capabilities are available from companies including D-Link, Linksys, and Netgear with a wide variety of prices. You can certainly buy one for as little as $30 or $40, but it is doubtful that a router at that price would have any very sophisticated firewall capabilities.

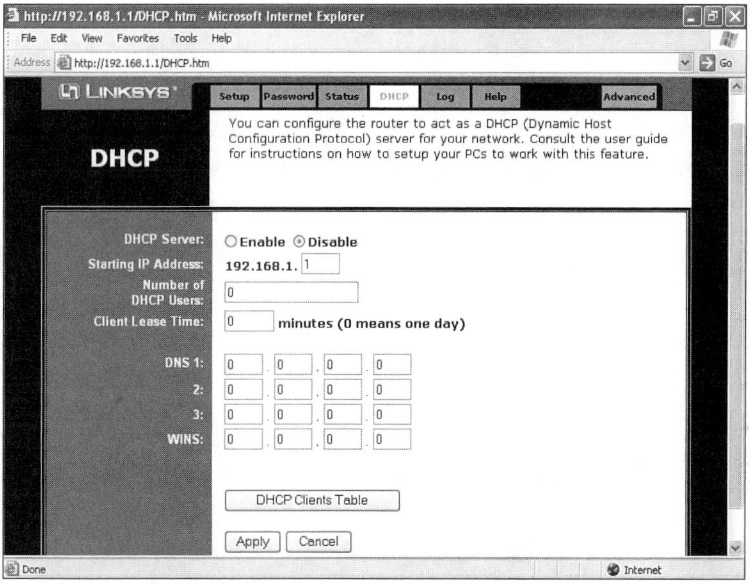

FIGURE 16.9

If you don't want to use an access point/router's routing functionality, you should set its DHCP server to Disabled.

Click Apply to keep the change disabling DHCP. If you need to, you can go ahead and set up the SSID and encryption password for your Wi-Fi broadcast.

Next, you can plug the Wi-Fi access point/router into your standalone router like any other device.

To test the standalone Wi-Fi access point, from a Windows XP machine, you can check to see that it is shown as active in the Wireless Network Connection Properties dialog, as shown in Figure 16.10.

Assuming that you've entered the correct Network key in the Wireless network properties dialog, shown in Figure 16.11, you can check the connection status using the Wireless Network Connection Status window, shown in Figure 16.12.

caution

With DHCP disabled, you may not be able to access the device's administration panel in the normal fashion by entering the appropriate IP in a Web browser. In fact, it may be necessary to use the reset switch on the device (which will re-enable DHCP) before you can access the administration panel again.

FIGURE 16.10

The SSID of the access point is displayed as active in the Windows XP Wireless Network Connection Properties dialog.

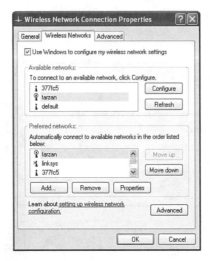

FIGURE 16.11

The Network key must be entered the way it appeared in the Wi-Fi access point.

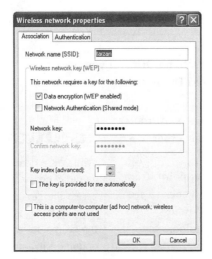

FIGURE 16.12

You can check the status of the standalone Wi-Fi connection using the Wireless Connection Status window.

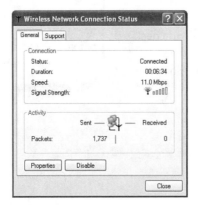

THE ABSOLUTE MINIMUM

Here are the key points to remember from this chapter:

- It's easy to share your Internet connection, and a very nice thing to do for ad-hoc Wi-Fi users.

- Dynamic IP addressing allows a variable IP to be used in place of a fixed IP, making the "bookkeeping" tasks involved in networks, and the Internet, much more manageable.

- A single IP address can be used to represent an entire local area network (LAN).

- If you want to use a standalone router, and plug your Wi-Fi access point into it, you should disable DHCP in the access point (if it provides this functionality).

17

ADDING WI-FI ANTENNAS TO YOUR NETWORK

Adding antennas to your Wi-Fi network—both to your access point and to the Wi-Fi cards in your computers—can greatly extend the range of your Wi-Fi network.

This chapter explains the ins and outs of antennas. What are the best kind to use and how do they connect? How should an antenna be positioned, and are there other configuration issues? What do antennas cost, and where should you buy yours?

I'll answer these questions and more in this "broadcast blast" of a chapter.

Why Use an Antenna with Wi-Fi?

In Chapter 9, "Wi-Fi on Your Desktop," I showed you an example of a Wi-Fi network interface card (NIC) that comes with an external antenna (the D-Link DWL-520). And, in Chapter 14, "Setting Up Your Access Point," I showed you an example of an external antenna attached to an access point (the Apple Extreme Base Station).

Antennas are used with Wi-Fi cards to give them a better connection to the access point broadcasting a signal.

Antennas are used with access points to add power (and range) to the access point's radio broadcast. They are also an integral part of a Wi-Fi network that covers a substantial area. The use of antennas with your access points can greatly reduce costs in deploying a wireless local area network because you can use fewer access points than you would need without the antennas.

If you are planning to use antennas as part of your Wi-Fi network deployment, it's important to understand the different kinds of antennas that are available. (You also need to make sure to buy access points that come with plugs for external antennas.)

An important part of deploying a Wi-Fi network is doing a site survey, which takes into account the topography and obstacles of the area that needs to be "unwired" and comes up with the best plan and layout for access points and antennas.

Antenna Basics

An antenna is a device that propagates radio frequency (RF) signals through the air. The transmitter (the Wi-Fi card or access point) sends an RF signal to the antenna, which amplifies the signal and sends it along through the medium of air.

When you are thinking about antennas, you need to think about the following characteristics:

- Radiation pattern
- Gain
- Frequency
- Power

Frequency

Antennas used with Wi-Fi need to be tuned to 2.4GHz (802.11b or 802.11g) or 5GHz (802.11a). The frequency of the antenna needs to match the frequency of the radio transmitter.

Power

Antennas are rated to handle a specific amount of power put out by a radio transmitter. In the case of Wi-Fi, this is not a great issue because most antennas are capable of handling the one-watt maximum transmission allowed by the FCC (see "Antennas and the FCC" later in this chapter for more information).

Radiation Pattern

The radiation pattern of an antenna defines the shape of the radio wave that the antenna propagates, or sends into the air. The radiation pattern that all other radiation patterns are compared to is called *isotropic*. In an isotropic radiation pattern, the antenna transmits radio waves in all three dimensions equally, so that the pattern represents a ball, or globe, with the antenna at its center. Figure 17.1 is a depiction of the isotropic radiation pattern.

Gain

The amount of gain an antenna provides means how much it increases the power of signals passed to it by the radio transmitter. The amount of gain is measured in decibels (dB), and bears a logarithmic relationship to the power input to the antenna. What you should keep in mind is that an antenna with a 3dB gain outputs double the power input to it, and an antenna with 6dB gain quadruples the power.

If you look at the specifications provided by antenna manufacturers, you will find gain measured in dBi, or gain in decibels relative to an isotropic radiation pattern. So dBi measures how much "better" a particular antenna is than if using a fictitious antenna with an isotropic radiation pattern, and it is a good measure of how effective an antenna is.

Different Kinds of Antennas

There are many different designs for antennas that Wi-Fi cards and access points can use.

Generally, antennas are either omnidirectional or directional.

Omnidirectional Antennas

Omnidirectional antennas are most commonly used with Wi-Fi cards and access points. These antennas send out radio waves in all directions equally on the horizontal plane but don't send out much in the way of signals vertically. The radiation pattern of an omnidirectional antenna looks like a doughnut, with the antenna in the center of the doughnut, as depicted in Figure 17.1.

FIGURE 17.1

An omnidirectional antenna sends out signals in all directions on the horizontal plane.

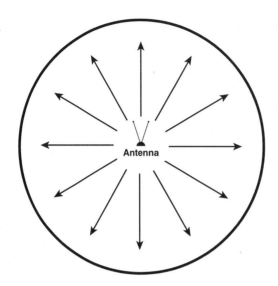

Figure 17.2 shows a fairly standard omnidirectional antenna made by Maxrad, Inc., which is intended to work with Wi-Fi and the 2.4GHz spectrum, and is mounted externally on a roof.

FIGURE 17.2

This omnidirectional antenna from Maxrad is intended for outdoor mounting on a roof.

Directional Antennas

In contrast to omnidirectional antennas, a directional antenna, which is also called a *yagi*, transmits radio signals in a focused beam, like a flashlight, or spotlight. Generally, the manufacturer's specifications give you some idea of the width of the radiation pattern of a yagi. For example, Figure 17.3 shows the radiation pattern for a yagi antenna from Cisco's Aironet division.

FIGURE 17.3

A yagi transmits RF signals in a focused single direction.

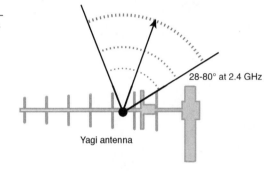

28-80° at 2.4 GHz

Yagi antenna

In general, directional antennas have much higher gain than omnidirectional antennas. Furthermore, the higher the gain of the directional antenna, the narrower is its beam.

High-gain directional antennas work best to facilitate point-to-point communications, for example, between two wireless bridges, each of which are located on top of a building on a campus. They also can be used to cover a long, but narrow area.

Intelligent use of directional antennas can cut down greatly on the number of access points required to cover an area.

Figure 17.4 shows a yagi (directional antenna) intended for use with 2.4GHz and 5GHz Wi-Fi broadcasts.

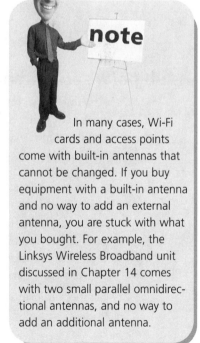

note

In many cases, Wi-Fi cards and access points come with built-in antennas that cannot be changed. If you buy equipment with a built-in antenna and no way to add an external antenna, you are stuck with what you bought. For example, the Linksys Wireless Broadband unit discussed in Chapter 14 comes with two small parallel omnidirectional antennas, and no way to add an additional antenna.

FIGURE 17.4

This yagi (directional) antenna is intended for use in situations that require high gain.

Multipolarized Antennas

Antenna development for Wi-Fi (and other wireless technologies) is a hot area right now, with many new developments. For example, a company named WiFi-Plus, Inc., has developed *multipolarized* antennas. According to the company's chief technology officer, Jack Nilsson, these antennas have the ability to propagate and receive signals that are both horizontal and vertical. These models are better than conventional models for going around obstructions. WiFi-Plus's multipolarized antennas can also be used in situations where Wi-Fi is being broadcast using a directional antenna to a deep valley. A conventional directional antenna might broadcast signals that would overshoot the valley, but a multipolarized antenna is capable of broadcasting signals that travel horizontally following the direction of the RF beam, but also can be received down in the valley.

For more information about multipolarized antennas, see the company Web site, www.wifi-plus.com.

Using an Antenna with a Wi-Fi Card

Connecting an antenna to a Wi-Fi card (or USB Wi-Fi device) requires a way to connect an external antenna to the card. If there is any kind of external connection at all for an antenna on the card, you can probably find a way to connect almost any antenna, although it may require a special adapter, sometimes called a *radio pigtail*. You can find lists of pigtails to fit most Wi-Fi cards (and buy them) at `www.wifi-plus.` `shoppingcartsplus.com/page/page/557856.htm`, or `www.hyperlinktech.com/web/cable_radio_` `pigtails_list.php`, or `www.jefatech.com/category/cable_assemblies/`.

Some cards come with sockets that will fit most antennas without any special adapter. For example, Figure 17.5 shows the D-Link DWL-520 card installed with the antenna that ships with the unit.

FIGURE 17.5

This card ships with a removable antenna.

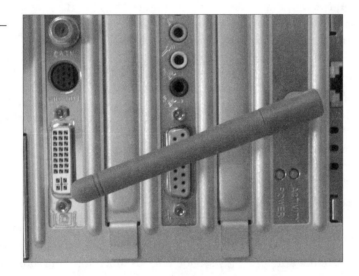

To install a more powerful antenna than the one that ships with this model, unscrew the original antenna so that you see the antenna socket, shown in Figure 17.6.

FIGURE 17.6

The antenna socket on this card can be used to plug in many Wi-Fi antennas.

With the antenna unscrewed, you can use the socket to connect many antennas with the connectors that ship with the antenna.

Adding an Antenna to an Access Point

As they say, some guys have all the luck. If your access point, like the Linksys Wireless Broadband Router does not have a connection for an external antenna, you can't add an external antenna to it (and you are out of luck!).

On the other hand, if your access point, like the Apple Extreme Base Station, comes with a connector for an external antenna, it is usually a simple matter to plug an antenna in (and you've got all the luck!).

Adding an external omnidirectional antenna to an access point is essentially a no-brainer. It will improve the range of your access point, and there are no trade-offs (you don't lose anything, except your out-of-pocket cost to buy the antenna).

More complex, directional antennas are a trickier story. If you are thinking of fitting your access point with one of these, you need to think carefully about how radio signals will propagate given the terrain you need to cover.

note

Although some Wi-Fi access points intended for home use don't have an external antenna connection, almost all Wi-Fi access point and bridge units that are intended for commercial applications have connections for (and are used with) antennas. Of course, these industrial-strength units do tend to cost more.

What the Antenna Should Cost

You should be able to buy an external Wi-Fi omnidirectional antenna for your NIC card for between $20 and $50. Believe it or not, the radio pigtail, if you need one for connecting to the antenna, may set you back as much (or more than) the card. This connector will probably cost between $20 and $30.

As you can imagine, there's a great range in price for antennas designed to work with access points. There's probably not much point in buying an omnidirectional external antenna for less than $50 because the antenna that ships as part of your Wi-Fi access point is just about as good.

For $50 to $100, you can get a good omnidirectional antenna intended for internal use.

Omnidirectional antennas intended for outdoor use start at about $50 and can run you $200 and up.

Directional antennas intended for external use run a little more than omnidirectional antennas. Highly specialized directional antennas can be very expensive indeed.

If you are interested in the multipolarized antennas mentioned earlier in this chapter, you can probably expect to pay a bit more for this feature. An omnidirectional multipolarized antenna intended for external use runs about $150. Directional multipolarized antennas, often used for point-to-point back haul traffic, cost between $200 and $900.

Of course, like everything else that is related to technology, many antennas can be found for sale on eBay. If you've read this chapter, and understand Wi-Fi antennas, you should be able to buy one safely on eBay, and save some cash.

The Antenna in a Can

If springing for a commercial antenna is too expensive for you, you can always consider building a "Cantenna." The total cost of a Cantenna, which uses an old tin can as its primary part, is under $5.

Besides the tin can, which should be between three and four inches in diameter, the only things you need to build the Cantenna are

- About 1.25 inches of 12-gauge copper wire
- Four nuts and bolts
- An N-type female connector

caution

If you build a Cantenna, and the FCC comes looking for you, please don't tell the Feds that you heard about it from me! Technically, using a Cantenna with your Wi-Fi equipment is probably illegal under FCC regulations.

The N-type connector is the standard connector for antennas, and will be used to connect it to your Wi-Fi equipment. The cost for this connector is $3–$5, which is where I got the original figure of less than $5. You can buy this connector from any of the sources I mentioned that sell radio pigtails (or go to your local Frye's or electronic hobby store such as Radio Shack).

You drill holes in the can for the connector and the nuts and bolts. Their placement is important, because it determines the propagation characteristics of the antenna.

The copper wire is attached to the back of the connector and soldered to the tin can.

The best how-to article that I've seen that describes creating a Cantenna, "How to Build a Tin Can Waveguide Antenna," is by Gregory Rehm and can be found at www.turnpoint.net/wireless/cantennahowto.html. The article includes a calculator to help you determine where to place the connector and nuts and bolts.

You can also purchase a premade Cantenna for $20 (this one meets FCC regulations) from Super Cantenna at www.cantenna.com.

Where to Buy Your Wi-Fi Antenna

As I mentioned earlier in this chapter, if you want to buy an antenna cheaply, you may have good luck on eBay. I recently tried the terms "RF antenna" and "Wi-Fi antenna" on eBay, and found quite a few items for auction, with almost none priced above $25.

If you decide to buy your antenna in a more conventional way, you should go to a company with a Web presence that specializes in RF antennas and related equipment. These companies include

- CushCraft Corporation: www.cushcraft.com
- Fleeman, Anderson & Bird: www.fab-corp.com
- HyperLink Technologies: www.hyperlinktech.com
- Jefa Tech: www.jefatech.com
- Maxrad: www.maxrad.com
- Til-Tek Antennas: www.tiltek.com
- WiFi-Plus: www.wifi-plus.com

THE ABSOLUTE MINIMUM

Here are the key points to remember from this chapter:

- Antennas are omnidirectional (all over the place) or directional (a focused beam).
- If your Wi-Fi card or access point has a connector, you can easily add an external antenna.
- Omnidirectional antennas don't cost very much, and they can add a great deal of range to your Wi-Fi network.
- Directional antennas are usually used to broadcast from one point to another point; you need to think carefully about deploying directional antennas with your Wi-Fi network.

PART V

Securing Your Wi-Fi Computer and Network

18

PROTECTING YOUR MOBILE Wi-Fi COMPUTER

Security is a big concern for mobile Wi-Fi users, as it ought to be. It's a fact of life, however, that most problems with mobile computing do not have to do with technology, but rather with human interactions. Perhaps someone sees you typing in confidential information while you are "Wi-Fi-ing" in a hotel lobby or a crowded airport waiting area. Or, it can be as simple as theft of an easily portable computing device. These issues are not much different because your mobile computing device is equipped with Wi-Fi (someone can still read confidential information over your shoulder even if you are not unwired). But it is a fact of life that mobile computers equipped with Wi-Fi do get out and about more—so security is an even bigger concern for them than for the run-of-the-mill non-Wi-Fi laptop.

This chapter explains the dos and the don'ts of traveling with a Wi-Fi–enabled laptop. I'll tell you what you can do to protect yourself and your equipment. I'll also tell you what software you should be running to Wi-Fi with the best of them—for fun and profit, but most of all, safety.

"Social" Engineering

Social engineering is a term for tricking a person into revealing their password or other confidential information.

A classic social engineering trick is to send email claiming to be a system administrator. The email will claim to need your password for some important system administration work, and ask you to email it back. Often, the email will appear to be from a real system administrator, and be sent to everyone on a network, hoping that at least one or two users will fall for the trick.

You can also be scammed for your password via telephone. In fact, theft of credit card information or identity information via "dumpster diving" (or from a restaurant credit card receipt) are examples of social engineering that do not involve technology or the Internet.

Another common trick used by social engineers is sometimes called "shoulder surfing." This is when someone reads your login information, password, or other confidential information over your shoulder.

Wi-Fi users are particularly vulnerable to shoulder surfing. The best defense is to be alert and very careful if you think someone may be looking over your shoulder. If you think someone has read your password, you should change it (or get it changed) immediately. For example, if you think someone may have read your T-Mobile Hotspot password over your shoulder as you entered it in a crowded hotel lobby, you can use the T-Mobile personal preference page to change your password, or contact T-Mobile technical support right away by email or telephone.

If somebody is watching you when you type in your password, you should move away, or ask them not to look while you log in. It's not polite to read someone else's password, so you shouldn't worry about being impolite yourself when you ask someone not to read it.

tip

The best passwords are long (at least six characters and digits) and contain both letters and numbers. If a password is very easy to remember, it is probably not that strong a password.

Another form of social engineering is guessing your password. You should try to use passwords for logging on to Wi-Fi networks, and passwords in general, that are hard to guess. You should realize that people can find out things about you from public records, such as your date of birth, the names of your children, and so on. So publicly available information about you should not be used for passwords because it can be guessed fairly easily.

Social engineering is the biggest threat to computer security, Wi-Fi–enabled and otherwise. The best defense is awareness of the problem, and alertness for possible security intrusions.

Physical Lockdown

The physical theft of mobile computers is a pretty big problem, with around 400,000 laptops a year stolen in the United States.

Like other kinds of computer crimes and security breaches, in a great many physical mobile computer thefts insiders are responsible. Typical insiders include employees, temporary workers, and contractors.

The moral is to be leery about leaving your laptop lying around, either in the office or when you are traveling. This sounds like pretty obvious advice, but what if you just don't want to lug it around with you—for example, to go on a bathroom break during a convention?

A common and relatively inexpensive security device to deal with this kind of situation is the cable lock. The manufacturer of the cable lock provides a way of attaching the lock to the computer. (Often the lock plugs into a port on the laptop, with a security mechanism preventing its removal without the key). The cable then loops around a stationary item, such as a desk leg.

Cable locks can be had for as little as $20 to $30. Probably the best known cable lock manufacturer is Kensington, www.kensington.com. In some cases, the manufacturer of the cable lock guarantees the laptop attached with the cable lock.

The problem with cable locks is that they can easily be cut using bolt cutters available in any hardware store. To add another level of security, you can use a cable lock alarm, such as the Defcon, made by Targus. Targus, www.targus.com, best known for its mobile computer cases, makes a number of different cable lock alarms for as little as $40. These alarms make a huge racket when the cable is tampered with.

Targus also makes a PC Card, the Targus Defcon Motion Data Protection (MDP) card, that slips into the PC slot on your laptop. This card, which sells for about $100, provides double-barreled protection. First, it sounds a loud alarm in response to motion (so it works as a physical theft inhibitor). The card also encrypts the computer, with PIN access (this encryption inhibits data theft as well as physical theft).

When the alarm has been triggered (because the card encounters unauthorized motion), a second, 16-digit PIN is required to gain access to the computer's operating system and files.

If you are going to be carrying around important, confidential data on your Wi-Fi–enabled mobile computer, this sounds like a pretty good investment to me!

There are quite a few solutions along the lines of the Targus MDP card that get more and more complex. Some of these schemes include biometric scanning devices—to authenticate you as the owner of your mobile computer. In other schemes, wireless technology is used to maintain a series of "leases" that keeps the mobile computer going. If the mobile computer fails to obtain a lease for a certain period of time, it stops working, and encryption is engaged. With these schemes, generally a cell phone call can also trigger arming of the defense mechanisms.

Companies that sell sophisticated defense systems along these lines include CoreStreet, Digital Persona, Keyware, RSA Security, and Vasco.

Typically, these are complex (and costly) solutions, more suitable for an enterprise than for an individual. But if you are involved in travel with mobile computers that store important and sensitive information, you might want to consider taking this next step.

Using Password Protection

In a mobile computer equipped with Wi-Fi, you can (and should) password-protect operating systems such as Windows XP. This makes it a great deal more difficult (although not always impossible) to boot up your computer without knowing the password.

You can also set a password in the BIOS of most computers. This provides a better level of security than an operating system password, but it is also not absolute.

To set a BIOS password, you must enter the BIOS screens for your computer. This is done during the boot-up process when you've turned the computer on, generally by pressing a key (such as the Delete key) or key combination while the computer is booting up.

I've already mentioned that you should take care to pick a password that can be easily guessed by someone who knows a little about you. In addition, proper password management requires some other steps, including

- Choosing passwords that meet certain technical characteristics

- Changing passwords on a regular basis

The long and short of this is that as an individual with a Wi-Fi–equipped mobile computer, you should certainly password-protect it before you take it on the road. (Don't forget the password!) But for an

note

Sophisticated data protection schemes may protect the data on a mobile computer, but they will not prevent the theft of the physical machine. Even if a machine is data-locked, the victim of the theft is unlikely to ever get the machine back.

note

For technical information about the security level provided by BIOS passwords, and what is involved in cracking them, see www.heise.de/ct/english/98/08/194/. The article also tells how the author used BIOS password protection as a disciplinary measure with his ten-year-old daughter ("We used to give them a slap on the wrist; now we lock them out of their computer!") and how easy it was for his daughter to circumvent the measure.

organization, there are real costs involved in password protection. These include implementing password management procedures, and also dealing with the inevitable user who loses his password.

In other words, even a seemingly easy security solution like password protection has its costs (at least for an organization). So with any security mechanism, it's worth toting up the value of the data that needs to be protected, and seeing if the trouble is worth it.

caution

If you set a BIOS password, make sure you don't lose it. Despite the various back doors described in the Web reference that I mentioned previously, retrieving a lost BIOS password can be very difficult (and impossible in some cases).

Creating a Password in Windows XP

You can easily password-protect your Windows XP computer. To do so, open the User Accounts applet from the Windows Control panel.

In User Accounts, click your logon name. Next, click Create a Password. Enter and confirm your password. You can also provide a password hint if you'd like (this will appear on the Windows welcome screen when your computer boots up).

Click Create Password to accept the new password.

File Sharing

We tell our children that sharing is good, but when it comes to computers, running with sharing turned on can pose a security risk.

If you are connecting to a Wi-Fi network—or any network—and sharing is turned on, anyone else on the network can read your files across the network. For that matter, your files can be altered or deleted across the network, as well.

If your folders are private, your files cannot be shared. This may not be very convenient when you are at home, but it certainly improves security when you connect to a network on the road.

note

You cannot lock the entire Documents and Settings folder, only the individual user's folders listed under Documents and Settings. Otherwise you would be able to lock out other users of the same machine.

Windows XP

In Windows XP, to turn file sharing off, and make your folders private, locate the top-level folder you want to make private (the folders beneath this one will also be private).

A good choice would be your entire hard drive, or your folder in the Documents and Settings folder, which contains your My Documents folder (among other things). With the folder you want to make private selected in Windows Explorer, right-click and select Properties to open its Properties window. Click the Sharing tab. On the Sharing tab of the Properties window for the folder, deselect the Share This Folder on the Network check box as shown in Figure 18.1.

Next, check the Make This Folder Private check box. Click Apply. The folder, folders beneath it within your computer, and the files in those folders are now private and not shared.

If you want to reverse the process when you get home, clear the Make This Folder Private check box, and check Share This Folder on the Network. Your files and folders are now public, meaning shared. If you really want to live dangerously, you can also check the Allow Network Users to Change My Files box, also shown in Figure 18.1.

note

Under Windows XP, you can only change the permissions on files and folders to make them private if the NTSF file system is being used. The NTSF file system is superior to the alternatives, FAT and FAT32 (which are used in Windows 9x/Me and optional in Windows XP), anyhow, so there is little reason not to be running it. If you can't make folders private, the reason is probably that your computer is not running NTSF. For information about how to convert to NTSF, open Windows Help and Support, and search for NTSF.

You should also know that the details of the process for setting sharing will differ from what I described if you are in a network with a domain controller, rather than in a workgroup network. For details of resetting permission in a network with a domain controller, see "Sharing and Security" in Windows Help.

FIGURE 18.1
The Sharing tab of the Properties window for a folder is used to make a folder (and its files) private.

MacOS

On an Apple computer, to disable sharing, open System Preferences from the Apple menu. Within System Preferences, in the Network group, open the Sharing application. Within Sharing, click the Stop button, shown in Figure 18.2, to stop sharing.

FIGURE 18.2

Click the Stop button within the Sharing application in System Preferences to turn off sharing on an Apple.

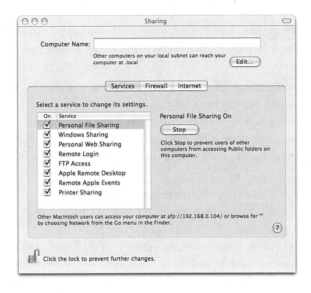

When sharing is turned off, a message will display that information as you can see in Figure 18.3. If you later decide to turn sharing back on, just click the Start button.

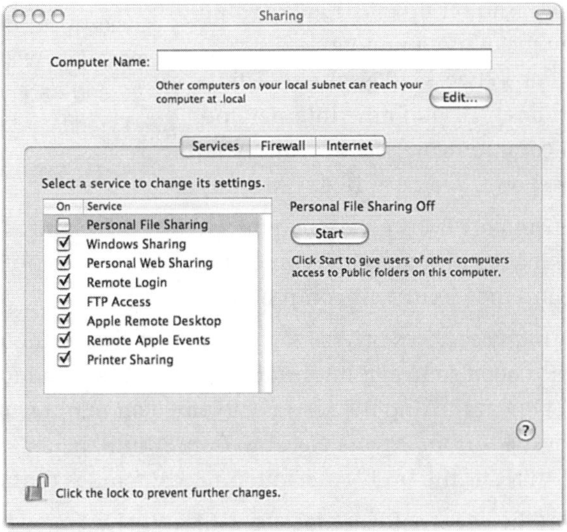

FIGURE 18.3

Sharing has been turned off; to turn it back on, click the Start button.

Using a Virtual Private Network (VPN)

You've logged onto a public hotspot at some great location. This time, let's say you're connected poolside at some great hotel in a warm location. So far, all is well and good.

When you connected to the Wi-Fi hotspot provider, say T-Mobile Hotspot or Wayport, you were probably authenticated. That means you had to provide a login identification and a password, in part so that the Wi-Fi provider would know who to bill for your time online.

But beyond this authentication, there is no security at a public Wi-Fi hotspot. Transmissions are not, for the most part, encrypted. Wireless networks are inherently less secure than wireline networks because anyone can pick up the signals. Without encryption, tapping into your Wi-Fi packets as they are transmitted is like reading plain text. It is not very hard to do from a technical viewpoint.

I don't want you to get the impression that the world is full of people who live to lurk and to pick up your Wi-Fi transmissions. But you should regard a public Wi-Fi hotspot as fundamentally insecure. If you need to work with information on your home (or, more likely, office) network, this can be problematic.

One solution that can be used to at least make a more secure connection from a public hotspot to your home network is to set up a Virtual Private Network (VPN) by installing a remote access server on your home network. VPNs use a dedicated server to "tunnel" through the Internet and provide a way to communicate securely with your home network as shown in Figure 18.4.

> **caution**
>
> As specific examples of security risks that may concern you, this means that someone with the know-how and right equipment could easily sniff passwords that you provide to Web servers, read your unencrypted email, note which Web sites you visit, and track your online banking and credit card transactions.

This means that using a VPN is a very helpful way to add security to a Wi-Fi connection. After you've logged into the VPN, you can use the resources of your home network without feeling that security is compromised.

There are a great many vendors of VPN server products, which are mostly geared at the enterprise. For a good source of information about VPNs, and to find the companies that are involved in making the server software, you might want to have a look at the Web site for the Virtual Private Network Consortium, better known as VPNC, www.vpnc.org. The VPNC is the trade association for companies that make VPNs.

It's good news that the client software for use with a VPN is baked into the Windows XP operating system.

FIGURE 18.4

A VPN tunnel
creates a secure
communications
channel across
the insecure
Internet.

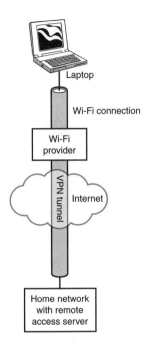

To make a connection to a VPN from Windows XP, open the Network Connections applet by double-clicking Network Connections in Control Panel. In Network Connections, click Create a New Connection (you can find this on the left under Network Tasks). When the New Connection Wizard opens, click Next.

Choose Connect to the Network at My Workplace, as shown in Figure 18.5, and click Next.

FIGURE 18.5

Choose Connect
to the Network
at My Workplace
to start the wiz-
ard that creates
the VPN client
on your remote
system.

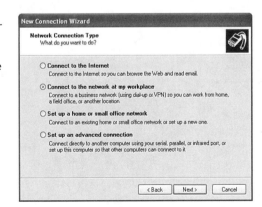

Choose Virtual Private Network Connection as shown in Figure 18.6, and click Next.

FIGURE 18.6

To create a VPN, choose Virtual Private Network Connection.

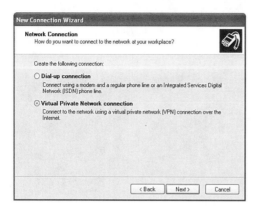

You will be asked to provide a name for the VPN, such as myVPN, and the host name or IP address of the VPN server.

Click Finish to close the wizard. The VPN will now appear in your Network Connections window, as you can see in Figure 18.7.

When you attempt to connect to the VPN, you will be prompted for your VPN user name and password so that the VPN remote access server can authenticate you, as shown in Figure 18.8.

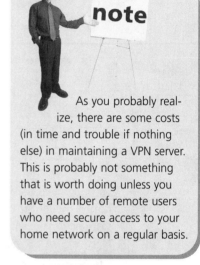

note

As you probably realize, there are some costs (in time and trouble if nothing else) in maintaining a VPN server. This is probably not something that is worth doing unless you have a number of remote users who need secure access to your home network on a regular basis.

FIGURE 18.7

The new VPN is shown in the Network Connections window.

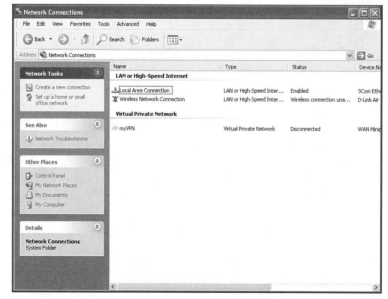

FIGURE 18.8

When you connect to the VPN, you will be asked to supply a logon and password so that the VPN's remote access server can authenticate you.

Personal Software for Protection

Any computer that connects to the Internet, or that connects to a network that connects to the Internet, should run some programs for general protection.

The most important category of program for protection is antivirus. Antivirus programs stop viruses from attacking your system, and help you recover if you are attacked by a virus.

The leading antivirus products are VirusScan from McAfee, www.mcafee.com, and Norton Antivirus from Symantec, www.symantec.com.

A firewall is another type of program useful for protecting your PC. A firewall program protects your resources by filtering network packets. If your computer is connected to a network that is not protected with a firewall, or if you are taking a computer on the road, you probably should use a personal firewall program for added protection.

There are a number of good personal firewall products on the market, including offerings from McAfee and Symantec that come bundled with their antivirus products. Other personal firewalls worth considering include Personal Firewall from Tiny Software, www.tinysoftware.com, Sygate Personal Firewall from Sygate Technologies, www.sygate.com, and Zone Alarm, from Zone Labs, www.zonelabs.com.

In addition, Windows XP comes with personal firewall software, with the grand virtues that it is free and (if you have Windows XP) you already have it.

To activate the Windows XP personal firewall, if you are using a wireless connection, first use the Control Panel to open the Network Connections applet.

caution

Because new viruses come on the scene so quickly, it is vitally important to keep your virus definitions up to date. If your antivirus program comes with an automatic update feature, you should make sure that this is turned on and operational. Otherwise, make sure to go online and update your virus definitions frequently. An antivirus program with out-of-date definitions is almost as bad as no protection at all.

In Network Connections, highlight the wireless device used for your Internet connection, and choose Properties from its context menu. The Wireless Network Connection Properties dialog will open.

On the Advanced tab of the Wireless Network Connection Properties dialog, as shown in Figure 18.9, check the box under Internet Connection Firewall, and then click OK.

The Internet connection will now be displayed as "firewalled" in the Network Connections window.

> **tip**
>
> You can also use the Network Setup Wizard to turn on the Windows XP personal firewall. The Network Setup Wizard can be started by clicking Set Up a Home or Small Office Network on the Network Tasks pane of My Network Places.

FIGURE 18.9

It's easy to turn on the personal firewall that ships with Windows XP.

THE ABSOLUTE MINIMUM

I hope this chapter has helped you learn how to practice safe computing with a Wi-Fi–equipped mobile computer.

Here are the key points to remember from this chapter:

- Protection from security problems is a mindset that requires awareness and alertness.

- Social engineering is the biggest security threat.

- Physical theft of laptops is a big problem, but there are some devices that can help with locking down your equipment.

- You can enhance your safety by password-protecting your computer and disabling sharing.

- If you need to access your home network from a public hotspot, setting up a VPN can enhance security.

- You should run antivirus and personal firewall protection on mobile computers equipped with Wi-Fi.

19

SECURING YOUR Wi-Fi NETWORK

We live in a world that can seem increasingly dangerous both to human beings and their computers. Wi-Fi networks are very convenient, wonderful to use, and easy to deploy (as I explained in Part IV, "Creating a Wi-Fi Network"). But running a wireless network does pose a substantial security risk.

This chapter will help you assess the risk that your wireless network poses, and create a game plan for dealing with these risks. I'll also show you how to work with some of the tools that can be used to minimize risks, including firewall and VPN servers, and MAC filtering.

How Real Is the Threat?

Make no mistake, the threat is real. If you compare a wireless network with a conventional wired network, essentially the security risks posed by the two are the same with one big exception. The big exception is that a wireless network provides no physical security. Essentially anyone can tap into a wireless network. In comparison, to hack a wired network you need a physical connection to the network's wiring.

Attacks from the Internet are a threat to both wired and wireless networks. But otherwise, no one can attack a wired network without gaining admittance to your premises. Wireless networks are vulnerable to attacks from people who are not on your physical premises. This means that protection cannot be obtained by physical security measures, but only by implementing appropriate internal management and security measures. A lock on your door should inhibit someone who would like to access your wired network, but it is meaningless to the security of your wireless network.

Another facet of the problem is that the default setup for a wireless access point/router, as I explained in Chapter 14, "Setting Up Your Access Point," just gets your Wi-Fi network up and running. It doesn't step you through the process of adding any security features, such as encryption, to your network.

An astounding percentage of private Wi-Fi networks—some estimates are as high as 80%—are run without any security features turned on.

It's also worth noting that public hotspots typically don't feature any security besides basic user authentication—because the people running the hotspot want to make it as easy as possible for people to log on.

I don't want to exaggerate the problem. You may quite rightly feel that you have no secrets, and that you don't care about giving away access to your files to strangers.

There's some merit to this position. It's likely that no one would really care about most of my files (or your files). In any case, it's worth a lot less effort to guard, say, Aunt Minnie's recipe for Tarheel pie than, say, the firing sequence for a nuclear warhead. Every security management issue comes down to a balancing act: Is that which is being secured worth the cost (in time, trouble, and money) of more stringent security? But everyone has something worth safeguarding. For example, you probably really don't want to hand out your Quicken or Microsoft Money data files to strangers.

The most stringent security of all would ban wireless networking, and indeed networking altogether—because whenever there is communication in and out, there is a potential risk. But, for most people taking that kind of step would not be worth the cost.

In order to more fully perform the security balancing act, I'd like to step back for a minute and look at just what the security threat to your Wi-Fi network is.

If your Wi-Fi network is completely unsecured, someone (whom I'll call the "nefarious evildoer"), within broadcast range of your access point but probably outside your physical perimeter, can become a node on your network. This is sometimes called *penetration*.

As a node (or client) on your network, the nefarious evildoer can access files on your network.

Access to the file systems on your computers means more than that the nefarious evildoer can read the files. The nefarious evildoer can also alter and delete them. If the nefarious evildoer is really malicious, your entire system could be wiped.

The nefarious evildoer, depending on how you have things set, can also change your network administrative settings. You could get locked out of your own network!

If you haven't changed the password in your access point, the nefarious evildoer could open its administrative panel, assuming (as most access points do) that it uses Web-based administration. The settings could then be changed to defeat whatever security measures are in place.

Of course, most penetration is relatively innocent, and is done to obtain Internet access. Yes, the nefarious evildoer may just not have Internet access and want to piggy-back (without paying) on yours.

Before you throw up your hands and say, "I don't care. I'm happy to share my Internet connection; it's not going to cost me any more. Besides, sharing is in the spirit of open source, Wi-Fi, and all those good things," you should think about a couple of ramifications.

tip

See Chapter 18, "Protecting Your Mobile Wi-Fi Computer," for information about turning file sharing off so that accessing files, even with network access, is harder to accomplish.

caution

Concerns about losing bandwidth are particularly valid in the case of file-sharers.

Another concern in this respect is that file-sharers are almost certainly trading in copyrighted information (songs) and the person who is the owner of the connection to the Internet is the one that the RIAA (Recording Industry Association of America) is going to track down.

In other words, if you leave your network open, you may be liable (both civilly and criminally) for the actions of freeloaders who use it.

By sharing your Internet access in this way, you are probably in violation of your agreement with your ISP. Okay, so I don't much care about this technicality either. But if some real nefarious evildoer does use your ISP account to launch a Web attack—such as a virus— you could be held responsible. At the very least, it could lead to the ISP shutting down your account. Also, if others are using your Internet connection, there's no doubt your connection speed will slow. I don't know about you, but even broadband isn't fast enough for me. I don't want freeloaders gumming up the works even more.

Before you say it's okay with you to have others use your Internet connection because it doesn't cost you anything more, think about whether you would leave the front door to your house open with a note saying, "Come in, use the phone, local and long distance minutes are free!"

What Steps Should You Take?

The steps you should take depend on how important the security of your personal network is to you. Some people will feel it more important than others to implement comprehensive security measures. But some of the basic security measures you can take are easy, and involve little (or no) trouble to set up and little extra trouble on the part of network users. So everyone should take at least some security measures.

This section will help you understand the security measures you can take, and how to implement them. It will also help you develop a security game plan in the context of your own requirements for security.

The security measures described in this chapter fall into three categories, or levels. I'll note each measure with which category it falls into, and explain any wrinkles related to the level.

The measures described in this section cover network security. Besides the measures explained in this chapter, you should also take steps to protect individual computers such as installing antivirus software and personal firewall software, as I explained in Chapter 18.

The levels for security measures that I use are

- **No-brainer:** I don't give a rat's bottom about security, and I've got nothing of any value on my network anyway, but this measure is easy to implement, and no trouble to use, so why not?

- **Middling:** I'm reasonably concerned about security, but I don't want to waste too much time on it. I'm willing to go to a little bit of trouble to make my network more secure.

■ **Red alert:** I am really concerned about security (perhaps I deal with confidential materi-
als belonging to clients). I can't take any
chances that my network is insecure, and
I'm willing to go to the additional trouble
and expense that this might imply.

In order to come up with a game plan for implementing security on your Wi-Fi network, you
should sit back for a moment and see which of
these security levels makes the most sense to you.

No-Brainer Security

The measures described in this section are the ones
that everyone with a Wi-Fi network should take
(that means you!):

■ Change the SSID, or network name, from its
default (see Chapter 14 for details).

■ Set the SSID not to broadcast (see Chapter
14 for details). If your SSID is not broadcast,
it will be harder for a nefarious evildoer to
log on (or even know your Wi-Fi network is
there).

■ Implement WEP (wired equivalent privacy)
encryption as explained in Chapter 15,
"Configuring Your Wi-Fi Network."

■ Make sure all the computers on your network are running antivirus software, and that
the virus definitions are updated weekly (see
Chapter 18 for more information). This has
more to do with general network protection
(and common sense) than it does with Wi-
Fi network security, but it is still very
important.

■ Change the default password for the
administrative application for your access
point. For example, to change the password for the Linksys Wireless Broadband
Router, open its administrative application
as explained in Chapter 14. Click the

note

The National Institute of
Standards and Technology,
which is a branch of the United
States Department of Commerce,
has prepared a comprehensive
white paper about wireless network security. The white paper
contains a very helpful and comprehensive wireless LAN security
checklist containing 45 items. The
items are characterized as "best
practice" (meaning it should be
done) and "may consider" (meaning for those who are a little more
concerned about security).

A draft of this white paper is currently available at http://csrc.
nist.gov/publications/drafts/
draft-sp800-48.pdf.

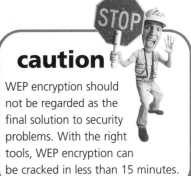

caution

WEP encryption should
not be regarded as the
final solution to security
problems. With the right
tools, WEP encryption can
be cracked in less than 15 minutes.

Password link to open the Password panel. Enter, and re-enter, the new password as shown in Figure 19.1. Click Apply to make the new password permanent.

FIGURE 19.1

You can use the administrative application for your access point to change its password, making it harder for intruders to take control of the access point.

PICK YOUR PASSWORDS WISELY

For security reasons, you should be careful about the passwords you pick. Never use as a password the name of your company, anyone in your family, or your pet hamster (these are all easy to guess). For the same reason, don't use your date of birth or street address.

The worst kind of password is one based on personal information that can be easily determined (or guessed). But you should also avoid passwords based on numerical sequences (such as 12345) or words (such as "password"). Better passwords are at least eight characters long, and include both letters and numbers: for example, "d31TY9jq".

Unless no one ever visits your home or office, don't jot down your important network passwords on a post-it, and then stick the post-it on your computer monitor.

caution

After you've changed the password on the access point, there may be no way to get it back short of doing a hard reset on the access point (which means all your settings will get lost). So keep the password in a safe place, and don't lose it.

Middling Security

You should consider using some of the middling security measures described in this section if you have some security concerns, and are prepared to take some trouble over security, but still don't want to go overboard.

These measures include the following:

- Plan to change your WEP encryption key regularly, perhaps once every week.

- Engage MAC filtering, as explained later in this chapter.

- Use the DHCP settings in your router (or access point/router combination) to limit the number of IPs that can be used in your network to the actual number of devices that you simultaneously connected to the network.

Red-Alert Security

Red-alert security measures are intended for use with networks that truly have confidential and proprietary information to protect and are willing to go to considerable trouble and expense. You should realize that protection at this level is not a one-shot affair: You have to constantly be on the lookout for new vulnerabilities. You'll need to keep surveying your wireless site, keep changing your passwords, and generally just keep on your toes. Expect red-alert security measures to take time and money, be trouble to maintain properly, and possibly to slow your network down!

If you really need a high level of security, you should consider not using a wireless network at all, or at the very least bringing in a qualified wireless network security expert.

> **caution**
>
> No wireless network can ever be completely secure. Keep any truly confidential information off a wireless network.

Red-alert security measures include the following:

- If your access point allows this, lower your broadcast strength. The lower your broadcast strength is, the less likely a nefarious evildoer outside your network is to be able to intercept it.

- Understand the range of your Wi-Fi broadcasts, and see if there are any obvious vulnerabilities (a parking lot? a neighbor who hates you?).

- Regularly review the DHCP logs provided by your router to see if there are any unauthorized connections.

- Turn off wireless access to the access point's administrative application (this is usually only available with enterprise-class Wi-Fi access points).

- Use a dynamic, per-session WEP encryption scheme. This is usually only available with enterprise-class Wi-Fi access points, and may require additional hardware such as an authentication server.

- Authenticate Wi-Fi connections with user names and passwords using a network directory server, or an authentication server.

- Encourage access to your Wi-Fi network via a VPN (see Chapter 18, and the section later in this chapter, "Setting Up a VPN," for more details about VPNs).

- Create a network topology that uses a DMZ with its own set of firewalls for the Wi-Fi access point (see Chapter 15 for more about DMZs and network topologies). This will isolate the access points from possible attacks. You can beef this up even further by making sure that the access point and the nodes on your wireless network can only communicate via a VPN. A good piece of equipment to use to implement this in the small office context is the Watchguard SoHo Firebox, which combines a firewall and a VPN, and costs about $300.

Understanding Firewalls

As I explained in Chapter 18, a firewall is a program that protects your resources by filtering network packets. Firewalls can be run as part of another piece of software. For example, your Wi-Fi access point/router almost certainly provides some kind of firewall capabilities. Firewalls can also be run as individual programs on computers (for example, the personal firewall programs explained in Chapter 18). Finally, sophisticated firewalls can be run on servers dedicated to that purpose, although this generally only happens in enterprise-class setups.

Firewalls enable a network administrator to determine which clients inside a network can access network resources, and which *ports* can be used from outside the network to access the network. In case you are wondering, a network port is a logical endpoint on the network. The port number identifies the kind of traffic that uses the port. For example, port 80 is used to connect to a Web server using the HTTP protocol.

Effectively, firewalls can be used to isolate portions of a network topology from the rest of the network, and from the Internet. This is another way of saying that you can use a firewall to limit access both to and from the Internet.

Figure 19.2 shows the administrative panel used by the Linksys Wireless Broadband Router. IP filtering is reached via the Advanced tab on the access point's administrative application.

FIGURE 19.2

Setting IP filtering using the firewall capabilities built into this access point allows you to control traffic into (and from) the network.

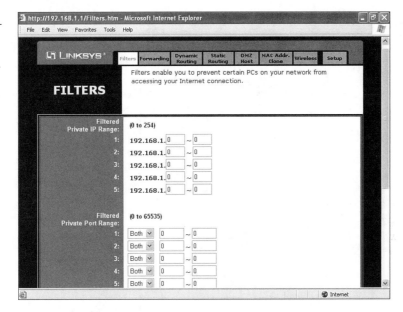

Setting Up a VPN

As I explained in Chapter 18, if you are connecting to a home network using a public Wi-Fi hotspot, using a virtual private network (VPN), which acts as a kind of tunnel through the Internet, is a great way to enhance security. In Chapter 18, I showed you the way to set up the VPN from the client (meaning the remote laptop).

Earlier in this chapter, I explained that using a VPN to isolate the Wi-Fi access point from the rest of the network, and to restrict access to authorized users, is a great way to beef up network security.

You can buy dedicated remote access servers that provide VPN functionality. For example, the Watchguard SoHo Firebox that I mentioned earlier is a good dedicated box for the SoHo class network that provides firewall and VPN capabilities. You can also buy sophisticated software to enable a VPN.

But why pay for it if it is available for free? Windows XP Professional already includes a VPN remote access server.

To set up your VPN using Windows XP Professional, open the Network Connections window by clicking on Network Connections in the Control panel. Next, click Create a New Connection in the Tasks pane on the upper left of the Network Connections window.

The New Connection Wizard will open with a welcome screen. Click Next to get started. In the Network Connection Type pane of the wizard, choose Set Up an Advanced Connection as shown in Figure 19.3.

FIGURE 19.3

Choose Set Up
an Advanced
Connection to
create a VPN in
Windows XP.

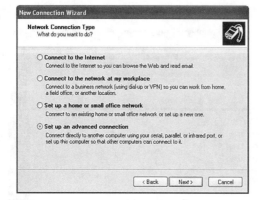

Click Next. In the Advanced Connection Options pane, choose Accept Incoming
Connections as shown in Figure 19.4

FIGURE 19.4

A VPN server
should be set to
accept incoming
connections, or
what is the
point?

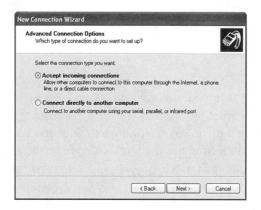

Click Next. The Devices for Incoming
Connections pane will probably show your parallel port (LPT1) and nothing else. Don't do anything in this pane. Just click Next to continue
setting up your VPN server.

In the Incoming VPN Connection pane choose
Allow Virtual Private Connections.

Click Next. In the User Permissions pane, shown
in Figure 19.5, you can specify the users who
have permission to use the VPN.

tip

Now that the VPN server
has been added as an
incoming connection, you
can edit it by selecting it in
the Network Connections
window and choosing
Properties from its context
menu. You don't have to run the
New Connection Wizard again.

There are a number of good features in specifying the users who can use the VPN in this way. First of all, access to the VPN is authenticated using the authentication controls baked into the operating system. Secondly, users who access the VPN have only the privileges on the network that they've been granted. So guests, for example, may only have the right to read certain files (and no right to delete files).

Click Next. The Networking Software pane, shown in Figure 19.6, will open.

FIGURE 19.5

In the User Permissions pane, specify the users who can use the VPN.

FIGURE 19.6

Select the networking software that should be enabled for incoming connections.

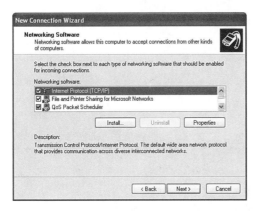

note

If the VPN is behind a router, as will often be the case, for this setup to work, the router will have to be configured to automatically forward communications from the appropriate ports to the VPN server, a process called *port mapping*. The ports used for VPN access are forwarded to the IP for the VPN server.

The ports used for VPN access depend on the VPN protocol used. Point-to-Point Tunneling Protocol (PPTP) uses ports 47 and 1723. Layer-To-Tunneling Protocol (L2TP) uses ports 50, 51, and 500.

In the Networking Software pane, with the Internet Protocol (TCP/IP) item selected, click Properties. In the Incoming TCP/IP Properties window, shown in Figure 19.7, determine whether IP addresses for VPN clients, or callers, should be assigned by DHCP, or provide a scheme for IP assignment.

FIGURE 19.7

In the Incoming TCP/IP Properties window, choose to have IP addresses assigned using DHCP, or designate an IP addressing scheme.

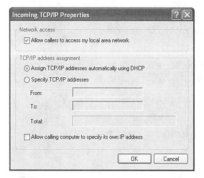

Click OK to close the Incoming TCP/IP Properties window. Click Next to move to the final wizard pane. Click Finish to create the VPN server, which will now be shown as an incoming connection in the Network Connections window, as you can see in Figure 19.8.

FIGURE 19.8

The VPN server is shown as an incoming connection in the Network Connections window.

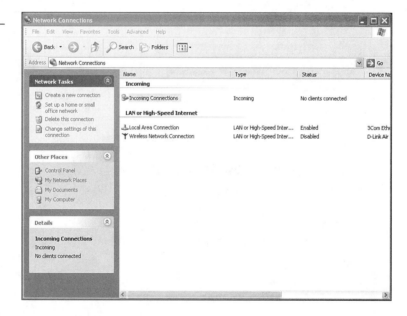

Using MAC Filtering

MAC filtering is a way to enforce security on a Wi-Fi network at a deeper level than WEP encryption.

Each device on a Wi-Fi network has a MAC (Media Access Control) address, or unique identification number baked into the hardware. (See Appendix A, "Wireless Standards," for more information about the MAC layer.)

The idea behind MAC filtering is to tell the Wi-Fi access point that it can only communicate with the devices on your network that are explicitly identified to it by their MAC address. You go into the access point/router's administrative application, and say, "Use these MAC addresses and no others!"

The only trick to this is that you've got to round up the MAC addresses for all the devices you want to be able to connect to your Wi-Fi network.

The good news is that the client software for most Wi-Fi cards will easily tell you the MAC address for the card.

Figure 19.9 shows the MAC address for an older Orinocco Wi-Fi card, which you can find on the Diagnose screen of the Client Manager software for the card.

note

MAC filtering is a great security tool. But as an administrative matter it would probably get out of hand if you have more than a handful of devices using the Wi-Fi network, or if you added and deleted devices regularly.

FIGURE 19.9

You can find the MAC address for this card on the Diagnose screen of the Client Manager software that ships with the card.

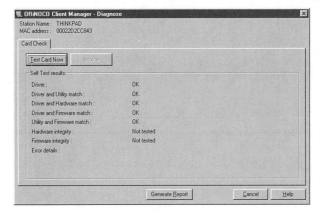

Figure 19.10 shows the MAC address for the D-Link DWL-520 card, which you can find on the About window of the D-Link Air Utility.

Windows XP Professional (but not Home) also provides a utility, getmac, that shows the MAC addresses of all the network devices on your system (it is a bit dicey knowing which is which if you have more than one).

To run getmac, choose Command Prompt from the Accessories group in the Start menu to open a command window. With the command window open, type `getmac` at the prompt and press Enter.

As you can see in Figure 19.11, the program will display the MAC addresses of the devices on your system.

FIGURE 19.10

The MAC address for the D-Link wireless card can be found on the About window of the D-Link Air Utility.

FIGURE 19.11

The getmac program displays the MAC addresses for the devices on your Windows XP system.

You can also use getmac to find the MAC addresses of devices running remotely on your network by supplying the program with the IP or network name of the remote device.

After you've gathered the MAC addresses for the wireless devices that will use your Wi-Fi network, the next step is to enter them into the Wi-Fi access point/router.

Obviously, this will vary depending on the specific piece of equipment.

Using the Linksys Wireless Broadband Router described in Chapter 12, "Working with National Wi-Fi Networks," you would open the administrative application by entering the address

note

Under Windows XP, to use the D-Link utility rather than the Windows XP wireless network configuration utilities, you need to uncheck the Use Windows to Configure My Wireless Network Settings box in the Wireless Network Connection Properties window.

If this box is checked, the D-Link Air utility will not run, and you won't see the MAC address for the device.

`http://192.168.1.1/` in a connected Web browser, followed by the password when prompted. Next click the Advanced tab.

In the Filters pane of the Advanced setup, go down to the Private MAC filter item, and click the Edit button. The MAC Access Control Table, shown in Figure 19.12, will open.

Enter the MAC addresses of the devices that are to be allowed access in the table, and click Apply when you are done.

FIGURE 19.12

The MAC Access Control Table is used to enter the MAC addresses of the devices that are allowed access.

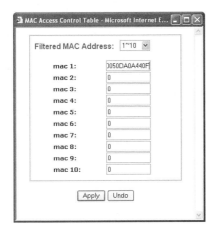

note

You can use Ipconfig, explained in Chapter 15, to find the MAC address of devices on your current computer. In contrast, getmac gives you a way to find the MACs for all active devices on your network.

tip

The MAC Access Control Table shown in Figure 19.12 uses a drop-down list to enter more addresses if you need to add more than ten MAC addresses.

THE ABSOLUTE MINIMUM

Here are the key points to remember from this chapter:

- Because Wi-Fi networks are not physically secure, some level of security protection is a good idea.

- The level of security protection that you require depends on the confidentiality of the information you are protecting.

- If you do nothing else, you should change the default SSID for your wireless access point, set it not to broadcast the SSID, set the access point to use WEP encryption, and change the default administrative password for the access point.

- Complete security for a wireless network is probably impossible, but there are many steps you can take to make your Wi-Fi network more secure.

PART VI

APPENDIXES

A

WIRELESS STANDARDS

Wi-Fi is a certified version of variants of the 802.11 wireless standards developed by the IEEE (www.ieee.org). Wi-Fi equipment is certified by the Wi-Fi Alliance (www.wi-fi.org) for compatibility and standards compliance.

The 802.11 wireless standards, also called *protocols*, are designed to use the so-called *free spectrums*, which do not require specific licensing. The spectrums currently used by 802.11 are 2.4GHz and 5GHz. (The 2.4Ghz spectrum is also used by household appliances such as microwaves.)

You don't need to know or give a fig about wireless standards or 802.11 to happily use wireless networking on the road or in your home network. That's why I've kept this material out of the body of *Absolute Beginner's Guide to Wi-Fi*: because you don't really need to know it unless you are practicing to be an engineer.

But in case you are curious, I've summarized the most important concepts that underlie 802.11 (and Wi-Fi) in this Appendix. Oh, and if you go into a store and a salesperson starts spouting "802.11 this and 802.11 that," you can check the summary of the 802.11 variants in "The Flavors of 802.11" and know exactly what is being talked about (perhaps better than the salesperson!).

Understanding 802.11 Wireless Standards

The IEEE (Institute of Electrical and Electronics Engineers) Standards Association, http://standards.ieee.org/, likes to designate standards using numbers rather than names. Within the IEEE schema, the number 802 is used to designate local area networks and metropolitan, or wide area, networks (LANs and WANs). 802.11 is the name for wireless LAN specifications in general. There are a number of different flavors of the 802.11 standards, such as 802.11b, 802.11g, and so on, that I'll discuss later in this Appendix in more detail. Each of these particular versions of the wireless LAN specification (802.11) runs on the 2.4GHz or the 5GHz spectrums at high speeds.

To understand 802.11, it's important to understand the purpose of the general wireless LAN standard. According to the original Project Authorization Request, "the scope of the proposed standard is to develop a specification for wireless connectivity for fixed, portable, and moving stations within a local area." In addition, "...the purpose of the standard is to provide wireless connectivity to automatic machinery and equipment or stations that require rapid deployment, which may be portable, handheld, or which may be mounted on moving vehicles within a local area."

The 802.11 standards specify a *Medium Access Control (MAC)* layer and a *Physical (PHY)* layer using *Direct Sequence Spread Spectrum (DSSS)* technology.

The MAC layer is a set of protocols that are responsible for maintaining order in the use of a shared medium. For example, data encryption is handled in the MAC.

The PHY layer handles transmission between nodes (or devices on the network). In other words, it is primarily concerned with hardware.

DSSS is a technique for splitting up and recombining information to prevent collisions between different data streams. Effectively, if my network is using DSSS and encounters other signals on the same spectrum it is using, my network can use DSSS to avoid interference from the other signals.

The MAC and PHY layers fit within the generalized OSI (Open System Interconnection) reference model. The OSI model is a way of describing how different applications and protocols interact on network-aware devices.

The primary purpose of 802.11 is to deliver MAC Service Data Units (MSDUs) between Logical Link Controls (LLCs). Essentially, an LLC is a base station with a wireless access point, which itself may be connected to a wire line network for hand-off to additional wireless LLCs.

802.11 networks operate in one of two modes: "infrastructure" and "ad hoc." The infrastructure architecture is used to provide network communications between wireless clients and wired network resources. An ad hoc network architecture is used to support mutual communication between wireless clients. It is typically created spontaneously, does not support access to wired networks, and does not require an access point to be part of the network.

The PHY layer of 802.11 defines three physical characteristics for wireless local area networks:

- Diffused infrared
- Direct Sequence Spread Spectrum (the primary technique for avoiding signal interference in today's 802.11 networks)
- Frequency Hopping Spread Spectrum (which is another technique for avoiding interference)

Okay! Enough jargon, acronyms, and theoretical engineering. Let's get on to the flavors of 802.11.

The Flavors of 802.11

This section briefly describes the variants of the 802.11 standard.

802.11b

Most Wi-Fi devices that are currently in operation are using the 802.11b flavor of 802.11 (although both 802.11a and 802.11g are up and coming).

The full 802.11b specification document is more than 500 pages long, but the most important things to know about 802.11b are that

- 802.11b uses the 2.4GHz spectrum.
- 802.11b has a theoretical throughput speed of 11 Megabytes per second (Mbps).

A speed of 11Mbps isn't bad (by comparison, a normal, wired Ethernet network only gets 10Mbps). However, for a variety of reasons Wi-Fi connections rarely achieve anything close to 11Mbps. You'll be lucky over an encrypted 802.11b connection to get transmission rates of over 6Mbps. This is fast enough for transferring Word documents, but probably not fast enough for applications such as streaming video.

802.11g

A newer version of 802.11, 802.11g, like 802.11b runs on the 2.4GHz spectrum. One of the best things about 802.11g is that it is fully backward-compatible with 802.11b. If your Wi-Fi laptop is equipped with 802.11b, you can connect to an 802.11g hotspot, although of course you will only achieve 802.11 throughput. Conversely, an 802.11g-equipped computer can connect to an 802.11b access point, once again at the lower speeds of 802.11b.

By comparison to 802.11b, 802.11g is blazingly fast, achieving throughput in the best conditions of 54Mbps. This is still slower than a sophisticated 100MBps wired Ethernet network, although a good bit faster than the 10MBps equipment used in most home networks.

802.11a

Unlike either 802.11b or 802.11g, 802.11a operates on the 5GHz spectrum. That's good news from the viewpoint of interference. There's simply less going on in the 5GHz band, and you are less likely to "bump into" other Wi-Fi networks, garage door openers, cordless phones, or what not. However, it is bad news from the point of backward compatibility because 802.11a systems are not compatible with 802.11b (or 802.11g) because they use a different spectrum.

Some vendors have solved this problem by creating tri-mode chipsets that run 802.11a, 802.11b, and 802.11g depending on the access point or hotspot they are connecting to. It's a good idea if you are considering purchasing an 802.11a Wi-Fi device to make sure it has this kind of standard-switching capability.

You can expect a throughput of something like 20Mbps with 802.a, so from a speed viewpoint it is midway between 802.11b and 802.11g.

802.11n

802.11n is a developing standard that has not yet been approved but promises to deliver greater than 100Mbps using both the 2.4GHz and the 5GHz spectrums. Despite the fact that the official standards approval process is likely to take several years, it seems likely that some companies, such as Broadcom Corporation, are likely to jump the gun and start producing "pre-standards approval" 802.11n chipsets and devices shortly.

This may in turn cause the IEEE to speed its approval of a new 802.11n standard. In effect, 802.11n is part of a process of better technology becoming more affordable. Right now, 802.11b is inexpensive. Equipment made using the 802.11g standard is faster, and on the market—but more expensive. It won't be all that long before 802.11g is inexpensive and what everyone is buying, with new, faster (but higher-priced) 802.11n equipment coming on the market.

802.11i

802.11i is the name given by the Wi-Fi Alliance to its proposed new security standard.

Products that successfully complete the test required for meeting the 802.11i standard will be called "Wi-Fi Protected Access" certified.

For more information about Wi-Fi and network security, see Part V, "Securing Your Wi-Fi Computer and Network."

B

Finding Wi-Fi Hotspots

In Chapter 11, "Where Can You Wi-Fi," I told you about the most commonly used online Wi-Fi hotspot directories. As a convenience, that list of sites is reproduced in this appendix. I've also included the list of Wi-Fi networks discussed in Chapter 12, "Working with National Wi-Fi Networks."

The problem is that, as they say, "you can't get there from here": An online source of information doesn't do you any good if you are not already online.

Besides online directories and Wi-Fi networks, this appendix lists the places where you are most likely to find a public Wi-Fi hotspot. Some of these are well known; for example, almost everyone knows that you can find a Wi-Fi hotspot at many Starbucks coffee shops. Others may surprise you.

Of course, no such listing can be complete (it would take an entire book). Also, the number of hotspots is expanding every day. But getting accurate information about the location of hotspots can be difficult, so this appendix is intended to give you a "leg up" on the task!

The categories I've included are "Retail Locations," "Hotels," "Airports," and "Free Public Networks"—meaning public noncommercial Wi-Fi hotspots that you don't have to pay for.

Online Directories

Provided you have online access, far and away the best way to find Wi-Fi hotspots is an online directory. The hitch, of course, is that you have to be online in the first place. These directories don't do you much good if you are wandering aimlessly around Podunk with your Wi-Fi laptop or PDA all ready to go. The moral is, do your research before you leave on your travels.

This section lists the best online directories. You can use them to find hotspots of all sorts (both free and for pay) in all locations.

- China Pulse: www.chinapulse.com/wifi (hotspot locator for China)
- HotSpotList: www.wi-fihotspotlist.com
- i-Spot Access: www.i-spotaccess.com/directory.asp (currently limited to Illinois, Iowa, Missouri, and Nebraska)
- JIWIRE: www.jiwire.com
- Ordinance Survey: www.g-intelligence.co.uk/wireless/wifimap.php (great for United Kingdom hotspots)
- Square 7: www.square7.com/hotspots (great for European hotspots)
- WiFi411: www.wifi411.com
- Wi-Fi-Freespot Directory: www.wififreespot.com (focuses on free—as in "you don't have to pay"—hotspots)
- WiFiMaps: www.wifimaps.com
- WiFinder: www.wifinder.com (one of the best all-round international hotspot directories)
- Wireless Access List: wirelessaccesslist.com/wireless/u.asp (categorized by state and ZIP code, also allows sorting by network, for example, T-Mobile, Wayport, and so on)
- Zagat Survey: www.subscriberdirect.com/the_new_yorker/zagat/ (lists and reviews restaurants and hotels with Wi-Fi access in five major U.S. cities)

Wi-Fi Networks

Because Wi-Fi is such a new field, networks of Wi-Fi hotspots are still relatively small. One implication is that incumbent telecommunication providers—such as AT&T Wireless, Sprint, T-Mobile, and Verizon—have a head start.

But I've also included "Mom and Pop" networks. After all, the sheer number of hotspots may not be what counts for you: You may be most concerned with particular locations. I've tried to include every commercial Wi-Fi network that currently operates 50 or more hotspots.

From a user's point of view, you should check the availability and cost of roaming features before you sign up with a Wi-Fi network—because no one network is likely to provide all the hotspots you want to use. See Chapter 12 for more tips and techniques related to working with Wi-Fi networks.

Table B.1 shows the biggest networks as of the date of this writing, their Web address and telephone contacts, and current number of hotspots.

The contact information in this table may be useful when you decide which network to sign up with. It could also help if you are traveling to an area that is particularly well served by a specific provider.

note

The hotspot counts in this section are based on the actual number of hotspots that I could locate using the directories listed earlier in this appendix.

The number of hotspots that I've noted are probably low now, and there will certainly be more by the time you read this book, but they do give an idea of the relative size of these networks.

You should know that most of the Wi-Fi networks claim a greater number of hotspots than I've shown in this section, but I'm sticking to the number that I can actually verify.

TABLE B.1   Wi-Fi Networks

Network	URL	Phone	Number of hotspots	Comments
Airpath Wireless	www.airpath.com	419-930-1500	83	Privately held operator based in Toledo, Ohio, that has hotspots in a wide variety of places.
AT&T Wireless	www.attwireless.com/ business/features/ communication/ servicehotspots.jhtml	888-290-4613	612	AT&T's Wi-Fi service is called "goport" and can be hard to find without the Web address shown in this table.
Azure Wireless	www.azure.com.au/	03-9572-8100	88	Australian Wi-Fi hotspot operator.

TABLE B.1 (continued)

Network	URL	Phone	Number of hotspots	Comments
Boingo Wireless	www.boingo.com/	800-880-4117	642	A pioneer Wi-Fi network, and still considered one of the best.
Hotspotzz	www.wifimetro.com	866-776-8991	88	Primarily provides hotspots in the Western US.
Metronet Wireless	www.metronet.at	43-1-8974685	58	Austrian Wi-Fi network.
Picopoint	www.picopoint.com	31-20-5210321	71	Wi-Fi network operator based in Holland with hotspots in South Africa and elsewhere.
Sprint PCS	www.sprint.com/ pcsbusiness/products_ services/data/wifi/ index.html	888-703-9514	1800	Rolling out quickly based on existing infrastructure.
Surf and Sip	www.surfandsip.com	415-974-6321	52	Based in San Francisco, this Wi-Fi network operator specializes in setting up hotspots for businesses that want to give access away to draw traffic.
SurfHere	www.csd.toshiba.com/ cgi-bin/tais/hs/ hs_home.jsp	877-429-6385	340	Affiliated with Toshiba, SurfHere provides access in stores including McDonald's and The UPS Store.
Telia Homerun	www.homerun.telia.com	020-22-11-50	55	Serves Scandinavian countries.
T-Mobile Hotspot	www.t-mobile.com/ hotspot/	800-981-8563	3590	The leading Wi-Fi provider, building infrastructure in Starbucks stores and elsewhere. T-Mobile is the one everyone else wants to beat.

TABLE B.1   (continued)

Network	URL	Phone	Number of hotspots	Comments
Verizon	`www.verizon.net/wifi/`	888-842-9275	254	Currently provides hotspots mainly in the metropolitan NY area; most are free to Verizon DSL customers.
Wayport	`www.wayport.com`	512-519-6000	54	An early pioneer in providing Wi-Fi hotspots, now providing infrastructure in hotels and elsewhere.
WLAN GmbH	`www.personalwlan.de`	040-88-88-55- 0	60	German Wi-Fi network provider.

Retail Locations

Here are some national chains that provide free Wi-Fi access in some or all of their stores:

- All Apple retail stores. See `www.apple.com/retail/` for locations.
- Panera Bread is aiming to have all their locations offer free Wi-Fi. In the meantime, many Panera stores already are "unwired." See `www.panera.com/wifi.aspx` for details.
- Many Schlotzsky's Deli locations. See `www.schlotzskys.com/wireless.html` for a list.

Here are a few of the national chains that provide Wi-Fi access in some or all of their stores using a paid provider (this means that you have to pay for your access):

- Barnes & Noble stores rely on different providers, including SurfHere. The best way to find a Barnes & Noble location that provides Wi-Fi access is to use one of the directories listed in the section "Online Directories."
- Borders bookstores are "unwired" using T-Mobile Hotspot's network. The best way to find a Borders location that provides Wi-Fi access is to use one of the directories listed in the section "Online Directories."
- Some McDonald's locations are being equipped with Wi-Fi access. The providers vary depending on the location (in many stores, it is SurfHere). See `www.mcdwireless.com/` for more information.

- Starbucks. Wi-Fi access is provided by T-Mobile Hotspot. See www.starbucks.com/ retail/wireless.asp for locations with this service.
- Many of the UPS Store branches provide Wi-Fi access using SurfHere or other network providers. Check with a local store, or use a Wi-Fi directory, to see if Wi-Fi is provided in a specific location.

Hotels

Many hotel chains offer Wi-Fi access on a paid or free basis in both hotel rooms and the hotel lobby. Wi-Fi is available in some or all or the facilities of a given hotel chain, so be sure to check with the hotel in which you will be staying to see if Wi-Fi is available.

Hotel chains with free service include:

- Best Western
- Comfort Suites and Clarion properties that are franchised by Choice Hotels International (370 Comfort Suites and 140 Clarions)
- Courtyard by Marriott
- Omni Hotels

Some hotel chains with paid access are shown in Table B.2. Please check with each individual hotel facility to determine the actual costs and network providers.

TABLE B.2   Hotel Chains with Paid Wi-Fi Access

Hotel Chain	Primary Network Provider
Doubletree	Wayport
Hilton	Wayport
Radisson	Wayport
Sheraton, W, Westin	Proprietary Starwood Hotels network
Wyndham	Wayport

Airports

Paid Wi-Fi access is available in many major airports, catering to stranded travelers. This kind of Wi-Fi service can be provided in special airline lounges, or it can be more widely available throughout passenger terminals.

Table B.3 shows some of the major American airports with widespread Wi-Fi access.

TABLE B.3   Airports with Wi-Fi

Airport	Network Provider
Atlanta (ATL)	T-Mobile Hotspot
Chicago (ORD)	T-Mobile Hotspot
Dallas (DFW)	T-Mobile, Wayport
Los Angeles (LAX)	The Gate Escape, a company with several facilities in LAX that rents office services to airport travelers
Newark (EWJ)	Telia Homerun
Oakland (OAK)	Wayport
Pittsburgh (PIT)	Free Access
San Francisco (SFO)	T-Mobile Hotspot
San Jose (SJC)	Wayport

Free Public Networks

As I noted in the listing of Wi-Fi directories, Wi-Fi-Freespot Directory, www.wififreespot.com, focuses on free hotspots. This is a good starting place if you are looking for no-cost Wi-Fi public access. It is also worth noting that some of the big telecom providers give free Wi-Fi access to users who subscribe to some of their other services. For example, Verizon provides free Wi-Fi hotspots in many downtown New York locations to their DSL subscribers.

Most of the free hotspots fall into one of three categories:

- Provided by a business in the hope of drawing traffic
- Provided by a library as a public service (see the following discussion)
- Provided by a local community (see the following discussion)

It's really worth browsing Wi-Fi-Freespot to see what local businesses you can find that provide free Wi-Fi. You'll probably be absolutely amazed at how many there are. (I know, I know, my community, Berkeley, California is not typical of anything, but there are literally hundreds here.)

Many public libraries provide Wi-Fi access that is free to the public (or at least to members of the community who have registered for a library card). The Wireless Librarian has a great directory of Wi-Fi availability in libraries:

http://people.morrisville.edu/~drewwe/wireless/wirelesslibraries.htm.

Wireless Communities, www.personaltelco.net/index.cgi/WirelessCommunities, provides information about community-maintained Wi-Fi hotspots all over the world. This is worth checking out. You'll be surprised at how many community-based providers of free Wi-Fi networks there are, and the passion and commitment of the people and communities that provide this public service.

Here are a few sample wireless communities:

- Bay Area Wireless Users Group (BAWUG) is one of the pioneering free Wi-Fi organizations. In addition to BAWUG's other activities, they maintain a number of free hotspots centered around the Presidio in San Francisco. www.bawug.org

- Detroit Wireless Project (DWP) helps maintain a number of free hotspots in downtown Detroit. www.dwp.org

- Personal Telco Project (PTP) has over a hundred hotspots in Portland, Oregon, and has contributed to Portland's being named the "hottest" city—or city with the most hotspots—in the United States for several years running. www.personaltelco.net/static/index.html

- Seattle Wireless, in addition to supported hotspots around the Seattle area, has pioneered an alternative public backbone for wireless networking. www.seattlewireless.net

note

Almost every university and college in the United States offers free Wi-Fi access to its students. This access is not, in most cases, available to the general public. However, if you are attending college, or plan to start next year, it is very likely that your alma mater will provide convenient Wi-Fi access for you. You should check with your school to learn the details of the Wi-Fi access provided, and to see if there are any special Wi-Fi equipment requirements.

Glossary

Symbols

10BASE-T Ethernet Standard for wired networks that use phone-like plugs.

3G A catch-all term used to refer to a proprietary high-speed wireless network using spectrums leased by telecommunications carriers that is proposed and/or has partially been developed.

802.11 The general standard for wireless networking, defined by the IEEE.

802.11a A relatively new version of the 802.11 wireless standard that is faster than 802.11b (it runs at speeds up to 20 Mbps) and uses the 5GHz spectrum. 802.11a is not backward-compatible with 802.11b, the predominant "flavor" of Wi-Fi.

802.11b Predominant current flavor of 802.11 wireless networking, or Wi-Fi. 802.11b uses the 2.4GHz spectrum and has a theoretical speed of 11 Mbps.

802.11g A version of the 802.11 wireless standard that is newer and faster than 802.11b. 802.11g runs on the 2.4GHz spectrum, is backward-compatible with 802.11b, and has a theoretical speed of 54 Mbps.

802.11i The name given by the Wi-Fi Alliance to its proposed new security standard, also called "Wi-Fi Protected Access."

802.11n A new 802.11 wireless standard that promises to deliver speeds of up to 100 Mbps using both the 2.4GHz and 5GHz spectrums. So far, 802.11n has not yet received IEEE approval, and the details of the standard are still up in the air.

A

access control layer Baked into the Wi-Fi standards; specifies how a Wi-Fi device, such as a mobile computer, communicates with another Wi-Fi device, such as a wireless access point. Also called MAC layer.

access point A broadcast station that Wi-Fi computers can communicate with. Also called AP, hotspot, and base station. Access points are used as the central point for a network of Wi-Fi computers.

access point/router This common hardware combination combines the functionality of a Wi-Fi access point with that of a network router.

ad-hoc mode   Wi-Fi computers in the ad-hoc mode communicate directly with one another in a peer-to-peer fashion without using an access point to intermediate network communication.

AirPort   Apple's version of 802.11b.

AirPort Extreme   Apple's version of 802.11g.

B

Bluetooth   A short-range connectivity solution designed for data exchange between devices such as printers, cell phones, and PDAs that use the 2.4GHz spectrum. Bluetooth is incompatible (meaning, does not work) with any of the 802.11 wireless networking standards.

bridge   Wireless bridges are used to connect one part of a network with another. They are often used to extend the range of a network, and to add non-PC devices to a network.

broadband   Fast delivery of Internet services. The predominant means for the delivery of broadband are cable and DSL.

C

cable   Broadband Internet delivery over the same cable that is used to bring in television content, primarily to residential subscribers.

Centrino   Notebooks with chips made by Intel that feature integrated Wi-Fi.

client   A device or program connected to a server of some sort. Typically, a client is a personal computer connected to a server computer that relies on the server to perform some operations.

client-server network   In a client-server network, a centralized server computer controls and polices many of the basic functions of the network, and intermediates the communications between the computers on the network.

closed node   A Wi-Fi broadcast that is protected by WEP.

CompactFlash (CF) card   Used to add memory (and in some cases other functionality, such as Wi-Fi connectivity) to PDAs, digital cameras, and other handheld devices.

D

DHCP   Dynamic Host Configuration Protocol, a standard for assigning dynamic Internet Protocol (IP) addresses to devices on a network.

Direct Sequence Spread Spectrum (DSSS)   Technology used to prevent collisions and avoid interference between devices operating on the same wireless spectrum.

directional antenna   An antenna used to focus a transmission in a specific direction, used in point-to-point Wi-Fi broadcasts, also called a yagi.

DMZ   Demilitarized zone, an isolated computer or subnetwork that sits between an internal network that needs to remain secure and an area that allows external access.

DNS   The Domain Name System (sometimes called Domain Name Service) translates more or less alphabetic domain names into IP addresses.

DSL   Digital Subscriber Line, a technology used to deliver broadband Internet services over telephone lines.

dynamic IP addressing   The provision of IP addresses to computers dynamically.

E

EIRP   Unit of measure (equivalent isotropically radiated power) for the strength of an antenna.

encryption   The translation of data into a secret code; used by WEP to achieve security for Wi-Fi networks.

encryption key   The key used to encrypt the transmissions of a Wi-Fi network protected by WEP; the password needed to access the Wi-Fi network.

Ethernet port   A socket that accepts a 10BASE-T Ethernet wire.

F

FCC   Federal Communications Commission. See www.fcc.gov for more information.

firewall   A firewall is a blocking mechanism—either hardware, software, or both—that blocks intruders from accessing a network or individual computer.

free radio spectrum   Bands of the radio spectrum, such as 2.4GHz and 5GHz, that do not require a license from the FCC. Wi-Fi uses these bands for its transmissions, as do other household appliances such as cordless phones and microwaves.

frequency   The oscillations, or movement from peak to trough, of the electromagnetic wave created by a radio transmission.

G

gain   The amount of gain provided by an antenna means how much it increases the power of a signal passed to it by the radio transmitter.

GHz   Gigahertz. One gigahertz equals one thousand megahertz (MHz).

H–K

hotspot   An area in which Wi-Fi users can connect to the Internet, whether for pay or for free.

hub   A simple wired device used to connect computers on a network.

IEEE   Institute of Electrical and Electronics Engineers. See www.ieee.org for more information.

infrastructure mode   A Wi-Fi network in infrastructure mode uses an access point to intermediate network traffic (as opposed to ad-hoc mode, which features direct peer-to-peer communication).

IP address   A hexadecimal tuplet that denotes a node on the Internet or other network.

isotropic radiation pattern   If an antenna has an isotropic radiation pattern, the antenna transmits radio waves in all three dimensions equally.

ISP   Internet service provider, such as the cable or phone company providing you Internet access using dial-up, cable, or DSL.

IT   Information technology department, usually in a large enterprise.

L

LAN   Local area network, such as the network in your home or small office.

latte   The beverage of choice to sip at a coffee shop while you are connected to the Internet via Wi-Fi.

logical topology   The logical data flow on a network.

M

MAC   Medium access control layer. See access control layer.

MAC address   Unique identification number of each Wi-Fi device.

MAC filtering   Creating a secure Wi-Fi network by using the MAC address of each Wi-Fi device on the network (and only allowing devices with a known MAC address).

Mbps   Megabytes per second.

MHz   Megahertz. In a radio spectrum, 1 megahertz means one million vibrations per second.

modem   Short for modulator-demodulator. A modem is a device that lets a computer transmit data over telephone or cable lines, and connects your cable or DSL Internet service to your computer or your network.

N

network   Two or more connected computers.

Network Address Translation (NAT) Translates local network addresses to ones that work on the Internet.

network name   See SSID.

NIC   Network interface card, used to connect a computer to a wired network.

O

omnidirectional antenna   An antenna that sends broadcast signals in all directions.

open node   A Wi-Fi broadcast that is not protected by WEP.

Open System Interconnection (OSI)   A general reference model that describes how different applications and protocols interact on network-aware devices. The MAC and PHY layers of Wi-Fi compliant devices fit within the OSI model.

P–Q

PC Card   Card that fits in the PCMCIA slot that is present on most laptops. Also called PCMCIA cards.

PCI Card   Card that fits into the PCI expansion slot inside a Windows desktop computer.

PCMCIA   Personal Computer Memory Card International Association, which is the name of the organization that has devised the standard for cards than can be added to laptops. For more information see www.pcmcia.org.

PCMCIA slot   Also called an expansion slot, used to add PC cards to a laptop.

PDA   Personal Digital Assistant, a handheld computer.

peer-to-peer network   In a peer-to-peer network, computers communicate directly with each other.

physical layer (PHY)   Baked into the Wi-Fi standards; handles transmission between nodes (or devices) on a Wi-Fi network. In other words, it is primarily concerned with connectivity at the hardware level.

physical topology   The way a network is connected.

PPPoE   Point-to-Point Protocol over Ethernet.

protocol   An agreed-upon format for transmitting data between devices. See also standard.

R

radio bands Contiguous portions of the radio spectrum, for example, the FM band.

radio spectrum The entire set of radio frequencies.

random access memory (RAM) Used to temporarily store instructions and information for the microprocessor of a computer or other device.

roaming The ability to use a Wi-Fi network provider other than your Wi-Fi network provider through your original account.

router A router is a device that directs traffic between one network and another, for example, between the Internet and your home network.

S

server A computer or device on a network that manages network resources.

shoulder surfing Reading confidential information on a computer over someone's shoulder.

social engineering Tricking a person into revealing their password or other confidential information.

SOHO Small office or home office.

SSID Service set identifier, used to identify the "station" broadcasting a Wi-Fi signal. Also called the network name, or wireless network name. Apple calls the SSID for their AirPort products the AirPort ID.

standard Used in engineering to mean the technical form of something such as a message or a communication. See also protocol.

static IP address An IP address that does not change.

switch An intelligent hub used to connect computers on a network.

T–V

TCP/IP Transmission Control Protocol/Internet Protocol, a protocol used by the Internet and other networks to standardize communications.

topology A network topology is the arrangement of a network.

USB Universal serial bus, used to connect peripheral devices such as a mouse to a computer.

VOIP Voice over IP, a technology that allows telephone calls to be placed over the Internet.

VPN Virtual private network, software used to "tunnel" through the Internet to provide secure access to remote resources.

W–Z

WAN Wide area network, such as the Internet.

WAP Wireless application protocol, used to provide Internet capabilities, such as Web browsing, to "thin" wireless devices, such as mobile phones.

War chalking The use of chalk markings on a sidewalk to identify Wi-Fi networks.

War driving Cruising in a car with a Wi-Fi laptop looking for unprotected Wi-Fi networks.

WEP Wired equivalent privacy, an encryption security standard built into the current versions of Wi-Fi.

Wi-Fi Short for *wireless fidelity*, is the Wi-Fi Alliance's name for a wireless standard, or protocol, used for wireless networking using the 802.11 standards.

Wi-Fi Alliance A not-for-profit organization that certifies the interoperability of wireless devices built around the 802.11 standard. See www.wi-fi.org for more information.

Wi-Fi directory A site on the Internet that provides tools to help you find Wi-Fi hotspots.

Wi-Fi finder A device that senses the presence of active Wi-Fi networks.

Wi-Fi network provider A company that provides access, usually for a fee, to multiple Wi-Fi hotspots.

Wi-Fi Protected Access See 802.11i.

Yagi See directional antenna.

Index